Praise for
Your Essential Guide to
Sustainable Investing

Larry Swedroe and his co-author Sam Adams provide an insightful guide for investors interested in the hottest investment today; namely sustainable investing (SI). Their book is not simply a "this is a wonderful opportunity," but a sober look at the reality that the plethora of SI funds are not particularly comparable and, in fact, the rating services provide radically different ratings for the same funds. Having set the framework and following up with details on the nature and attributes of the SI market, they conclude with a comprehensive guide on "How to Invest Sustainably" (and the warning that it will take work). If this is an investment universe you have an interest in entering, *Your Essential Guide to Sustainable Investing* is indeed an essential book to own and read.

—Harold Evensky, Founder, Evensky and Katz

Sustainable investing is a complex subject. The investing industry, as it always does, has made it even more so. Here is a book that spells out what the data and peer-reviewed academic evidence tell us. The truth is, we simply don't know whether ESG portfolios will outperform or underperform mainstream portfolios in the future. Ultimately, though, there are far more important things at stake. Adams and Swedroe have produced the go-to guide for anyone who wants to understand the issues involved.

—Robin Powell, Editor, The Evidence-Based Investor

Demand is booming for mutual funds that specialize in ethical investing—helping you put your money into companies that support the environment, workers, and society in general. But some apparently "green" funds are merely "green-washed," only pretending to invest ethically. How can you find investments that truly reflect your principles? This excellent book will tell you. You'll learn the nuances of social investing as well as discover your likely investment returns. Highly recommended!

—Jane Bryant Quinn, Author, *How to Make Your Money Last:*
The Indispensable Retirement Guide

You may have noticed that there's currently a lot of buzz in the investing world about ESG and SRI. If you don't have a clue what all this buzz is about, then this book is a must-read, since Larry and Sam get down in the weeds, explaining exactly what these investing styles are and how they may or may not be right for you. This book will bring you up to speed on these latest trends and help you become a better-informed investor.

—Mel Lindauer, Co-Author, *The Bogleheads' Guide to Investing* and *The Bogleheads' Guide to Retirement Planning*

Larry and Sam present a comprehensive view of today's ESG investing landscape. Both have a vast experience in investments and client interactions. Larry has been a prolific writer on financial topics and Sam has been a globe-trotting champion for the environment. Together they bring clarity to an evolving investment world full of acronyms, making it accessible to all interested investors.

—Eduardo Repetto, CIO, Avantis Investors

Sustainable investing is paramount for values-driven investors; yet, it is neither well-understood nor easily implemented by many investment professionals. Sam and Larry elucidate the dynamic landscape of sustainable investing and empirically demonstrate the impact of sustainable investing on firm characteristics such as cost of capital, valuations, and profitability, and on the performance of stocks and bonds. Moreover, they demonstrate that ESG investors, through their impact on asset prices, generate societal benefits by rewarding investments in green technologies and the reduction of gas emissions. Finally, Sam and Larry share robust investment principles and practical suggestions for building sustainable investment programs by clearly defining investment objectives, developing asset allocation methodologies, selecting underlying investments, and actively managing investment portfolios. This book is an essential resource for investment professionals who seek to understand sustainable investing and implement sustainable investment programs.

—Marat Molyboga, Chief Risk Officer, Director of Research at Efficient Capital Management

Adams and Swedroe have delivered a comprehensive review of the state of sustainable investing. They cut through the jargon, which is inconsistent and confusing at best, and misleading at worst, to help investors identify strategies aligned with their financial, societal, and personal goals. The book is essential reading for anyone seeking to put their money where their values are.

—Tobias Carlisle, Founder and Portfolio Manager, Acquirers Funds

An eye-opening guide to the opportunities and consequences of sustainable investing. I admire the thorough discussion of recent developments, the crisp bottom lines, and Burton Malkiel's wise Foreword. Required reading for my Duke investment strategies course.

—**Ed Tower, Emeritus Professor of Economics, Duke University**

Read this book! After doing so, you'll know more about Sustainable Investing than anyone you know, including your financial advisor. In *Your Essential Guide to Sustainable Investing*, Sam Adams and Larry E. Swedroe dive deeply, making sense of the subject's academic research while explaining how capitalism, itself, doesn't have to destroy our planet. This should be required reading for every investor and investment professional.

—**Andrew Hallam, Bestselling Author,** *Balance: How to Invest and Spend for Happiness, Health and Wealth* **and** *Millionaire Teacher*

Sam and I were together at Dimensional Fund Advisors for a number of years, so he is well aware of my role in co-founding Dimensional and my "analytical data-driven" view of investment management. Sam and Larry's book reflects on the evolution of asset management and the challenges and opportunities ESG data analysis brings.

—**John 'Mac' McQuown, Co-Founding Dimensional Director, and Co-Proprietor, Stone Edge Farm**

Experienced financial practitioners are typically wise enough to approach financial product innovation with healthy skepticism. Sam and Larry cut through the noise of "greenwashing" and marketing jargon to offer a genuine roadmap investors can use today to achieve the long-term returns stakeholders require while effecting a sustainable positive impact on the world.

—**Adam Butler, Chief Investment Officer, ReSolve Asset Management**

If you really want to understand the research, risks, returns, ratings, and reasons to own ESG funds this is the book to read. Evidenced-based investing information at its best!

—**Paul Merriman, Author,** *We're Talking Millions! 12 Simple Ways to Supercharge Your Retirement*

Is there a choice between values and value in investing? Not always. Adams and Swedroe answer this question and many others that all investors must ask about ESG and sustainable investing. This impressive summary dispels myths and simplifies an evolving investment landscape with clear definitions and evidence. I hope many investors will read it, discover the power in the paradox, and use the principles to reclaim prosperity for all.

—Tammira Philippe, CFA, President and CEO,
Bridgeway Capital Management

As investors increasingly look to align their holdings with their ESG preferences, it's important to look beyond ESG branding and evaluate whether a fund focused on environmental, social, or governance objectives meets specific, individual goals and desires. *Your Essential Guide to Sustainable Investing* by Sam Adams and Larry Swedroe provides key tools to help optimize this evaluation process and guide investors to their preferred destination.

—Dave Butler, Co-CEO, Dimensional Fund Advisors

A central question facing investors is whether to embrace so-called environmental, social, and governance (ESG) investment products. The temptation to have a positive impact on societal problems like climate change and social justice is overwhelming. Virtually every asset manager has responded with ESG-labeled products. Swedroe and Adams have carefully analyzed this difficult decision and whether the costs to investors outweigh the psychic and monetary benefits of ESG investing.

—Robert Huebscher, CEO, Advisor Perspectives

YOUR ESSENTIAL GUIDE TO
SUSTAINABLE
INVESTING

Every owner of a physical copy of this edition of

YOUR ESSENTIAL GUIDE TO
SUSTAINABLE
INVESTING

can download the eBook for free direct from us at
Harriman House, in a DRM-free format that can be read
on any eReader, tablet or smartphone.

Simply head to:

**ebooks.harriman-house.com/
essentialguidetosustainableinvesting**

to get your copy now.

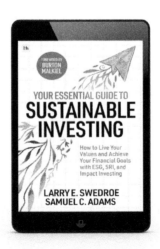

YOUR ESSENTIAL GUIDE TO
SUSTAINABLE INVESTING

How to Live Your Values and Achieve Your Financial Goals with ESG, SRI, and Impact Investing

LARRY E. SWEDROE
SAMUEL C. ADAMS

HARRIMAN HOUSE LTD

3 Viceroy Court
Bedford Road
Petersfield
Hampshire
GU32 3LJ
GREAT BRITAIN
Tel: +44 (0)1730 233870

Email: enquiries@harriman-house.com
Website: harriman.house

First published in 2022.

Paperback ISBN: 978-0-85719-904-1
eBook ISBN: 978-0-85719-905-8

British Library Cataloguing in Publication Data
A CIP catalogue record for this book can be obtained from the British Library.

Larry dedicates this book to the memory of Larry Goldfarb, the best friend one could have

CONTENTS

ACKNOWLEDGMENTS

I would like to thank the management team at Buckingham Wealth Partners for all their support in educating investors. I also thank the love of my life, my wife, Mona, for her support and encouragement throughout our 48 years together. Walking through life with her has truly been a gracious experience. And finally, I would like to thank all those who have given so graciously of their time in sharing their investment wisdom. There are too many to mention, so my apologies if your name is not on this short list. Special thanks to my friend and co-author Andrew Berkin, Wes Wellington and the entire research team at Dimensional, Vladimir Masek, and Cliff Asness and the entire research team at AQR. I cannot thank you enough.

Larry Swedroe

I would like to thank my wife and business partner, Sarah, for being my inspiration, my support, and my go-to resource for this book. Her expertise in sustainable investing and her editing assistance has made this a better book. I'd also like to thank Dan Wheeler, Professor Brad Barber, and John Elkington, collectively the Vert Advisory Board, for keeping my thinking up to date, evidence-based, and clear. A big thank you to my mom, Nancy, for reading every word to excise the industry jargon. I also give thanks to every individual making sustainable choices, and my deepest appreciation to those making sustainability their cause. Finally, I'd like to thank Larry for partnering with me and teaching me the art of writing.

Sam Adams

Sam and Larry would like to thank Sandy Hickman for her editing efforts. She was such a pleasure to work with. We also thank Nick Ledden for his editing work, and Nick Fletcher at Harriman House for his outstanding work and contributions editing the numerous drafts. We also want to give specific thanks to CNote for the use of their "History of SRI" for Appendix A, and to the Plan Sponsor Council of America (PSCA) for the use of their excellent ESG Resource Guide for Appendix D. And finally, we would like to thank Craig Pearce, our editor at Harriman House, for believing in our project and providing his support.

FOREWORD BY
BURTON MALKIEL

URING THE FIRST half of 2021 there were robust flows of investments
into funds with sustainable objectives, bringing the total amount of such
funds to approximately $25 trillion according to Morningstar. Interest from
investors in funds with presumptive environmental, social, and governance
(ESG) objectives continues at record highs, both in the United States and
abroad. The financial industry has responded by providing a plethora of new
ESG funds and by rebranding existing funds. Bloomberg Intelligence estimates
that by 2025, over $50 trillion (more than a third of the total funds under
management) will be invested with an ESG mandate. Such funds are advertised
as helping to achieve a more sustainable world while enhancing investment
returns as well.

There is clearly a strong demand by investors to ensure that their investments
are consistent with their ethical principles. In addition to meeting financial
goals, there are potential emotional benefits from investing. People want to
align their investment strategies with their societal values. It would also be
unambiguously advantageous if they could push the firms in which they
invest to improve societal outcomes while simultaneously enhancing their
financial returns. But do the investment products that advertise themselves as
ESG-compliant actually deliver? How do you know if your investments will
have the desired social impact? And is sustainable investing really a way to
assure investors they can do well by doing good?

Amid all the hype concerning sustainable investing, there has been far too
little attention paid to careful analysis of exactly what such investing really
entails and what the evidence shows about its effectiveness. There is also far
too little serviceable advice for investors who wish to invest sustainably. Adams
and Swedroe have brilliantly fulfilled these needs with their highly readable and
evidence-based guide for investors. Here they show what sustainable investing
is, why one might want to do it, what financial returns have been achieved, and
what its impact has been, as well as the pitfalls that exist. They also provide
practical investment advice for individuals wishing to build ESG portfolios.

We learn that meritorious investments are in the eye of the beholder. The objectives of faith-based investment funds are far different from those that prize enhancing the goals of fair pay and inclusiveness. The most common and popular of such funds are those with explicit ESG objectives. But even then, the term means different things to different people, and it is difficult for investors to understand exactly what the ESG portfolios actually achieve. To make matters worse, the ESG scores for different companies published by the professional rating services provided to portfolio managers differ materially. Correlations of ratings between different rating services are as low as 0.42. To put that number in perspective, the correlations between the bond ratings of S&P and Moody's are more than 0.99. ESG raters cannot even agree when they are considering the same attribute, such as carbon intensity. Within the electric utility industry, a company with one of the biggest carbon footprints is Xcel Energy. Xcel is ranked poorly by some raters because it generates a substantial share of its power from coal. But Xcel is the first U.S. utility committed to going 100 percent carbon-free by 2050 and is a leader in building wind-generation facilities.

ESG ratings also differ markedly for companies for which carbon footprint is not a major factor. Apple gets a high ESG rating of 73 percent from Refinitiv. S&P Global rates them only 23 percent and close to the bottom of their 22-company industry. Even on the identical ESG component of governance, ratings are not even close to one another. Sustainalytics considers Apple's management among the most compliant with the best governance criteria, while MSCI considers Apple's governance score second to last in its peer group.

If carbon footprint and governance are major factors in excluding companies from a broad ESG portfolio, what kinds of companies are favored for investment? Examining the top holdings in the largest ESG mutual funds and ETFs, we find Alphabet (Google's parent) and Facebook, as well as Visa and MasterCard, prominently featured. These companies have had their fair share of controversies. Would all ESG investors really have their social consciences assuaged by investing in companies that have been found to breach individual privacy and impose exorbitant interest rates?

What about the returns from sustainable investing? The authors do a masterful job of meticulously documenting the existing empirical studies. There is no better survey of the returns from ESG investing. Again, the studies do not suggest a clear conclusion. Some studies report market-beating risk-adjusted returns, while others come to the opposite conclusion. There is no unambiguous evidence that sustainable investing enhances long-run financial performance. Moreover, sustainable funds have higher management expenses than traditional index funds. The authors do believe, however, that avoiding certain companies can reduce so-called *tail risk*—the risk, for example, that a company that cannot or will not curtail its polluting activities could be severely harmed by government fiat. Thus, ESG investing can be a risk-reducing strategy.

One of the very important insights in this book concerns the differences we should expect between short- and long-run returns. This insight can help explain some of the different empirical results. A heightened demand for ESG-compliant investments can cause share prices to rise and thus enhance the returns of sustainable funds. But then so-called *green* stocks will sell at higher valuation multiples and lower long-run required rates of return. Thus, any short-term benefits will be realized at the expense of long-run performance. Investors who wish to invest sustainably should have reasonable expectations, including a willingness to accept lower long-run returns.

A further important insight concerns the likelihood that an ESG influence on share prices will affect corporate behavior. If ESG-compliant companies enjoy higher share prices and a lower cost of capital, then they will be incentivized to improve their ESG ratings. Thus, a focus on sustainable investing can cause companies to behave in a more positive manner.

Adams and Swedroe then turn to a survey of the empirical evidence on whether sustainable investing is actually making companies more responsible. They cite a number of studies that suggest that ESG concerns by investors have had a positive effect in encouraging firms to take actions that have positive societal impacts, such as reducing their greenhouse gas emissions. There is no clear evidence, however, that disinvestment from unsustainable firms has interfered with their ability to raise capital. It would also be a mistake to conclude that increasing the investments to sustainable companies will be sufficient to allow the country to meet its environmental goals. The most effective way to reduce an economy's carbon intensity is to change the economic incentive to pollute. This could be accomplished with carbon taxation. Or the government could auction off a limited number of tradable pollution permits. Companies could reduce emissions to avoid the cost of a permit or buy permits if they faced especially high pollution-abatement costs. For those who question the morality of a government selling rights to pollute, there is a good answer: It's better than giving such rights away.

So what is the best practical advice we can give investors who would like to put their money where their mouth is and would be delighted if they could feel that their investments had a positive social impact? An easy solution would be to purchase one of the broad-based ESG investment mutual funds or ETFs that advertise the claim that you can help save the world and increase your return simultaneously. The problem is that it is far from clear that the holdings in these funds are all worthy of merit. Moreover, such funds are less diversified and more expensive than pure index funds and may well underperform in the long run. In trying to do well by doing good, you may achieve neither objective.

In their final chapter, Adams and Swedroe provide useful practical advice for investors who wish to build portfolios that are consistent with their individual values. While such an undertaking requires hard work, they clearly show the necessary steps and the framework required. The criteria are provided for the selection of ESG investments, keeping in mind the difficulties and pitfalls involved.

My own preference is to favor what they call a *patient approach* of making changes *around the edges* rather than having investors alter their entire portfolios. For example, the core of the portfolio could consist of low-cost, broadly diversified index funds. Then investors could add an allocation to a renewable energy fund or some other funds consistent with the particular themes that are important to them. Whichever alternative is chosen, the authors remind us that due diligence is of overriding importance. It is not easy to be good.

Burton G. Malkiel
Author of *A Random Walk Down Wall Street*

INTRODUCTION

The Education of a Climber

I WAS FORTUNATE TO grow up in Northern Italy, in a family that loved to ski. We went skiing almost every weekend. Our first trip would be for Thanksgiving and the last one after Easter. I have my own kids now. We have never been skiing at Thanksgiving. Lately, in fact, it has been hard to find snow to ski at Christmas. This has been a wake-up call. The ski season used to stretch over seven months. Now it is down to four. Should I teach my kids to ski, knowing that when they are older, they might not be able to?

In college, I transferred to the University of Colorado at Boulder so I could start climbing. Rock climbing became my main passion. Later I added snow, ice, alpine, and mixed climbing. I even moved to Chamonix, France, the birthplace of alpinism and home to some of the most classic climbs in the world.

Another wake-up call. Many of those classic routes are no longer possible to climb. The snow and ice have receded so much that the climbs are too dangerous. In some cases, they no longer exist.

If you are thinking that my skiing and climbing is the least of our worries when it comes to climate change, you are right. In the grand scheme of things, it is inconsequential. However, it is precisely because it is personal and it is my passion that it is so motivating. I know from first-hand experience that climate change is real. And I am not alone.

One of my good friends was a commercial tuna boat captain. Catching big fish was his passion. But there are not enough fish to catch anymore, so he has had to find another line of work. Another friend's kids have embraced his passion for ice hockey. He laments that they have never played it outside on a pond, like he did growing up.

When my sister moved to Charleston, South Carolina, a few years ago, nobody warned her that she would have to shelter in place several times each fall during hurricane season. They didn't use to, but the storms are stronger now. When I moved to Northern California four years ago, we were unaware that PG&E, the local utility company, would start shutting off the power for everyone in our region for three to five days at a time every fall. They didn't use to, but the risk of wildfire is greater now. We also didn't know we would have to keep our kids inside for several weeks due to poor air quality from those wildfires. My neighbor grew up in Paradise, California. His mother lost her home, and the family business, in the fire of 2018.

Most people in the world now believe that climate change is real. In fact, according to a 2021 survey of over half a million people across 50 countries conducted by the UN 64 percent believe it is an emergency.[1] I believe that more people were convinced of this by their personal experience rather than by reading some scientific paper. What has changed in your life because of climate change?

The Education of a Capitalist

I graduated from college with a philosophy degree, which is another way of saying I was going to be unemployed for a while. Luckily, I met Dan Wheeler, who was working on a twin revolution in financial services.

Dan taught me what stocks and bonds are, what a mutual fund is, and how financial advice is delivered. And he taught me that the traditional Wall Street firms' investment advice, and the products that come with it, are designed to enhance their own wealth, not that of their clients. Dan had a better model, a fee-based advice model using low-cost passively managed funds.

This model of investment advice was better for the client because lower commissions and management fees meant more money in the client's pocket. Almost nobody was doing it at the time, since Wall Street dominated the field, but I liked being the underdog, so I joined Dan. Twenty-five years later, index funds are king, and fee-based advice is the standard around the world. This experience has given me an enduring faith in the power of capitalism to improve outcomes.

No Army Is Stronger Than a Good Idea Whose Time Has Come

My experiences taught me that large-scale change is possible, even probable, when you have a better way of doing things. It takes time and some hard work to convince people to change their minds, especially when it requires upending their business models. And it takes time for the disruptive innovators to overcome the power of the status quo, which is held in place by those who work hard to protect their vested interests. But if markets are working correctly, truth wins in the end, and the better way will eventually overcome the conventional method.

The wake-up calls I received about climate change and capital markets were not alarm bells. They were more a slow-rolling series of realizations that culminated in a growing sense of dread. We have known about climate change and that it is caused by burning fossil fuels since the 1970s. Yet, we have only begun to adjust course.

When it came to climate change, capitalism wasn't changing the game—certainly not on any meaningful scale, and certainly not quickly enough. It was easy to criticize capitalism. And many thought leaders and authors were having a go at it. In 2002, the 30-year update to the 1972 book *The Limits to Growth* made a compelling case that their original predictions were coming true—humanity was using more resources than the planet could sustainably provide.[2] The implications were clearly stated. In order to avoid catastrophe, we needed to turn off the exponential growth model of capitalism.

I found this line of thinking—that capitalism was flawed beyond repair and needed wholesale replacement—difficult to accept. After all, I was working with Dan, and the twin revolution in financial services was gaining traction, providing better advice and better investment solutions. Capitalism seemed to be working toward a better solution here, although change was slow. It helped that we worked at a firm loaded with Nobel laureate economists from the University of Chicago, a school known for its full-throated defense of free-market capitalism. And it was hard to miss the geopolitical message of the day. The Berlin Wall had only recently come down, signaling the complete failure of communism, capitalism's main competitor.

With that in mind, I kept looking for ideas that used capitalism as the solution. I eventually discovered the work of Paul Hawken and two of his books, *Natural Capitalism*[3] and *The Ecology of Commerce*.[4] I realized, with great relief, that there is an alternative way of thinking about climate change and capitalism. This way sees capitalism as flawed, but not fatally so. It also sees capitalism as probably the only force strong enough to create massive change in scale and at the required pace. After all, capitalism is what replaced the horse and buggy with the automobile in just a few years.

Paul and his co-authors suggested that with some admittedly significant shifts in mindset, capitalism could be our solution to climate change. Most importantly, investors would need to learn to be patient as it would take time and effort for businesses to adjust. Companies would need to replace the linear, extractive, polluting approaches (i.e., *take, make, waste*) with circular business models—ones that strive to eliminate waste by using outputs as inputs in a *regenerative* system. In addition, the shareholder primacy model would need to become a more inclusive stakeholder model. This resonated with me. I realized that I wanted to work within the capitalist system and help transform it into a new and improved version, just as we did with financial services. I just did not know how.

Then I learned about ESG investing, and how it was different from socially responsible investing (SRI). ESG is the acronym for environmental, social, and governance. It is a system of investing that incorporates *extra-financial* criteria into analyzing the risks and opportunities of companies. This data is called extra-financial or even *nonfinancial* because it is not disclosed by companies in their standard financial reporting. It includes the natural resources that firms use as inputs, some of which are mostly free (such as fresh water, clean air, and nutrient topsoil) and some that are almost free (such as mature trees, minerals, and deposits). It also includes a company's negative outputs (such as pollution, waste, and greenhouse gases) as well as their positive outputs (such as jobs, training, services to the community). Thus, while SRI is about aligning a portfolio to one's personal values, ESG is an attempt to attach economic value to things we believe have worth but are not priced by the market.

Capitalism is great at allocating resources. Resources are allocated based on the price signals the free market provides. However, it can only count that which has a price. And clean air, fresh water, and soil, as well as waste and pollution, do not come with price tags. If it doesn't have a price, the model thinks it is free. The result is that firms, in their best interests, don't limit the use of a free input, nor do they curtail the production of *free* waste. By pricing in *externalities*, capitalism could turn around one key problem: the linear extraction model of take-make-waste. If the taking and the wasting were expensive, firms would develop regenerative circular business models because they would be more profitable.

ESG investors (at least some) strive to be long-term investors. After all, they are looking for sustainability. If enough investors have multiyear time frames, company leaders could look beyond quarterly earnings cycles and invest in more high-returning projects. ESG investors also prize the multi-stakeholder approach, where companies look after people and planet, not just profit.

An Engine for Change

Sustainable investing has the chance to change the three main problems with our current capitalist system: the shareholder primacy model, the linear extraction model, and short time frames. I became excited about the idea that sustainable investing could be the engine for change. And with that, I was ready to shift my career to promoting sustainability full time. I thought there might be real opportunity to do good by doing good work in this emerging arena. If I could help shift billions of dollars to sustainable investing, capitalism would begin to adjust. Like the twin revolution in financial services, we would be on our way to improving outcomes.

The Three Questions

There is a big difference between an idealistic movement and a robust business model. With that in mind, before launching Vert, I researched whether sustainable investing had legs. I had three main questions:

1. Is there real demand for ESG investing?
2. Is ESG a robust investment strategy?
3. Does it make a difference?

My initial research led me to believe that the answer to each question is a resounding yes. So Vert Asset Management was launched. Our mission is to educate as many people as possible about sustainable investing so that more money moves into ESG investing, and capitalism evolves as a result.

When it comes to educating investors and financial advisors, Larry Swedroe is everywhere. Thus, it was not long before we crossed paths. I had known Larry for decades as one of the most prominent voices in that twin revolution in financial services we both worked on. It was great to reconnect with him at the intersection of evidence-based investing and ESG. Larry was getting inundated by all the ESG research coming out, reviewing the papers, and publishing summaries for advisors. When he told me we needed a book to synthesize all the information, I jumped at the chance to collaborate with him.

The purpose of this book is to share with you what Larry and I have learned about these questions. It is also a guide for those who choose to embrace sustainable investing.

The Journey

You are about to embark on a journey that will provide you with the knowledge you need to develop your plan for sustainable investing. The journey has three parts.

In the first part, we define sustainable investing. We then provide clear distinctions between ESG, SRI, and impact investing. We provide some historical context and cover who is doing it, and why.

In the second part, we summarize the empirical research and what it says about risk and return. We cover what happens to firms' cost of capital when they integrate sustainability, and what investors can expect in terms of performance from ESG and SRI strategies.

The third part is our how-to guide, where we provide frameworks for choosing an asset allocation strategy and for selecting managers and funds.

It is our hope that this book will provide not just a how-to guide to invest for sustainability, but that it will impress upon you the role you play in capital markets. Capitalism, after all, shapes our world, and investor choices matter. With a bit of care and intention, you can choose how your money impacts the world. Larry and I hope you enjoy the journey.

Sam Adams

CHAPTER 1

What Is Sustainable Investing?

S USTAINABLE INVESTING HAS grown significantly, with global investments now at $35.3 trillion. This amounts to 36 percent of all professionally managed assets according to the Global Sustainable Investment Alliance.[1] The financial services industry has responded to this demand with a dizzying array of product launches. Seventy-one new sustainable mutual funds and exchange traded funds were launched in the U.S. in 2020 alone.[2]

This is good news for sustainably minded investors, who now have more options. There are even custom solutions (such as separately managed accounts) to match each individual's unique values. The bad news is that fund sponsors are not using consistent terms to describe their products. Managers use ESG and SRI interchangeably, or call the whole field *impact investing*. Others use terms such as *values-based investing, mission-driven investing, ethical investing*, or even just *responsible investing*. The lack of a common nomenclature makes it difficult for investors to understand what investment choices are available, what the purpose of an investment product is, and what the performance might be. (See *What's in a Name?* at the end of the chapter.)

Unfortunately, it is common for popular forms of investing to suffer from this malady. Many disagree over what the term *value investing* means, even though it has been around for 100 years. More recently, terms like *factor* and *fundamental* have lost much of their original meaning as more and more investors adopt the terms for different uses. It is therefore helpful to review the original use of the terms before they became widespread and watered down. While the historical definition may no longer be the only one in use, it often contains useful information about the type of investing it refers to.

Three Types of Sustainable Investing

While there are dozens of forms of sustainable investing, we can categorize most of them into three general categories: ESG, SRI, and impact. As illustrated in Figure 1, these three forms of sustainable investing span the spectrum of opportunity between conventional investing, where financial returns are the priority, to philanthropy, where social and environmental outcomes are the goal.

Figure 1: The Spectrum of Sustainable Investing

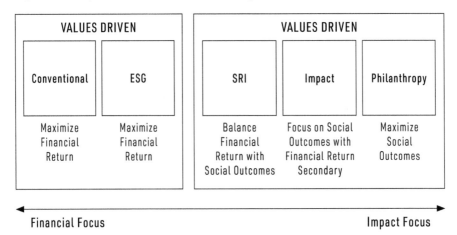

VALUES DRIVEN		VALUES DRIVEN		
Conventional	ESG	SRI	Impact	Philanthropy
Maximize Financial Return	Maximize Financial Return	Balance Financial Return with Social Outcomes	Focus on Social Outcomes with Financial Return Secondary	Maximize Social Outcomes

Financial Focus ⟵⟶ Impact Focus

> The Values Driven categories on the left include the investment approaches that are designed to not compromise on risk and return. Both conventional and ESG strategies aim to maximize financial return for the risk taken. They put financial return first, before other issues are addressed. The Values Driven categories on the right include strategies that consider financial return only after the investors' values have been satisfied.

We will now review the three types of sustainable investing in turn, beginning with SRI.

1. Socially Responsible Investing

SRI, or socially responsible investing, was for decades the dominant term to describe sustainable investing. Just like the conventional investor, the socially responsible investor seeks to maximize total return for a given level of risk. However, given their personal values, they avoid investing in certain companies because of the products the companies make, or the way they conduct business.

Commonly ascribed to religious or deeply ethical investors, SRI strategies typically exclude problematic companies or even whole industries from portfolios. One oft-cited example is the Quakers, who published an investor guide more than 100 years ago, exhorting their followers to avoid any companies that profited from slave labor.

Some of the original SRI funds appealed to the ethical investor by the blanket avoidance of *sin* stocks—stocks of companies in the alcohol, tobacco, gambling, and pornography industries. Some of these strategies also excluded gun manufacturers and/or nuclear power. As another example, in the 1980s SRI investors began divesting from South Africa to protest apartheid.

SRI strategies have become more sophisticated than just employing a negative screen of certain industries or companies. Some SRI strategies now seek to invest using positive screens, investing in companies providing solutions. Others try to engage with problematic companies to change their behavior. In general, these strategies are trying to accommodate investors' personal values when constructing portfolios. As such, SRI is a balanced approach—pursuing economic value while incorporating deeply held personal values.

Building a portfolio to match one's values is easier said than done. If you have the resources, you can hand-pick the stocks and bonds that reflect your values. However, to build a well-diversified portfolio requires a lot of time for research and a lot of data. You can hire professionals who create separately managed accounts (SMAs) tailored to your unique values. Typically, an SMA provider would ask you to fill out a questionnaire about your views on issues from A (abortion, alcohol, animal welfare…) to Z. The SMA manager would then construct a portfolio optimized for those values, excluding any problem areas and perhaps overweighting solutions the investor likes. SMA managers typically have minimums of several hundred thousand dollars.

For those with more modest means, or more commonly held values, a portfolio of SRI funds might appeal. To attract broad audiences, SRI funds typically organize their strategy to appeal to the common values held by certain groups. For example, Catholics can choose from fund families like Ave Maria, Aquinas, and Knights of Columbus. These funds typically exclude companies that are involved in abortion and contraception, and perhaps even stem cell research.

Many of the early SRI funds charged high fees and excluded so many companies they lacked diversification, leading to the generally poor results that we discuss in Chapter 6. The good news is that, in general, fees have come down and funds are more diversified. Unfortunately, it is not always clear what an SRI strategy is and what an ESG strategy is. As we discussed, what the SRI investor cares about most is whether the investment matches their personal values—as long as they can get clarity on the risk and return implications, they can go into the investment with proper expectations.

Example: SRI Fund

The US Vegan Climate ETF is a good example of an SRI strategy because it strikes a balance between striving for market returns and avoiding companies at odds with the vegan or animal lover's values.

Name	US Vegan Climate ETF
Provider	Beyond Investing
Investment Vehicle	Exchange Traded Fund
Investor Availability	Anyone
Asset Class	U.S. Large Company
Minimum Investment	None
Liquidity	Intraday
Number of Holdings	268
Expenses	0.60 percent
Primary Goal	Balance Financial Return with Social Outcomes

This fund attempts to address the concerns of vegans, animal lovers, and environmentalists by avoiding investments in companies whose activities directly contribute to animal suffering, destruction of the natural environment, and climate change. It excludes companies that engage in the following activities:

- Animal testing.
- Animal-derived products, animal farming, and other exploitation activities.
- Animals in sport and entertainment.
- Research, development, and use of genetically engineered animals.
- Extraction or refining, or services principally related to the extraction or refining, of fossil fuels.
- Burning of fossil fuels for energy production.
- Other activities having a significant negative environmental impact.
- Tobacco products.
- Armaments and products specifically designed for military and defense uses.
- Contributions to the abuse of human rights.

2. Impact Investing

While impact investing has also been around in principle for hundreds of years, the term is thought to have been coined at a meeting hosted by the Rockefeller Foundation in 2007.

Impact investing has common cause with philanthropy—the primary objective of both is to address a social or environmental problem. The nonprofit approach, using donations to deliver goods and services to areas of need, works well in many cases. However, some large philanthropists realized that their donations were only alleviating a problem in the short run, not solving it for the long term. They sought to create permanent solutions. Perhaps the most famous of these is Bob Geldof, the musician behind *We Are the World*, the initiative that raised hundreds of millions of dollars to alleviate hunger in Africa. A few years after shipping in money, food, and supplies, Geldof returned and saw that the kids were still suffering. Experiences like these led some philanthropists to wonder if a for-profit model would have more long-term success than a nonprofit model.

The for-profit model replaces the philanthropic donation with an investment of capital that is used to establish a business with recurring revenue. The primary service of the business would be to solve the particular environmental or social need. For example, rather than donating food, the impact investor might contribute capital to start a farm. The food from the farm would feed the local community. Any profits would be reinvested to expand the business, thus feeding more people, creating more jobs, and increasing the resiliency of the community. In some cases, for-profit investment models are more sustainable and can be more impactful than philanthropic ones.

Impact strategies can be difficult to invest in, as most are available only to institutions, foundations, and high-net-worth investors. Equity investments are often made in private companies, whose shares are unlisted. Unlike a listed company, or a regulated fund, there is little public information available. Thus, extra due diligence is necessary. Since these opportunities typically are not registered for sale to the public, investors might need to qualify for an exemption based on their income or net worth with high minimum-net-worth requirements. In addition, most such investments are highly illiquid, with lock-up periods between 5 and 10 years during which you cannot sell or take proceeds. These are some of the reasons why impact investing is still a small part of the sustainable investment landscape overall.

Example: Impact Investing

The conventional agriculture system in the U.S. has been able to increase yields by adopting factory farming methods. This has not been kind to family farms, to soil health, or in fact to human health. Iroquois Valley provides secure land access through long-term leases to family farmers that practice organic and regenerative farming. Its mission is to scale organic agriculture. To date, they have invested in more than 60 farms in 15 states comprising nearly 13,000 acres.

Name	Iroquois Valley Farmland REIT
Provider	Iroquois Valley
Investment Vehicle	Private Unlisted Company
Investor Availability	Qualified Investors Only
Asset Class	Real Estate Investment Trust
Minimum Investment	$10,115
Liquidity	5-year minimum investment period
Number of Holdings	1
Expenses	N/A
Primary Goal	Focus on Social Outcomes; Financial Return Secondary

Iroquois Valley is one of the more accessible impact investments because the founders worked hard to make investing in their company available to ordinary investors. They converted their company to a private REIT (real estate investment trust) in 2018 so that qualified investors could participate. You are a qualified investor if you have a net worth greater than $1 million or annual income greater than $200,000, or as long as you invest no more than 10 percent of your annual income or net worth.

3. ESG

While ESG (environmental, social, and governance) investing is a relatively new form of sustainable investing, it has become the most popular, dwarfing the others in terms of assets. The term is believed to have been first defined in 2005 in the landmark report "Who Cares Wins."[3] This report was an initiative launched by former UN Secretary Kofi Annan.

Ultimately, 20 major banks, asset managers, and financial institutions joined with the UN Global Compact to create the framework for integrating environmental concerns, social issues, and corporate governance into capital markets. The report argued that integrating these factors would lead to "better investment markets and more sustainable societies." The UN followed up the report with the 2006 launch of the Principles for Responsible Investment (PRI) to advance the integration of ESG.

In 2017 the PRI launched its Blueprint for Responsible Investment, setting the direction of its work for the next 10 years. The blueprint stated that the PRI should focus its efforts on nine priority areas.[4]

- *Responsible Investors*: We will strengthen, deepen and expand our core work to lead responsible investors in their pursuit of long-term value and to enhance alignment throughout the investment chain.

  1. Empower asset owners.
  2. Support investors incorporating ESG issues.
  3. Foster a community of active owners.
  4. Showcase leadership and increase accountability.
  5. Convene and educate responsible investors.

- *Sustainable Markets*: We will address unsustainable aspects of the markets that investors operate in, to achieve the economically efficient, sustainable global financial system that responsible investors and beneficiaries need.

  6. Challenge barriers to a sustainable financial system.
  7. Drive meaningful data throughout markets.

- *A Prosperous World for All*: We will enable signatories to improve the real world—now and in the future—encouraging investments that contribute to prosperous and inclusive societies for current and future generations.

  8. Champion climate action.
  9. Enable real-world impact aligned with the SDGs (sustainable development goals).

The PRI now has more than 3,000 signatories representing over $100 trillion in assets managed. While not all of those assets are managed sustainably, the asset managers have signed on to the principles in support of more ESG disclosure and integration. ESG has quickly become the largest category within sustainable investing. The Global Sustainable Investing Alliance estimates that, of the global total of $35.3 trillion of sustainably managed assets, over 70 percent, or $25.2 trillion, is managed with ESG integration.[5]

Traditional security selection employs fundamental ratios like price-to-earnings (P/E) or dividend yield (D/P) to identify companies to either invest in or avoid. ESG integration does that as well, but adds environmental, social, and governance factors into that analysis. This process requires collecting additional data. Portfolio managers will buy ESG ratings from large data providers, obtain them from in-house ESG analysts, or conduct their own fundamental research. The manager uses E, S, and G data alongside financial information to make investment decisions.

The idea is to create more in-depth analyses of companies by providing fund managers with a better understanding of overall risk—both financial and nonfinancial. Every fund manager has their own proprietary approach to portfolio construction. It is no different with ESG. The weight managers put on different criteria varies widely.

Data and research companies, such as Bloomberg, MSCI, and Sustainalytics, collect and distribute data on dozens of ESG criteria. Examples of these criteria can be found in Figure 2.

Figure 2: Examples of ESG Criteria

Environmental	Social	Governance
Conservation of the natural world	Consideration of people & relationships	Standards for running a company
• Climate change and carbon emissions • Air and water pollution • Biodiversity • Deforestation • Energy efficiency • Waste management • Water scarcity	• Customer satisfaction • Data protection and privacy • Gender and diversity • Employee engagement • Community relations • Human rights • Labor standards	• Board composition • Audit committee structure • Bribery and corruption • Executive compensation • Lobbying • Political contributions • Whistleblower schemes

Source: CFA Institute, ESG Factors, www.cfainstitute.org/en/research/esg-investing.

The environmental factor E captures data on the natural resources that a firm consumes and how much it pollutes. Until recently, it was difficult to obtain this data. However, more than 9,600 global companies now voluntarily report to CDP (formerly known as the Carbon Disclosure Project), a data provider that advocates disclosure of greenhouse gas emissions, water use, and other metrics. This represents a 70 percent increase since the Paris Agreement was signed in 2015.[6] In some markets, such as the U.K., all listed companies are required to report their greenhouse gas emissions. Thus, this data is now part of the standard reporting package.

The social factor S looks at how well companies are managing their human relationships, in particular employees, customers, and suppliers. But it also examines how the company affects its local community. By its nature, the S factor can be highly qualitative. For example, how an employer treats its workers and contributes to the local community can be subjective. Investors should be cautious with these scores. Some social metrics are more quantifiable than others, including safety records, number of human rights violations, and employee access to health care and benefits. The events of 2020 have raised the profile of many S issues. Health, safety, and well-being became critical during the COVID-19 crisis. And many companies chose to make additional efforts on diversity, equity, and inclusion after the murder of George Floyd and the subsequent Black Lives Matter protests.

The governance factor G captures issues such as board independence, executive pay, and employee ownership. Governance is the most well-researched factor. The data has been reported in company filings for decades. The abundance of good data has allowed researchers to compare thousands of companies over long periods of time. Many studies indicate that poor corporate governance can adversely affect corporate financial performance.[7]

The vast majority of sustainable investments are now categorized as ESG strategies. ESG investors have a wide array of options across most asset classes. Though there are still more offerings in large-cap equities, there are increasingly more choices in small caps, in bonds, and even in alternative asset classes. Investors can choose from broadly diversified to highly concentrated strategies, from low cost to high cost, and from passive to active. In the last few years, investors have shown a growing appetite for low-cost passive investment vehicles over higher-cost active ones. This is also the case within ESG. Since 2018 over $54 billion has been invested in passive ESG vehicles compared to $23 billion in active funds.[8]

Example: ESG Investments

The market leader for ESG strategies is iShares. Of the 10 largest ESG exchange traded funds, they manage seven. Most of the iShares ETFs track an MSCI index, of which there are many types, with different construction methodologies. They offer four different ETFs in the U.S. large-cap asset class alone. An investor might choose the iShares ESG Aware MSCI USA ETF (ESGU) profiled in the following table. Its stated objective is to "track the investment results of an index composed of U.S. companies that have positive environmental, social and governance characteristics as identified by the index provider while exhibiting risk and return characteristics similar to those of the parent index."

Using a portfolio management technique called *optimization*, the ESG Aware fund managers eliminate weapons, tobacco, and coal companies, and then prioritize more sustainable companies over lesser ones, all while keeping adequate diversification across sectors. They target a performance variance (referred to as *tracking variance* or *tracking error*) within 0.5 percent of the benchmark on average, making it almost a substitute for the conventional index.

Alternatively, an investor could target a deeper tilt to ESG with the iShares MSCI USA Select ETF (SUSA), also profiled in the following table. This fund uses the same optimization technique but holds fewer companies that are more highly rated on ESG performance. It is designed to perform within 1.8 percent of the benchmark on average. The tradeoff is clear: A light ESG tilt results in index-like performance with less sustainability; a stronger ESG tilt delivers performance with more variation.

Name	iShares ESG Aware MSCI USA ETF(ESGU)	iShares MSCI USA Select ETF (SUSA)
Provider	BlackRock	BlackRock
Investment Vehicle	Exchange Traded Fund	Exchange Traded Fund
Investor Availability	Everyone	Everyone
Asset Class	U.S. Equity	U.S. Equity
Minimum Investment	None	None
Liquidity	Intraday	Intraday
Number of Holdings	347	223
Expenses	0.15 Percent	0.25 percent
Return Expectation	Returns within 0.5 percent of Index	Returns within 1.8 percent of Index
Primary Goal	Maximize Financial Return	Maximize Financial Return

Summary

This chapter provided definitions of sustainable investing. We defined the three main types of sustainable investing: ESG, SRI, and impact. With this foundation, we are ready to proceed to Chapter 2, where we discuss the most common methods of sustainable investing.

What's in a Name?

Sam handed the customs official his passport and mentally prepared his responses for the usual questions, like "Where have you visited?" or "Do you have any fruits or vegetables?"

This time, the agent asked what business he was in. Sam responded, "My wife and I run a sustainable investing firm." The agent tilted his head, paused, then asked, "Shouldn't all investing be sustainable?" Sam beamed and responded, "Of course!" However, he quickly realized that for the official, sustainable meant the investments wouldn't go under, not that they were environmentally and socially responsible.

Later that week, Sam had an electrician come to his house to wire in an electric car charging station. The electrician asked what business he was in. Recalling the conversation with the customs official, Sam said, "We run a green investing firm." Nodding enthusiastically, the electrician said: "Yeah, now that California has legalized marijuana, the cannabis business is where it's at!"

Sam decided to go back to calling it sustainable investing and be ready for further explanation. It's a confusing term and, as it gets more popular, seems to become even more so.

CHAPTER 2

Methods of Sustainable Investing

S USTAINABLE INVESTORS HAVE an array of options on how to construct and manage their portfolios. In this section we look into the most common methodologies.

In doing this, we make use of the Global Sustainable Investment Alliance's categorization of sustainable investing strategies. The Alliance publishes a biannual study on the growth of sustainable investing. Since 2012 it has grouped sustainable investing strategies into the following seven styles based on the methodologies they employ:

1. *Negative/Exclusionary Screening*: The exclusion from a fund or portfolio of certain sectors, companies, or practices based on specific criteria.
2. *Positive/Best-in-Class Screening*: Investment in sectors, companies, or projects selected for positive characteristics relative to industry peers.
3. *Norms-based Screening*: Screening of investments against minimum standards of business practice based on international norms, such as those issued by the OECD, ILO, UN, and UNICEF.
4. *ESG Integration*: The systematic and explicit inclusion by investment managers of environmental, social, and governance factors into financial analysis.
5. *Sustainability-themed Investing*: Investment in themes or assets specifically related to sustainability (e.g., clean energy, green technology, or sustainable agriculture).
6. *Impact/Community Investing*: Targeted investments aimed at solving social or environmental problems and including community investing, where capital is specifically directed to traditionally underserved individuals or communities, as well as financing that is provided to businesses with a clear social or environmental purpose.

7. *Corporate Engagement and Shareholder Action*: The use of shareholder power to influence corporate behavior, including through direct corporate engagement (i.e., communicating with senior management and/or boards of companies), filing or co-filing shareholder proposals, and proxy voting.

We find this list represents the most common methodologies investors use in constructing sustainable portfolios.

These methodologies may be applied in ESG, SRI, and impact strategies. Many investors employ more than one form simultaneously—they are not mutually exclusive. For example, an ESG integration strategy could also use negative screens to eliminate from consideration any company not meeting some minimum ESG standard. Or an SRI fund might dedicate a portion of the portfolio to an impact investment. And many investors increasingly expect their managers to employ some level of corporate engagement and shareholder action regardless of their specific methodology.

Figure 3 shows the GSIA's estimates of assets managed by methodology, and their corresponding growth rates since 2016.

Figure 3: Global Growth of Sustainable Investing (2016–2018)

	2020	2018	2016	GROWTH 2016–2020	COMPOUND ANNUAL GROWTH RATE
Impact/community investing	$352	$444	$248	42%	9%
Positive/best-in-class screening	$1,384	$1,842	$818	69%	14%
Sustainability-themed investing	$1,948	$1,018	$276	605%	63%
Norms-based screening	$4,140	$4,679	$9,195	−33%	−10%
Corporate engagement and shareholder action	$10,504	$9,835	$8,385	25%	6%
Negative/exclusionary screening	$15,030	$19,771	$15,064	0%	0%
ESG integration	$25,195	$17,544	$10,353	143%	25%

Note: Asset values expressed in billions.

Source: Global Sustainable Investment Review 2020, Global Sustainable Investment Alliance

We will now look at each of the Global Sustainable Investment Alliance's seven styles of sustainable investing in turn.

1. Negative/Exclusionary Screening

Negative screening is the process of excluding from a portfolio companies, or entire sectors, based on specific criteria. It is a ubiquitous approach—a large percentage of sustainable investment strategies use some form of negative screening. The SRI example mentioned in the previous chapter, the US Vegan Climate ETF, uses negative screening to exclude companies unfriendly to animals and those in the business of tobacco, fossil fuels, and weapons. Similarly, both the ESG examples, the iShares USA ESG Aware, and Select ETFs exclude coal, tobacco, and weapons.

Exclusions are not always based on what the company does. Sometimes they are based on how they do it. Many strategies exclude any company with a significant controversy (such as a human rights violation), or for having received a fine for environmental pollution. Another way portfolio managers use negative screens is to exclude companies that fall below a certain threshold of ESG performance (e.g., they fall in the bottom quartile of ESG scores for their industry).

Negative screening sounds straightforward in principle. However, it can be tricky in practice. It is easy to say you want to exclude alcohol, but what does that actually mean? Do you exclude just the manufacturers, or the liquor stores as well? What about the bars that serve alcohol? Restaurants? And what do you do with the global conglomerate that generates most of its revenue from food sales but derives a small percentage of its revenues from selling beer? Or the advertising firm that has large contracts with the beverage industry?

2. Positive/Best-in-Class Screening

Positive screening is the process of including in a portfolio companies based on specific criteria. Inclusion could be based on whether a company provides a desirable product or service (such as organic food, renewable energy, or affordable housing). It could be determined by membership in a particular group or campaign. For example, companies in the RE100 (a global initiative bringing together the world's most influential businesses) have committed to procuring 100 percent of their electricity from renewable energy. Some strategies include any company that scores higher than a minimum ESG rating.

Another form of positive screening is known as *best-in-class*. This approach buys the companies that score better on ESG criteria than their peers. This strategy is often used to ensure adequate diversification across industries and sectors. For example, if a portfolio goal is to lower the carbon footprint, you could end up with a heavy concentration in tech stocks and financials while having low or no exposure to energy, mining, or manufacturing. By holding the best in each sector rather than the best overall, the portfolio can maintain a balanced exposure. This approach also appeals to some investors who want to reward the leaders and omit the laggards.

Investment strategies using positive screens can dial in the degree to which they want to focus on more sustainable companies. If you buy all the companies scoring average or above, you have a well-diversified strategy that might perform much like the overall market. If you only buy the top 10 percent of performers, you get a true leaders portfolio. However, it will be less diversified and could differ markedly from the market in performance.

The iShares ETFs in our ESG example use a version of positive screening to choose the companies they hold. The Select strategy is pickier, looking for higher scores than the Aware version. Thus, it has fewer holdings and a greater emphasis on sustainability. However, it will experience greater tracking variance relative to the market portfolio.

3. Norms-Based Screening

Norms-based screens use the principles or standards set by a third-party organization to define what companies should be included or excluded from a portfolio. For example, one popular approach is to use the 10 principles from the UN Global Compact:

Human Rights

1. Businesses should support and respect the protection of internationally proclaimed human rights; and
2. make sure they are not complicit in human rights abuses.

Labor

3. Businesses should uphold the freedom of association and the effective recognition of the right to collective bargaining;
4. the elimination of all forms of forced and compulsory labor;
5. the effective abolition of child labor; and

6. the elimination of discrimination in respect of employment and occupation.

Environment

7. Businesses should support a precautionary approach to environmental challenges;
8. undertake initiatives to promote greater environmental responsibility; and
9. encourage the development and diffusion of environmentally friendly technologies.

Anti-Corruption

10. Businesses should work against corruption in all its forms, including extortion and bribery.

Any business that does not conform to these norms would be excluded from a portfolio. A challenge with the norms-based approach is determining which companies don't make the grade. What exactly qualifies as the "effective recognition of the right to collective bargaining"? Do the employees have to have a union? What constitutes "elimination of discrimination"? Does a policy count? Or does the company need to meet some diversity threshold?

4. ESG Integration

ESG integration is a methodology whereby the investor incorporates environmental, social, and governance metrics in their evaluation of securities in an integrated approach, along with other factors. What that means in practice varies widely as there are now hundreds of strategies that claim to use this approach. It can include strategies where the manager primarily focuses on traditional financial analysis of firms and only considers an ESG issue if they believe it is particularly pressing. Or it can describe a process that selects securities first and foremost on ESG characteristics but also considers some traditional analysis.

So many strategies now claim to use ESG integration that the label itself has become largely meaningless. Investors need to dig deeper into the actual methodology to understand what process is employed. Compounding the complexity is that the lines between traditional analysis and ESG are blurring. In 2010 it was fairly clear what traditional financial analysis was and what nonfinancial or ESG analysis was. Over time, ESG metrics have become more a part of standard risk analysis. After all, a conventional investor is as worried as the sustainable investor about financial losses due to an environmental fine, a data breach, or a corruption charge.

A good example of where ESG and conventional analysis are merging is climate risk. Climate risk is defined by *transition risk* and *physical risk*. Transition risk describes the issues companies face due to the transition to a low-carbon economy. Are companies prepared for the ascendance of renewable energy as it becomes cheaper than fossil fuels? Are they prepared for the electrification of vehicles? Physical risk describes the impact that rising sea levels, flooding, heat, drought, and storms might have on businesses as the climate changes. Are the company's facilities in harm's way? Can they operate effectively in higher temperatures or in a drought? All investors, conventional and sustainable, should be concerned about these risks. Thus, it is not hard to imagine a time when all investment analysis integrates some ESG considerations.

5. Sustainable-Themed Investing

More and more investors are choosing to invest in themes or assets related to specific sustainable products or processes. Dozens of funds and ETFs invest solely in renewable energy. For example, you can invest in strategies that purchase the stocks of companies in the electric vehicle space or those that are focused on battery storage. There are water funds, sustainable agriculture funds, and green technology ETFs.

Some investors are forecasting high returns from these companies as they scale up. Others see their capital as a catalyst to accelerating the development of new technologies. Many view a themed approach as a way to participate positively in the massive transformation of business as the transition to a low-carbon economy gets going.

6. Impact/Community Investing

Impact investing, as we defined it at the beginning of Chapter 1, is one of the three main types of sustainable investing, along with ESG and SRI. Iroquois Valley Farms is an example of a single impact investment. Impact investing can also be seen as a methodology, akin to a focused version of a positive screening process by only targeting investments that solve a particular social or environmental problem. Some portfolio managers reserve a portion of an overall allocation to private impact investments in order to boost the overall sustainability of a public market fund.

Community investing refers to impact investing that is specifically directed to traditionally underserved individuals or communities. Good examples of community investing are community development financial institutions (CDFIs). CDFIs provide financial services and loans in low-income communities and to people who lack access to financing.

Both of these strategies are methods for investors to catalyze positive change in a direct manner. By focusing the investment narrowly on a specific issue or location, the investor's capital can be transformational. Another benefit is that the investor might even be able to see the direct effect of their capital at work.

7. Corporate Engagement and Shareholder Action

Engagement is the use of shareholder power to influence corporate behavior. It takes many forms but is grounded in the fact that shareholders are the actual owners of the company. As such, the shareholders have influence over it. Public company ownership is usually dispersed across thousands of shareholders, few of which hold more than a fraction of a percent of the company. Investors and investment managers can amplify their influence by forming and joining coalitions. Some of these coalitions focus on direct engagement at the company level, while others push for regulatory changes or standardization in disclosure.

An example of these coalitions is the Climate Action 100, an investor initiative to ensure the world's largest corporate greenhouse gas emitters take action on climate change. There are 545 investors with a collective $52 trillion in assets under management engaged in this initiative. The size and breadth of that coalition makes it hard for companies to ignore their requests.

Active shareholder engagement is important to many sustainable investors. They want their manager to use their voice and vote to push for positive change. Engagement is a method that many ESG, SRI, and impact strategies employ.

Summary

In this chapter we outlined the seven most common methodologies investors use in constructing sustainable portfolios. In Chapter 3 we take a look at who is investing in these ways.

CHAPTER 3

Who Is Investing for Sustainability?

ACCORDING TO THE Global Sustainable Investment Alliance, at the beginning of 2020 there was $35.3 trillion invested on a sustainable basis across the globe.[1] The group of investors that invest for sustainability is large and diverse, ranging from early pioneers to those working on the cutting edge today. They have developed different strategies and methodologies depending on who they are, and for whom they invest. In this chapter we will look at each of the following types of investors:

1. Sovereign Wealth Funds
2. Pension Plans
3. College and University Endowments
4. Faith-based Investors
5. Family Offices and Foundations
6. Financial Advisors and Wealth Managers
7. Individual Investors
8. Institutional Asset Managers
9. Investor Coalitions

1. Sovereign Wealth Funds

A sovereign wealth fund (SWF) manages the surplus assets of a national government. They are not the assets of a central bank, which are used for liquidity provision or currency stabilization. Rather, they are the assets the country has developed (often through natural resources such as oil) and monetized, and which they plan to rely on to provide for their citizens' future needs. As such, these funds have long-term investment horizons and thousands, if not millions, of beneficiaries.

25

In 2017 Abu Dhabi, Kuwait, New Zealand, Norway, Saudi Arabia, and Qatar formed the One Planet SWF Working Group. The Group created an ESG Framework around three principles: alignment, ownership, and integration. The principles focus on climate change as a risk to portfolios—significant given that all the members are states that derive a substantial portion of their wealth from oil and gas (with the possible exception of New Zealand):

> *Principle 1: Alignment.* Build climate change considerations into decision-making.
> *Principle 2: Ownership.* Encourage companies to address material climate change issues.
> *Principle 3: Integration.* Integrate the consideration of climate change risks and opportunities into investment management to improve resilience of long-term investment portfolios.[2]

The largest SWF is the Norwegian Government Pension Fund Global (GPFG). It was established in 1990 to manage revenues from the oil that Norway extracts from the North Sea. With more than $1.1 trillion in assets (at the time of writing), the fund is so large it holds more than 9,000 stocks from 73 countries and is estimated to own more than 1 percent of all public equities globally. Norway's Ministry of Finance is responsible for the assets and has appointed Norges Bank Investment Management as the fund manager.

The Norwegian pension fund is a leader in sustainable investing. In 2004 the Norwegian Parliament adopted ethical guidelines for the GPFG, specifically prohibiting investments that would put the fund at risk of contributing to systematic human rights violations, serious environmental damage, and gross corruption. The GPFG now also excludes investments in companies that make or sell certain weapons, produce tobacco, or derive more than 30 percent of their revenue from thermal coal. In March 2019 it announced plans to sell most of the holdings in oil and gas. The GPFG also reserves a 3 percent allocation of the portfolio for social (impact) investments.

2. Pension Plans

A pension plan is an employer-sponsored retirement plan that provides income during retirement or upon termination of a worker's employment. Traditionally, these assets were managed collectively by employers in defined benefit plans— so called because they would provide the retiree with a set benefit (such as 40 percent of base pay for the rest of their life). Pension funds for big companies can grow to be large—IBM, Ford, Boeing, and GE all have plans with more than $50 billion in assets.

The real pension behemoths are those managed for national and local government employees. Dozens of these pension funds have assets in excess of $100 billion, with many that consider sustainability in their investment process. In fact, 10 of the largest 15 pension funds in the world have committed to integrating ESG principles. The Japan Government Pension Investment Fund (GPIF), the largest pension fund in the world—with more than $1.5 trillion in assets—leads the way in Asia. Its ESG approach focuses on stewardship and managing externalities:

> "We at Government Pension Investment Fund (GPIF) are responsible for providing stable income to multiple generations of retirees, and thus our investment horizon spans several decades. Within such a long timeframe, the latent risks associated with negative externalities generated by individual companies—that is, environmental, social, and governance (ESG) issues—will very likely materialize. This has the potential to significantly impair the value of the assets we invest in. Similarly, since our portfolio includes virtually all investable assets, the sustainability and stable expansion of the market as a whole is critical in protecting and growing the pension reserves entrusted to us by beneficiaries. We work to limit these externalities and promote the holistic growth of the market through ESG investment."[3]

In Europe the two largest Dutch pension funds, ABP (with more than $500 billion worth of assets) and PFZW (with more than $200 billion) are credited with driving much of the innovation in ESG investing. In 2008 they teamed up with their asset managers to develop GRESB (Global Real Estate Sustainability Benchmark), enabling them to measure the sustainability performance of their real estate companies.

In the United States, California has the two largest pension funds: the Public Employee Retirement System (CalPERS), at $426 billion in assets, and the State Teachers' Retirement System (CalSTRS), at $259 billion. New York State's Common Retirement Fund and New York City's Retirement System are the next largest, with $225 billion in each fund. All four of these pension plans use an ESG approach to their investment strategy.

CalPERS was a leader in sustainable investing before the term ESG was coined. As far back as the 1980s, CalPERS was using its position as one of the world's largest shareholders to influence company behavior. It was a founding signatory of the UN Principles of Responsible Investing in 2006. In 2015 CalPERS began requiring all their third-party managers to identify and articulate ESG in their investment process. Since they employ dozens of managers, and dozens more apply each year, this requirement pushed many managers into developing an ESG process.

It is the work of these large pension funds that has made ESG the dominant form of sustainable investing. Their early focus on data collection, standardization, and application has paved the way for other investors. Their sheer size encouraged the companies they own shares in to respond to their requests for disclosure and better sustainability performance. And their role as fiduciaries has given other investors comfort that integrating ESG is a prudent risk-based investment process.

3. College and University Endowments

Colleges and universities often have endowments that help fund their educational programs. These endowments can be extraordinarily large, particularly in U.S. Ivy League schools such as Harvard and Yale, each with assets in the tens of billions of dollars. Several of these schools have earned reputations for being proactive on social issues through their investment portfolios. The fossil fuel debate has featured prominently on college campuses, as a large student movement led by 350.org called for school endowments to shed oil and gas holdings. Elsewhere, many credit the ultimate success of the South African divestment movement to student movements on college campuses.

Endowments can find it challenging to invest sustainably because of their unique set of stakeholders. The source of the capital (the alumni) and the beneficiaries of it (the students and professors) do not always see eye-to-eye on investment policy. The administration, at which the students usually direct their ire, are caught in the middle and frequently have limited influence on how the trustees and investment committees make decisions. 350.org's success, as evidenced by hundreds of institutions of higher education committing to divestment, is all the more surprising when one considers that many of these institutions' alumni are leaders of the fossil fuel industry. Perhaps because of the varying interests of their stakeholders, endowments invested for sustainability more often adopt an ESG approach as opposed to focusing on SRI or impact.

Yale University's endowment, under the direction of its legendary CIO, the late David Swensen, came to set a trend for investing in general. Many investors emulate its approach to asset allocation and diversification. Yale was one of the first institutions to formally address the ethical responsibilities of institutional investors. In 1969 a small group of Yale faculty and graduate students convened a seminar on the ethical, economic, and legal implications of institutional investments. This eventually led to the 1972 publication of the book *The Ethical*

Investor: Universities and Corporate Responsibility,[4] which offers guidelines on how a university should factor in requests from members of its community (in addition to considerations of economic return) when making investment decisions and exercising rights as a shareholder.

When the Yale Corporation adopted the book's guidelines, it became the first major university to resolve this issue by abandoning the role of passive institutional investor.

Yale's new approach put them at the forefront of the South African and Sudan divestment movements and later led to their divestment from assault weapons retailers and private prisons. In 2014 Swensen wrote a letter about climate change that was sent to every investment manager that Yale employed to manage their endowment. In the letter he gave explicit instructions on how the managers should incorporate climate change into their portfolio decisions:

"Yale asks that when making investment decisions on the University's behalf, you assess the greenhouse gas footprint of the prospective investments, the direct costs of the consequences of climate change on expected returns, and the costs of policies aimed at reducing greenhouse gas emissions on expected returns. Simply put, those investments with relatively small greenhouse gas footprints will be advantaged relative to those investments with relatively large greenhouse gas footprints."[5]

This letter effectively forced all of Yale's managers to begin adopting ESG methodologies. The managers began divesting from the dirtiest fossil fuel producers, namely thermal coal producers and tar sands operators, and began proactively searching for companies working on climate solutions.

4. Faith-Based Investors

Faith-based investors are often considered the pioneers of socially responsible investing. Historically, people of faith have sought to avoid companies profiting from issues to which they object. Quakers steered clear of slave labor, Muslims spurned interest income, and Catholics avoided contraceptives. This negative screening approach became synonymous with SRI. However, the religious community was doing more than just excluding companies.

In 1971 Paul Neuhauser, a lawyer and member of the Episcopal Church, drafted the first religious shareholder proposal with a social theme and filed it at General Motors. The proposal requested that GM withdraw its business from South Africa until apartheid was abolished. This precipitated the founding of the Interfaith Center on Corporate Responsibility (ICCR) and a shareholder advocacy movement. The ICCR comprises 64 faith-based members, including Catholic, Presbyterian, Methodist, and Unitarian organizations. They also have more than 100 members who, though not faith-based, join the ICCR in active shareholder engagements with companies. Many of the issues the ICCR espouses (such as climate change, health, and human rights) are not necessarily religious ones.

In June 2015 Pope Francis published his second encyclical, *Laudato si'*, with the subtitle *On Care for Our Common Home*.[6] The pope wrote about how the pursuit of short-term economic gain is exacerbating climate change, waste, biodiversity loss, and poverty. With this powerful publication, the pope effectively announced that the faithful SRI investor and the ESG investor have common cause across many issues.

5. Family Offices and Foundations

Wealthy families often set up a family office, which is effectively an investment advisor for the family's assets. A family office might start a foundation to direct their philanthropy efforts and reduce taxes. Unlike many of the previous categories of investors, the family office, or family foundation, is normally not beholden to other stakeholders. They can do what they want with their money, and they can choose to invest in low- or high-returning assets as they see fit. This flexibility allows them to pursue a sustainable investing program with more emphasis on solving social and environmental issues they care about through impact investing and philanthropy.

In 2010 Bill Gates and Warren Buffett started The Giving Pledge, whereby extremely wealthy signatories commit to giving over half their money to charity and philanthropic causes. There are now more than 220 global signatories representing more than $1 trillion. This commitment builds on a long tradition of U.S. philanthropists, such as Carnegie, Ford, Rockefeller, Kellogg, and Stanford.

Some of the wealthiest families have foundations that are so large they are making significant impacts on their philanthropic causes. The Bill and Melinda Gates Foundation has granted more than $50 billion since inception—mainly toward improving health and education and combating poverty. Although their goal to eradicate malaria has not yet been achieved, they have helped prevent 1.5 billion cases and saved 7.6 million lives.[7] Michael Bloomberg's foundation has helped fund a series of critical climate organizations, including Beyond Carbon—an initiative to get the U.S. on a path to 100 percent clean power by electrifying buildings and transportation, and replacing coal and gas in electricity production.

By law foundations are required to donate 5 percent of their assets each year. The remaining 95 percent of the assets remain in the foundation and need to be invested. Some families have begun to invest their foundation assets based on impact investing principles in order to align their investments with the family's mission statement. Foundation assets are in some ways the perfect vehicle to create impact. Because the assets have already been donated, the family is not relying on them for future liabilities. Thus, they can choose to invest in high-risk projects such as a speculative renewable energy technology. Or they could choose to provide capital to a bank to finance microloans to the poor and accept low expected returns. The flexibility foundations have on risk and return can provide opportunities for outsized impact.

6. Financial Advisors and Wealth Managers

Financial advisors and wealth managers have been slower to adopt sustainable investing. There are a host of reasons for their reluctance, some valid, some less so. Typically, advisors want to see many years of strong financial performance before they place client assets into an investment strategy. Since many of the traditional SRI funds from the 1980s and 1990s tended to underperform, few advisors embraced this form of investing. When ESG funds generating market-like returns became available in the 2010s, there were limited offerings, usually only in the large-cap equity asset class.

The number of advisors offering sustainable investing grew slowly and steadily for decades, primarily through word of mouth and community building. In 1988 the First Affirmative Financial Network was founded. First Affirmative is a nationwide network of financial advisors who specialize in SRI and help customers build portfolios aligned with both their values and their financial goals. In 1990 First Affirmative convened The SRI Conference. It became one of the first gatherings of its kind, bringing socially responsible investors and asset managers together with the common goal of directing the flow of capital in more positive, healthy, and transformative ways. By 2019 this small grassroots group of independent advisors had grown considerably, and more than 1,000 attended that year's conference.

More recently, the large wealth management firms have used their abundant resources and scale to get into sustainable investing quickly. UBS is the world's largest wealth manager and has almost 10,000 advisors on staff around the globe. In 2020 it became the first major global financial institution to make sustainable investments the preferred solution for all private clients. By the end of 2020, core sustainable investments had already reached $793 billion, or 19 percent of all client-invested assets at UBS.[8]

7. Individual Investors

When surveyed, individual investors expressed keen interest in sustainable investing (see Figure 4). Morgan Stanley's Institute for Sustainable Investing has been tracking this issue, and demand seems to be increasing on an already substantial base.

Figure 4: Interest in Sustainable Investing

How interested are you in sustainable investing (also known as impact investing), which is the practice of making investments in companies or funds which aim to achieve market-rate financial returns while pursuing positive social and/or environmental impact?

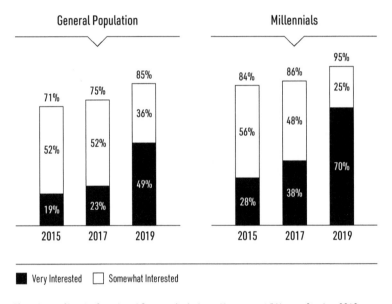

Source: "Sustainable Signals: Growth and Opportunity in Asset Management," Morgan Stanley, 2019.

Until the last few years, individual investors found it difficult to source sustainable investments. For example, there were only a small number of SRI funds, and finding those that fit the individual's personal values was challenging. It was only recently that a diverse selection of ESG mutual funds and ETFs across many asset classes became available. Their advisors also needed education programs to learn how to invest sustainably as well as ESG research tools to select investments. Thankfully, both have emerged with the proliferation of ESG funds. Advisors still reluctant to offer sustainable investing may not be aware of the resources newly available to them. It is also possible that many are underestimating how many of their clients are interested in sustainable investing (an issue we will address in the next section). And impact investing was, and is, hard to do for most given the high minimums and extra due diligence required.

Fortunately, some of these challenges have been alleviated by the explosion in ESG investment products. In the U.S. in 2020 alone, 70 funds and ETFs were launched that emphasized sustainable investing.[9] U.S. investors can now choose from more than 400 ESG funds and ETFs across most asset classes, in active and in passive form, with weak or strong tilts to sustainability. There are even thematic funds that allow an investor to express their preference for issues like social justice, climate change, and biodiversity. It is also easier for the SRI investor who wants a portfolio attuned to their specific individual values. The minimum account size for separately managed accounts has dropped from the millions to the tens of thousands of dollars.

However, in another sense the challenge has become thornier. As we discussed in Chapter 1, the investment product providers are not using a common language to describe their offerings. That makes it difficult to determine what's what. Compounding this issue is the fact that many of the original SRI funds, and now even many conventional funds, have rebranded or recharacterized their process as ESG. Fortunately, investors and advisors also have more research tools at their disposal. For example, both MSCI and Morningstar now publish free ESG data and ratings on mutual funds and ETFs. We will look at some of these tools in more detail in Chapter 8.

8. Institutional Asset Managers

Institutional asset managers consider all the previous categories of investors their clients. In fact, every one of the world's top 25 asset managers now offers ESG products. For example, BlackRock is the largest asset manager in the world, with more than $7 trillion in assets under management. It offers an abundant array of sustainable options in equity, fixed income, real estate, and alternative asset classes. It has ESG funds and ETFs, thematic options, and impact strategies. Of the 10 largest ESG ETFs, BlackRock manages seven. Clearly, it is committed to providing an array of sustainable investment products.

Being the largest manager, BlackRock receives an extra share of scrutiny. Many activist investors have questioned its commitment to sustainability. These activists feel BlackRock could be using its heavyweight status to influence companies more. Given that BlackRock is the largest shareholder of many public companies, often owning several percent, they feel the firm should use its voice and shareholder votes to influence change.

Every year since 2012 the CEO of BlackRock, Larry Fink, has exercised the voice option by publishing an open letter to all the public companies in which it invests. In 2018 he encouraged all companies to articulate their purpose and how they benefit all stakeholders, not just shareholders. In 2020 he wrote that "climate risk is investment risk."[10] And in 2021 he called on companies to prepare for the transition to net-zero emissions.[11]

BlackRock's historical proxy voting record is less convincing. From 2015 to 2019, it voted on 1,033 ESG-related resolutions and voted in favor of only 3 percent of them, whereas other managers, such as PIMCO, AQR, and Nuveen, supported more than 60 percent.[12]

9. Investor Coalitions

Many sustainable investors share a desire to get companies to behave more responsibly to people and planet. For some, it is the primary goal, and they use their voice and vote as shareholders to promote change through engagement. Companies are more likely to be swayed by larger numbers of shareholders, so many investors have formed coalitions to amplify their influence. The following table shows a few of the larger coalitions represented.

Organization	Members	Assets (USD)	Example Member
Principles of Responsible Investing (PRI)	3,038	103 trillion	Nuveen
Climate Action 100	545	52 trillion	CalPERS
Net Zero Asset Owners	35	5 trillion	Allianz
Net Zero Asset Managers	73	32 trillion	BlackRock
Global Investor Coalition on Climate Change	515	35 trillion	UBS
Interfaith Center on Corporate Responsibility (ICCR)	203	N/A	Presbyterian Church (USA)

The original—and still largest—of these bodies is the Principles of Responsible Investing (PRI). The PRI is a very broad tent, with more than 3,000 signatories representing more than $100 trillion in assets. Other coalitions have formed to provide a more targeted approach. For example, the Climate Action 100 group has 545 members who concentrate their engagement efforts on the 100 or so companies with the largest carbon footprints and greenhouse gas emissions. Signers take proactive action together to encourage these companies to reduce their carbon footprints.

Investors also form coalitions to address specific issues or companies. Green Century Funds has led multiple investor initiatives since 2012 to encourage more responsible palm oil production. Frequently, investors coalesce around regulatory proposals. In 2020 hundreds of investors submitted comment letters and signed petitions protesting the Department of Labor's proposed change to proxy voting rules. In 2021, 43 investors signed on to an ultimately successful effort to stop Barclays Bank from funding a private prison.

The US SIF estimates that one-third of all professionally managed money in the U.S. and one-half of all managed assets in Europe are managed with sustainability criteria. The vast majority of these assets are categorized as ESG.[13] The biggest SWFs, pension funds, endowments, family offices, financial advisors, and asset managers employ ESG and are driving large sums into it. SRI remains a niche reserved for the wealthier individual investor who has a portfolio large enough to warrant an SMA, and a financial advisor adept at providing a bespoke solution. Impact investing is done by both institutions and individuals, but since it usually involves private placements, it only commands a couple percent of an overall portfolio.

Summary

A broad array of investors, both individual and institutional, from small to large, have chosen to invest sustainably. It is no longer a niche, but a mainstream approach. Why have so many investors made this choice? What is their motivation? That is what we turn to next, in Chapter 4.

CHAPTER 4

Exploring Motivations

MANY SURVEYS SHOW that a majority of today's investors are interested in sustainable investing. For example, Morgan Stanley's 2019 annual survey of individual investors found that more than 75 percent state a preference for sustainable investment strategies, and more than 90 percent of millennials say they are interested.[1] Investors are putting their money where their mouth is: Flows into ESG mutual funds and ETFs in the U.S. doubled in 2019, and doubled again in 2020. Having established that today's investors are interested in sustainable investing, we turn now to addressing the questions this raises:

- Why are they so keen to invest for sustainability?
- What do they hope to achieve?

The Three *Returns* of Sustainable Investing: Financial, Societal, and Personal

The goal of investing is to earn a financial return commensurate with the risk taken with your capital. However, while money alone may be motivation enough for the conventional investor, the sustainable investor is looking for other sources of return as well—above and beyond the financial. Sustainable investors also seek to promote a better world, through the societal return achieved by improving outcomes for both people and the planet. In addition, many are looking to feel better about how their capital is employed. The personal return shows up in the form of emotional benefits for the sustainable investor.

While some investors might think that investing is only about making the greatest financial return possible—with other considerations being irrational—that is not the way normal investors behave. Meir Statman, a leading expert in behavioral finance, begins his excellent book *Finance for Normal People* with the following example.[2] He imagines a man trying to decide whether to buy his beloved a rose for $10 or to just give her the $10. After all, a rose has no utilitarian benefits—she can't eat it, save it, or trade it. But the gift of a rose says and means much more than $10. It has expressive benefits; it sends a clear signal to his sweetheart. And it has emotional benefits, generating warm feelings. Statman makes the point that normal people understand this. Normal people consider not only the utilitarian benefits of a decision but also the expressive and emotional benefits.

When you buy a car, you examine the utilitarian benefits, such as gas mileage. However, it is likely that you would also consider the car's expressive benefits, such as what it says about you to drive that car. You might also think about how the car makes you feel.

As another example, if you are thinking about renovating your kitchen, you would probably evaluate how that investment will increase the value of your home. However, you would also consider how much more you would enjoy your new kitchen, how inviting it would be, and how your family and guests would feel about it.

We do this with many of our decisions, investing included. With investing, the utilitarian benefit is your financial return. However, there can also be a host of expressive and emotional benefits. There are too many of these to compile an exhaustive list here (and everyone is different), so we limit our review to some of the more common motivations of sustainable investors.

The Financial Returns of Sustainable Investing

Many investors, both individual and institutional, remain confused about what to expect in terms of financial returns from sustainable investing. The money management industry, seeking to sell more products, routinely claims that sustainable investing has lower risk, or higher returns, or both, while also allowing you to align your investments with your values and save the planet at the same time. We have heard these promises before. And we remain skeptical of such claims. As you will learn in Chapter 6 where we review the findings from academic research, it is not hard to find examples of sustainable funds that have underperformed, or sin stocks (such as tobacco companies) that have outperformed.

The reality is that when investing you have to make a choice, because the type of sustainable investing you employ can have a large impact on both your risk and your returns. Whether you choose impact investing, socially responsible investing, or ESG investing has perhaps the greatest implications for your range of outcomes.

The Financial Returns of Impact Investing

Impact investing, as we define it, is putting your capital into private equity or private debt, or even individual projects. The private markets can be like the Wild West: Anything can happen. Financial returns on impact investing can be extreme. Losing 100 percent of your capital, or making 10 times your investment, are both possible. And it can take a long time to know which it will be, as many of these investments have long lock-up periods, typically between 5 and 10 years. You may not be able to access your capital during the lock-up period. And you might only receive an estimated value of your investment once a year. While there are some impact funds that provide an experience closer to market-like returns, in private markets it is incumbent upon the investor to perform robust due diligence so they are able to understand all the risks. The impact investor is willing to accept these risks, and the extreme range of returns, as they are first and foremost seeking social return. They want to produce an improved environmental or social outcome—the financial return is secondary. And it should not be surprising that there are large variations in returns, because returns are not the primary focus and risks are concentrated in a small number of individual investments.

The Financial Returns of Socially Responsible Investing

Unlike impact investing, SRI can be easily implemented through public markets. Thus, the range of return outcomes is narrower than in private markets and more akin to conventional investing in that regard. However, SRI investors seek to balance the pursuit of financial return with the incorporation of their values. Incorporating their personal values changes the security selection process and can override return considerations. For example, many SRI investors will exclude tobacco, gaming, alcohol, and gun company stocks regardless of their return potential. If the investor has many no-go areas (i.e., their personal values preclude holding many stocks, or even entire industries), they should expect greater variation in returns because their portfolios are less diversified. As you will see in Chapter 6, SRI funds tend to underperform. While it is not necessarily the case that the values exclusions create underperformance in and of themselves, less diversified portfolios with higher management fees (you are paying a fund manager to perform the screening process) tend to struggle to provide returns earned by similar index funds. However, SRI investors are often willing to accept financial returns below that of the market because they also place importance on the personal return.

The Financial Returns of ESG Investing

ESG investing is different from the preceding categories. Most modern ESG strategies are not based on what is individually important to the investor. Instead they are about what is important to the investments—companies are selected based on how they are dealing with the environmental, social, and governance issues most likely to affect them financially. It is more an investment-led strategy rather than the client-led strategies of SRI and impact investing. As a result, ESG strategies can be used by many people because they are not tailored to any individual in particular.

In addition, the concept of sustainability is not as black and white as an individual's values—there are lots of grays. Most companies exist on a spectrum between poor performance and good performance on ESG issues. As a result, strategies can be built with varying degrees of tilt toward sustainability. You can have an ESG strategy built to deliver returns close to a market benchmark (minimizing what is referred to as tracking error, or tracking variance, risk). Many ESG index funds and ETFs do just that. An investor that chooses one of these ESG strategies, compared to the SRI or impact investor, will more often achieve market-like rates of return. However, the ESG investor could also choose a strategy with more focus, perhaps investing in only sustainability leaders. Such funds tend to have more variable performance.

The bottom line is that the financial returns you get from sustainable investing depend largely on what kind of sustainable investing you pursue. We now turn to examining the social returns sustainable investors look for.

The Social Returns of Sustainable Investing

One of the most common questions about sustainable investing is whether it has any impact. If you invest your money in a sustainable strategy, does anything happen? Does the world become a better place? Do companies get the message? Do they respond? These questions are about the social return. The answer is less definitive than with the financial return: At the end of the day, you can count your money; a number is published for the return. On the other hand, some social outcomes (like cleaner air, better health, happier employees) are hard to measure, and it can be even harder to determine to whom or what they should be attributed. In many cases we are unable to directly link causality between the investment and the outcome. We delve into the research on this issue in Chapter 7 where we explore how sustainable investors are changing the world. In the current chapter we describe the levers of influence the sustainable investor employs—how their investment choices direct companies, and capitalism overall, to change for the better.

Many sustainability-minded people choose greener products, eco-friendly alternatives, organic food, or fair trade products because they believe that doing so makes the world a better place. With consumer products, the logic is straightforward. The more people buy sustainable alternatives, the more the providers will profit, at the expense of less sustainable ones. The laws of supply and demand apply. How does this work with investing?

Unlike consumer products, if you do not buy a stock, it does not just sit in inventory. By avoiding investing in a company's stock, you are not preventing capital from flowing to the company—because the stock is already owned by other investors. (We explore the effects in greater detail in Chapter 6.) With that said, when sustainable investors buy an ESG fund, they are demonstrating demand for sustainability and sending a signal to the markets that they want more. This has many downstream effects, including:

- Building capacity for sustainable investing.
- Changing what investors demand.
- Supporting active shareholder engagement with companies.

Through their actions, sustainable investors are causing capitalism to evolve. In Chapter 7 we will explore the research on how sustainable investors are forcing companies to change behavior. For now, we will show how the trend to sustainable investing is causing the providers of investment products to react.

Building Capacity for Sustainable Investing

Investing in a sustainable fund over a conventional one is much like purchasing any green product—the laws of supply and demand apply. The sustainable investor sends a signal to the marketplace that there is demand for sustainable investment products. When more investors signal their intention to invest sustainably, investment managers launch more products in the space, making it easier for further investment. Through their actions, sustainable investors act as catalysts for others to do the same. And competition in the space leads to lower costs, creating more demand—and a virtuous circle evolves.

While sustainable investing is growing rapidly, we are still at an early stage. When you ask for a sustainable investment solution from your financial advisor, they notice. They might say no to you, and to the next person, but if more than a few clients ask, they will recognize that they need to create a solution. The same thing happens when you ask your bank, brokerage firm, custody platform, retirement plan, or wherever you invest. You are sending a signal—a catalyst.

Sustainable investors tend to pay more in management fees. These fees pay for the research, the data, and the systems that go into selecting more sustainable companies. This has become a big business. Gone are the days when ESG research was done primarily by nonprofits, academics, and small think tanks. The largest market research companies, including MSCI, Morningstar, Bloomberg, Reuters, and S&P, have bought up many of the early entrants. They have also developed in-house capabilities. As more and more investment management firms buy this research, it funds further development, creating a virtuous circle as the data gets better and better. Today it is easier than ever for investors to make distinctions between companies on sustainability performance. This has important ramifications for companies.

Changing What Investors Demand

Much has been made of the predatory and rapacious nature of capitalism. At its worst, the economic system we have chosen does create some poor outcomes. When corporations are caught spoiling the environment, mistreating workers, or building unsafe products, sometimes their defense has been that they did it in the name of profit. They *had to,* because the market demands rising profits. And it demands profits frequently, asking companies to report their financial results each and every quarter.

Who *is* the market? Who is demanding profits in such fashion? It is Wall Street, the analysts working for the big investment banks harassing companies on their quarterly earnings calls, examining every penny earned and spent. If a company fails to deliver good numbers, or the analysts dislike the results, they will sell or issue a negative rating, causing other investors to sell. The stock price will suffer and management will be punished. If you ask the analysts why they are so demanding, they will say it is because they are protecting their clients' capital. Who are their clients? They are the investment managers who manage the trillions of dollars in pension funds and mutual funds. For whom are they managing those assets? It is you and me—whether the money is in your retirement plan or Sam's, or in Larry's IRA, it is our money.

It is a bit shocking to realize that collectively we are this so-called market—the market driving companies to do all manner of things, good and bad, in the name of profit. We doubt you asked British Petroleum to cut corners on the safety inspections of their offshore oil wells so they could save a few dollars and make their quarterly earnings estimate. It is not hard to understand that taking such shortcuts could lead to the Deepwater Horizon disaster, the biggest oil spill ever, and record fines of $65 billion. No investor asked Volkswagen to cheat on emissions tests so they could advance their goal of becoming the world's largest car company. However, it is also not hard to have foreseen that their stock might drop sharply if they were caught. (The stock fell 25 percent on the announcement.)

While investors did not send those messages (at least not directly), they might have inadvertently sent a message to investment managers to maximize profits at all costs over the short term. By not speaking up they were accepting this model of capitalism without objection. More and more investors are desirous of sending a different message. They want sustainability. They want their investment managers to consider all costs, including the costs to people and the planet. And they prefer companies to focus on building value over the long term.

As you will learn in Chapter 7, as more investors demand sustainability, more investment managers and more companies are responding. This is how capitalism evolves. By becoming a sustainable investor, you join the growing chorus of investors clamoring for more sustainability. How many investors are sending this message now? It is currently estimated that 33 percent of all professionally managed assets in the U.S. consider sustainability criteria. In Europe, it is 50 percent. Investment managers, as well as companies, have noticed.

Supporting Active Shareholder Engagement with Companies

Public companies are noticing because they are now being asked about sustainability from the investment community. Many sustainable investors expect their investment managers to engage with the companies in which they invest. Engagement takes many forms, but at its core it is an effort by investors to encourage companies to perform better on sustainability.

Most public companies have an investor relations department. Much of their work is supplying the market with financial reports, such as balance sheets and income statements, and explaining what this or that footnote means. They prepare quarterly presentations and set up the calls where their company executives explain results to analysts and investment managers. Their job is to present the company in the most favorable light possible so that it is more attractive to investors. Historically, this was all about making a financial case. But investment managers are starting to ask questions about what the company is doing for people and the planet, in addition to profits. Sustainable investment managers start with the questions and then use several approaches to encourage companies to do better. These efforts generally start out friendly and then increase in pressure. They include, ranked from low commitment to high:

- Letter-writing.
- Proxy voting.
- Meeting with company representatives.

- Group dialogue.
- Sign-on letter.
- Meeting with the board or CEO.
- Filing a shareholder resolution.
- Book and records request.
- *Vote No* campaign against director re-election.
- Running a candidate for the board.
- Lawsuit.

Most companies don't want lawsuits. Most board members prefer to keep their positions. And dealing with a shareholder resolution is quite taxing for a public company. If the investor request is reasonable, most companies would rather acquiesce than fight it to the end—especially when many of their peers have already begun doing what the investors are asking. It's difficult to claim an inability to report greenhouse gas emissions when thousands of public companies already do so.

The Personal Returns of Sustainable Investing

Research into investor behavior has found that investing is an emotional endeavor. Profits can elicit euphoria, and losses can generate despair. Unfortunately these emotions often cause us to trade the wrong stocks at the wrong time. Subject to recency bias, we tend to buy the winners and sell the losers, and we buy after the market has gone up and sell after it has gone down. Buying high and selling low is not exactly a prescription for investment success. Yet it is what so many investors do. That is why much effort goes into tempering the emotions of investing. We hire investment advisors to keep us on track, we use index funds to maximize diversification, and we study market history to learn from the past. It works, but much like dieting works. As Michael Mauboussin, author of *More Than You Know* stated, "A quality investment philosophy is like a good diet: it only works if it is sensible over the long haul and you stick with it."[3]

A few megatrends have actually added to the emotional component of investing. Many of us are paying more attention to our investments. As we do so, we are becoming more aware of our capital, where it is going, and what it is doing:

- Our financial capital is becoming more important in our lives. Retirement lasts longer than it used to, and college education is more expensive than ever. Our investments are critical to our future, so we pay more attention to them.

- Who we entrust our capital to has changed. Our parents may have been able to rely on a company pension or Social Security. Today our 401(k)s and IRAs are our own responsibility. Whereas mom and dad trusted stockbrokers to select a few stocks, we use financial advisors that likely use index funds holding thousands of firms.
- The role of the company in society is changing. It is no longer as acceptable to maximize profits at all costs. Many of us want companies to look after people and the planet too.

Increased awareness leads many to want to be more intentional with their capital. There are millions of people who invest for sustainability, and there might be just as many personal reasons why they do so. Everyone has their own definition of the personal return they are looking for. We have identified some common themes around why people want to shift their capital to sustainability. What is your motivation? Do any of these resonate with you?

- Aligning your values.
- Voting your capital.
- Being part of the solution.
- Leaving it better than you found it.

Aligning Your Values

Sustainable investing has been described as *aligning your values*. In the broadest terms, it means your money is invested according to your beliefs and wants; you support companies doing things you approve of and avoid investing in those doing things you disapprove of. How does an investor align their money with their values? Let's look at some examples in impact investing, SRI, and ESG.

Some professional athletes, after becoming successful, want to regenerate the poor neighborhoods they grew up in. These generous souls can maximize their contributions through impact investing. By placing their money directly into the local community, perhaps by building more affordable housing or funding an after-school care program, their capital becomes a catalyst for real, immediate, impactful change.

Other investors have strong objections for certain products, like alcohol or tobacco. Maybe their family suffered from alcoholism or lung cancer. Maybe their religion shuns these habits. These investors are SRI investors. They can invest broadly in public equities and bonds while excluding only the offending companies. There are mutual funds that cater specifically to these investors. There are funds for Muslims, for Catholics, and for Presbyterians. There are LGBTQ-friendly and vegan-friendly funds. These funds can help an investor align at least some of their money to their individual concerns without having to build a portfolio from scratch, stock by stock. The main challenge is finding the fund that most closely aligns with your values.

Then there are investors who generally want to be part of the solution rather than part of the problem. They may want to push companies, and capitalism, in a better direction. Or they might be concerned about what kind of world they are leaving for future generations. The investment solution for these investors is ESG. As we mentioned earlier, since ESG strategies aren't normally tailored to individual taste, there are many more options for these investors. They can choose an ESG fund in almost every asset class now, so they can invest most of their portfolio for sustainability.

Voting Your Capital

Dan Esty, a professor at Yale and author of several books on sustainability, has described how concerned citizens are expanding their view of their role in society. For much of the 20th century, the citizen who wanted change focused on their role as a voter. Back then, the mechanism of change was influencing the policy or the politicians. Activism meant organizing, campaigning, writing letters to elected officials, and of course voting.

In contrast, concerned citizens of today also see opportunity in their roles as consumers, savers, and investors. While they vote with their ballots on election day, they vote with their capital every day. They have come to believe that where they spend, save, and invest their money has impact.[4]

In the late 1980s some college students built shantytowns on their university quads to protest apartheid in South Africa. They wanted their schools to divest from companies doing business there. Specifically, they wanted Coca-Cola, and others, to feel pressure from their investors to terminate business activities in the country until apartheid ended. This was a new form of political activism, the point of which was to isolate and delegitimize the government in South Africa, and ultimately change the politicians. However, the vehicle wasn't voting—it was capitalism. It was the power of the purse, not politics. Money was the lever. And it worked.

In the 1990s activists turned their attention to Nike for using sweatshop labor, and even child labor, in their Asian factories. Nike's initial response— tantamount to "it's not our problem because we don't own those factories"— was widely criticized and resulted in a consumer boycott. Eventually, Nike, and the broader apparel and footwear industry, developed supply chain standards and monitoring protocols to ensure compliance. Again, it worked.

Today we can choose organic produce, fair trade coffee, and ethically sourced and sewn apparel. In many instances these products are not demonstrably superior, and yet they cost a bit more. NYU Stern publishes a study each year of growth in sustainable brands. From 2013 to 2018 sustainability-marketed products grew seven times faster than conventional ones.[5] Consumers are voting with their wallets.

Being Part of the Solution

The environmentalist community has made it painfully clear that we should drive less, fly less, eat less red meat, stop using plastic, etc. The message is that we are part of the problem. It's not a pleasant message to hear over and over again. So we recycle and take our own reusable bags to the store. We carry our own water and coffee containers. We ride a bike or use public transportation. We buy organic and sustainable products. We would rather be part of the solution than part of the problem.

When it isn't too difficult, many of us will choose the sustainable option. Not many folks can stop driving altogether. However, electric cars are now competitive with gas cars, both on price and performance. The result is that more people are making the switch. The same is happening with sustainable investing. As more options become available, with lower prices and better performance, more and more investors are making the sustainable choice. They like to know their money is part of the solution, not part of the problem.

Leaving It Better than You Found It

Since the Industrial Revolution human progress has seen rapid growth. Whether you measure success by higher GDP, longer life spans, improved health, increased literacy, or greater wealth, mankind has benefited from capitalism to an extraordinary degree. Progress does not move in a straight line, and there certainly have been dark times. However, for the past 200 years it was generally assumed the next generation would have much to look forward to.

That might be why it is such a shock to realize this may no longer be the case. The threat of climate change, in particular, has called into question the idea that the future is bright. The science certainly suggests that we are at risk of entering a darker tomorrow. The increasingly dire predictions we hear and read about invariably come with an important admonition—humanity has brought this upon itself. We are going to leave it worse than we found it. However, along with the admonition comes a caveat: We can still change course and mitigate the worst-case scenarios.

The most oft-cited definition of sustainability is from the Brundtland Report of 1987: "Development that meets the needs of the present without compromising the ability of future generations to meet their own needs."[6] It is a simple definition. Yet it is profoundly motivating. Tom Steyer, the billionaire hedge fund manager turned political activist, was asked why he had committed his life to fighting climate change. His response? "Because I have kids and I can read."

Summary

In this chapter we explored what motivates the sustainable investor. Sustainable investors seek three types of returns. They want financial returns, like conventional investors. They seek a societal return, measured through positive change or impact. And they want a personal return, comprising a set of emotions they get from putting their money to work for good.

Part of the Solution

Sam banked at Wells Fargo for more than 20 years and was generally satisfied. In 2016 news broke that Wells Fargo employees had opened 1.5 million fake bank accounts and a further 500,000 fake credit card accounts in order to meet the aggressive sales targets their managers set for them. Sam wasn't happy about this, but he figured he wasn't directly affected, so he did nothing. In 2017 he learned that it was actually 3.5 million fake accounts and that the bank leadership fired 5,300 employees who opened the accounts rather than take responsibility for the unachievable sales targets they had set. This made Sam uncomfortable. Every time he went into the bank, he wondered what kind of pressure the employees were under and what they would have to try to sell him. Every time he saw an ATM, he felt bad that he was contributing to the bank's awful practices by virtue of being a client. Finally, it became too much, so he closed his accounts and moved his money to a local credit union. Now he no longer feels like part of the problem. When he goes by an ATM or a branch, he gets a little boost. His money isn't feeding more scandal. Instead, it is helping his credit union make loans to the local community and he now feels he is more a part of the solution.

CHAPTER 5

The Evolution of ESG Investing

A CCORDING TO THE US SIF Trends Report, of the $17.1 trillion invested on a sustainable basis as of the beginning of 2020, $16.6 trillion (more than 97 percent) was put into ESG strategies.[1] ESG's dominance in sustainable investing is remarkable given that it has only been around for about 15 years, whereas SRI has been in existence for several hundred. Even within that relatively short period, ESG has undergone important transformations. In this chapter we will examine the history of ESG and take a sneak peek at its potential future.

Before ESG There Was SRI

The foundations of ESG investing come from SRI. The earliest records of responsible investing are found in ancient religious texts, and clearly demonstrate that humans have been working on the intersection of money and values for a long time. SRI has a rich and well-documented history. You can find a summary of this history in Appendix A.

By the 2000s the foundational strategies for responsible investing were well established. Sustainable investors were employing negative screens to exclude problematic companies, positive screens to include companies making positive impacts, and engagement to encourage companies to behave more responsibly.

However, sustainable investors lacked the critical ingredient needed to raise their responsible investing to the next level, across more companies, and across more asset classes: data. Without a consistent set of metrics to compare companies, investors were left to cherry-pick them in an unsystematic manner from a limited number of firms on which they had information—it is difficult to apply robust investment management techniques across portfolios when you only have scattered information on a handful of companies.

Organizations were forming to solve these data and reporting issues, but they were just getting started. Among the first was CDP, founded in 2000 as the Carbon Disclosure Project. In 2002, the first year it asked companies to disclose their environmental footprint, only 245 companies responded. Such was the appetite for responsible investing in the years that followed, that by 2020 more than 9,600 companies reported to CDP.[2]

How ESG Began

The 2004 Environmental Program Finance Initiative Report, published by the United Nations, was the first to use the phrase "environmental, social, and corporate governance analysis."[3] The UN followed up this report with The Principles for Responsible Investment (PRI):

1. We will incorporate ESG issues into investment analysis and decision-making processes.
2. We will be active owners and incorporate ESG issues into our ownership policies and practices.
3. We will seek appropriate disclosure on ESG issues by the entities in which we invest.
4. We will promote acceptance and implementation of the principles within the investment industry.
5. We will work together to enhance our effectiveness in implementing the principles.
6. We will each report on our activities and progress toward implementing the principles.

As of March 2020 the PRI had 3,700 signatories representing more than $100 trillion in assets under management.[4] While not all of those assets are currently managed sustainably, the managers entrusted with them have signed onto the Principles. With so many investors signing on, the acceptance of responsible investing has grown, and so have the tools, techniques, and data available to practitioners.

ESG 1.0: The Ratings Era

In the earliest days of ESG, not many public companies reported on their environmental, social, and corporate governance performance. To be fair, they had not yet been asked by many investors for that kind of information. The prevailing model at the time was to report only what was legally required. The disclosures required comprised almost entirely financial information. For those companies that wanted to publish more, there was little guidance and few frameworks on how to report. And investors didn't know where to get the information, or how to compare one company to another.

Institutional investors typically bought information on companies they were considering investing in from equity research firms such as Goldman Sachs, Morgan Stanley, Merrill Lynch, and other investment banks and brokerage firms. The information was presented in analyst reports, which typically contained the analyst's opinion of whether the stock was a buy, hold, or sell. This rating summed up the analyst's overall impression of the stock based on the data they collected, their own research, speaking to management, and visiting the companies.

Thus, it isn't surprising that when ESG research firms, such as MSCI and Sustainalytics, began publishing information on company sustainability, they took a similar approach. They would collect environmental, social, and governance data from companies, usually by sending each company a survey with dozens or even hundreds of questions, and sometimes speaking with management and/or visiting the companies. Then they would publish a summary with a headline rating. The ratings often came in the form of letter grades (MSCI rates firms A to E) or a numerical score (Sustainalytics uses a range of 1–100). The idea was to summarize all the E, S, and G data on a company into a single rating that was simple, convenient, and easy for investors to use. And use them they did. Many of the early ESG funds used these ratings to determine whether to include or exclude companies from their portfolios. And they also used the ratings as a basis to publish scores on how sustainable their funds were.

Until around 2015 the use of ratings was the dominant form of ESG security selection and portfolio construction. It was considered best practice because it was believed the ESG research houses had the most information on ESG issues. Who better to decide which firms were sustainable than the researchers collecting the data?

ESG 2.0: Materiality to the Fore

As ESG investing grew in popularity, investment firms launched more sustainable investing strategies. It wasn't long before some of these professional investors discovered some shortcomings in the use of ratings.

For starters, the ESG research houses often disagreed on which firms were sustainable. A firm might get a high sustainability score from MSCI and a low one from Sustainalytics. Initially, it was thought these disagreements were aberrations. However, a 2020 study, "Aggregate Confusion," showed that raters only agree about half the time.[5] The divergence of ratings poses a challenge for investors: It is difficult to build a more sustainable portfolio if you don't know which are the more sustainable companies.

In retrospect it should not be surprising that ratings from different firms do not agree. Many of the research firms are using dozens of E, S, and G metrics to evaluate companies, and there are several ways in which these might diverge:

1. The metrics may not be the same across research firms. Researcher A might measure a firm's pollution risk by counting environmental fines, while Researcher B is counting tons of waste created.
2. Even if the metrics are similar, how they are measured may differ. Researcher A might evaluate a firm's greenhouse gas emissions based on the firm's disclosure, while Researcher B might use a model or estimate.
3. The researchers have different methodologies for calculating their ratings. For example, Researcher A might give environmental issues a higher weighting than Researcher B, while Researcher B might emphasize corporate governance.

Another problem was that companies with good overall ratings might have a serious deficiency in one area that gets lost in the average score. When Volkswagen got caught cheating on diesel emissions tests, it became clearer in retrospect that their poor corporate governance structure might have said more about their risk profile than their average overall score suggested.

Examining the problems with overall scores reveals not so much a failure on the part of the ESG research houses as it does the problem of creating comprehensive overall ratings from dozens of metrics in the first place. Companies are complex organizations. Summarizing all their impacts on the world and society into a single letter or number might not be the most informative way to present data.

Many investors, in their enlightened self-interest, are also concerned with the financial return on their capital. For them, the most relevant ESG issues are the ones that impact the firm financially. This is the concept of materiality. In 2010 Harvard University's Initiative for Responsible Investment published "From Transparency to Performance: Industry-Based Sustainability Reporting on Key Issues."[6] It was a call to refocus the goal of maximum disclosure to one of material disclosure.

What this report and others recognized was simple enough in concept. Some ESG issues are very important in some industries, and much less so in others. Workplace health and safety is more critical for miners than for bankers. A poor health and safety track record at a mining company indicates to investors the presence of material financial risk. For a bank, the risk that a workplace accident could impact the bottom line is far lower.

It was becoming increasingly apparent that the prevailing approach to ESG research needed modification. It might have been simpler for the ESG researcher to send the same questionnaire to 5,000 companies, collate the results, and present a uniform set of scores. But that process failed to provide decision-useful information for investors. It also put a large burden on companies to collect and report information that wasn't relevant to their business. Investors don't want companies spending money and manpower on reporting that isn't informative.

In 2011 the Sustainability Accounting Standards Board (SASB) was founded. SASB is a nonprofit organization that takes on the mission of standardizing sustainability information. They have developed a set of standards that guides the disclosure of financially material information by companies to investors. The goal is to surface sustainability information in a way that is cost-effective for companies and decision-useful for investors. The first thing SASB did was rationalize the hundreds of potential sustainability metrics down to the most relevant risks, as pictured in Exhibit A.

Exhibit A

In developing its standards, the SASB identified sustainability topics from a set of 26 broadly relevant sustainability issues organized under these five sustainability dimensions.

Environment
- GHG Emissions
- Air Quality
- Energy Management
- Water & Wastewater Management
- Waste & Hazardous Materials Management
- Ecological Impacts

Leadership & Governance
- Business Ethics
- Competitive Behavior
- Management of the Legal & Regulatory Environment
- Critical Incident Risk Management
- Systemic Risk Management

Social Capital
- Human Rights & Community Relations
- Customer Privacy
- Data Security
- Access & Affordability
- Product Quality & Safety
- Customer Welfare
- Selling Practices & Product Labeling

Human Capital
- Labor Practices
- Employee Health & Safety
- Employee Engagement, Diversity & Inclusion

Business Model & Innovation
- Product Design & Lifecycle Management
- Business Model Resilience
- Supply Chain Management
- Materials Sourcing & Efficiency
- Physical Impacts of Climate Change

Source: Value Reporting Foundation, SASB Standards. www.sasb.org/standards/materiality-map/

Once the most critical and financially material topics were defined, SASB engaged in a lengthy consultative process with companies and industry participants to develop their materiality matrix, a partial snapshot of which is in Exhibit B. The essential insight that led to the development of this matrix was the recognition that different industries face different risks, and that investors want to focus on the information that affects value.

In November 2021 SASB was consolidated into the International Sustainability Standards Board. This merger brought together several of the leading organizations at the forefront of ESG disclosure and will create a uniform set of standards to be adopted in over 70 countries by companies and investors alike.

Exhibit B

Dimension	General Issue Category	Consumer Goods	Extractives & Minerals Processing	Financials
Environment	GHG Emissions		■	
	Air Quality		■	
	Energy Management	▦	▦	
	Water & Wastewater Management		■	
	Water & Hazardous Materials Management		■	
	Ecological Impacts		▦	
Social Capital	Human Rights & Community Relations		▦	
	Customer Privacy	▦		▦
	Data Security	▦		▦
	Access & Affordability			▦
	Product Quality & Safety	■		
	Customer Welfare	▦		
	Selling Practices & Product Labeling			■
Human Capital	Labour Practices	▦	▦	
	Employee Health & Safety		■	
	Employee Engagement, Diversity & Inclusion	▦		▦
Business Model & Innovation	Product Design & Lifestyle Management	■		■
	Business Model Resilience		▦	▦
	Supply Chain Management	■	▦	
	Materials Sourcing & Efficiency	▦		
	Physical Impacts of Climate Change			▦
Leadership & Governance	Business Ethics		▦	■
	Competitive Behaviour		▦	▦
	Management of the Legal & Regulatory Environment			
	Critical Incident Risk Management		■	
	Systemic Risk Management			■

Sector Level Map

■ Issue is likely to be material for more than 50% of industries in sector

▦ Issue is likely to be material for fewer than 50% of industries in sector

☐ Issue is not likely to be material for any of the industries in sector

Source: Value Reporting Foundation, SASB Standards. www.sasb.org/standards/materiality-map/

The efforts of SASB, the IIRC, and others are helping to improve sustainability disclosures. The end goal is for investors to be able to trust sustainability data, use it to make direct comparisons between companies, and thereby illuminate differences in risk and potential reward.

ESG 3.0: A Peek at the Future

In 1973 the Financial Accounting Standards Board (FASB) codified and standardized the way companies report their financial performance. Prior to this, companies could report their earnings, expenses, and profits in almost any manner they saw fit—making it difficult for investors to understand how companies were actually performing relative to their peers. Because of FASB, and other reporting standards such as the Generally Accepted Accounting Principles (GAAP), investors can now use a P/E ratio or an earnings figure with greater confidence. Financial reporting has been standardized, and the market is better for it.

Similarly, market participants are working on standardizing ESG data. The hope is that in the near future ESG data will be on par with financial data in terms of quality, consistency, and comparability. Exhibit C, a graphic from the World Economic Forum, illustrates just some of the entities developing standardization for ESG data:

Exhibit C

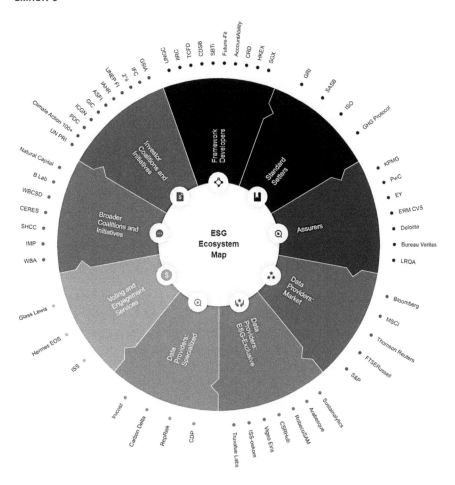

Source: World Economic Forum ESG Ecosystem Map. https://widgets.weforum.org/esgecosystemmap/index.html#/

Investors are looking forward to the day when all companies report ESG performance like they do financial performance. In the meantime, investors are looking at validating their information from other sources. Because firms are incentivized to report their performance in the best possible light, obtaining second opinions can often be illuminating. Increasingly, information is coming from outside the firms. Let's look at some examples.

If an investor wants to understand how well a company is treating its employees, they can get a sense of that through employee retention statistics, number of labor disputes, and even absenteeism rates. They can also review the firm's employee surveys. But now they can go to Glassdoor, a publicly available website, and look at actual employee reviews.

Oil and gas companies are meant to report how much methane they leak into the atmosphere. Until recently investors had to trust the energy firms on these figures. A few researchers would spot-check certain sites by hand, and not surprisingly, there were often discrepancies. It's hard to capture every leak and hard to hold companies accountable. However, today there are satellites that can detect methane from space. Companies can no longer hide. And investors get data in real time rather than having to wait until the end of the reporting year.

ESG data used to be referred to as *externalities* because the information was not incorporated into stock prices. The market could not factor this information in; thus, it was *external*. There was not sufficient standardized data that could be relied on. It was also called nonfinancial information. The link between that data and materiality, and thus a direct link to financial outcomes, could not be made.

Both the availability of data, and the materiality of it, are changing. More ESG information is available than ever before, and more companies are reporting along standardized frameworks. Researchers are also making the connections between ESG risks, such as emissions, and stock prices.

Unfortunately, we have not yet arrived at a place where all ESG data is high quality, standardized, and material. And we may never actually get there because the market is always searching for more information. What is clear is that investors now have better data on which to base their decisions. The day is coming when ESG data is contained within the regular reporting that companies do, and will be an important part of the information set that all investors, not just sustainability-minded ones, use to evaluate companies. For some information, in particular climate risk data, that day is already here.

Climate Risk

The climate is changing. Today this is a statement of the obvious for many. However, it was quite contentious up until recently, so much so that NASA still maintains a web page listing the scientific societies, agencies, and academies that have come to this consensus.[7]

The 2010s put climate risk on the front burner. We experienced hurricanes Sandy, Irma, and Harvey as well as the massive California, Colorado, and Australian wildfires. A recent ice storm incapacitated the power grid in Texas for more than a week. As we write this, Portland, Oregon, is experiencing 117-degree temperatures, well above previous highs and about 40 degrees above normal. All of these were expensive events. The connection is clear. Climate risk is investment risk. Thus, even conventional investors, heretofore uninterested in sustainability, are paying attention. They want information, data, and models so they can properly assess these developing risks.

Recognizing the need, in 2019 Moody's (one of the world's largest credit rating agencies) announced that they were purchasing Four Twenty Seven, a climate risk consultant that assesses threats from sea level rise, flooding, heat stress, drought, hurricanes, and wildfires. In 2020 Moody's began providing Four Twenty Seven's climate risk data on properties for all their investor reports, not just for ESG investors. They also began factoring Four Twenty Seven's analysis into their assessments of the risk of sovereign debt (the ability of countries to repay their loans).

Summary

Climate risk is changing the narrative on sustainable investing for many who had lumped in ESG investing with SRI. These investors might have thought that ESG was not relevant to them because they were not trying to align their values with their money. However, because they have been confronted with example after example of how ESG risk affects their own conventional portfolios, they are no longer dismissing ESG concerns. Instead, they are trying to determine which metrics are relevant and material to their assets. In particular, professional investors, charged with looking after other people's money, have begun asking tougher questions of companies about their exposures to these risks. Many of these institutional investors now use climate risk data in conventional risk analysis.

The line between conventional and sustainable investing seems to be blurring as more investors adopt ESG risk analysis. In December 2020 Larry Fink, the CEO of BlackRock, the world's largest asset manager with over $7 trillion, stated that they will make climate change central to their investment strategies beginning in 2021.[8] It is conceivable that all conventional investors will begin incorporating ESG to the extent that ESG is material and relevant. However, there will also be investors who want to align their portfolios more closely to their values. The choice between conventional and sustainable investing will often come down to what investors expect in terms of performance. We turn to that question now, with a look at what the research says on the financial performance of sustainable investing.

CHAPTER 6

The Performance of
Sustainable Investing

A**S WE HAVE** discussed, the 2010s have seen a dramatic increase in sustainable investing. Does this trend influence company valuations, and thus their cost of capital, and by implication the returns investors can expect?

When seeking answers to such questions, investors are best served by learning what the academic research has to say rather than relying on opinions. With that in mind, in this chapter we take a deep dive into what the research has found. We will examine the findings on questions such as:

- Is there consistency in ESG ratings across providers?
- Is the market factoring carbon risk into stock prices?
- Are returns to green and brown stocks well explained by asset pricing models?
- What is the impact of exclusionary screens versus *best-in-class* strategies?

Reviewing the research findings will allow you to make an informed decision. We begin with a discussion on what economic theory has to say about the impact of sustainable investment strategies on valuations and expected returns.

Economic Theory on Taste, Risk, and Diversification

While sustainable investing continues to gain in popularity, economic theory suggests that if a large enough proportion of investors choose to favor companies with high sustainability ratings and avoid those with low sustainability ratings (sin businesses), the favored company's share prices will be elevated and the sin stock shares will be depressed. In equilibrium, the screening out of certain assets based on investors' taste should lead to a return premium on the screened assets.

The result is that the favored companies will have a lower cost of capital because they will trade at a higher P/E ratio. The flip side of a lower cost of capital is a lower expected return to the providers of that capital (shareholders). And the sin companies will have a higher cost of capital because they will trade at a lower P/E ratio, the flip side of which is a higher expected return to the providers of that capital.

The hypothesis is that the higher expected returns (a premium above the market's required return) are required as compensation for the emotional cost of exposure to offensive companies. On the other hand, investors in companies with higher sustainability ratings are willing to accept the lower returns as the cost of expressing their values.

There is also a risk-based hypothesis for the sin premium. It is logical to hypothesize that companies neglecting to manage their ESG exposures could be subject to greater risk (that is, a wider range of potential outcomes) than their more ESG-focused counterparts. The argument is that companies with high sustainability scores have better risk management and better compliance standards. The stronger controls lead to fewer extreme events such as environmental disasters, fraud, corruption, and litigation (and their negative consequences). The result is a reduction in tail risk in high-scoring firms relative to the lowest-scoring firms. The greater tail risk creates the sin premium.

Diversification has been called the investor's best friend. Yet, sustainable investors sacrifice some of the benefits of diversification relative to a broad-based market index fund because their investments are limited to the universe of stocks that meet a sustainable investing screening process. In theory, less diversified portfolios are less efficient ones.

That's the economic theory, but is the evidence consistent with it? Before reviewing that evidence, it is important to understand some of the limitations of the research, in particular around the length of ESG studies, and in the consistency of ESG ratings.

ESG investing, as we defined in Chapter 1, has only formally existed since the mid-2000s. Asset pricing researchers like to have multiple decades of data to study. For example, the comparative studies on the performance of small versus large and value versus growth stocks now have more than 90 years of data to analyze. The more data, the more robust the interpretations. With less than two decades of ESG data, and not much more for SRI studies (e.g., sin stock performance), investors should consider the findings from these studies to be preliminary.

It is also a problem that ESG ratings from different providers disagree dramatically. For example, the authors of the 2020 study "Aggregate Confusion: The Divergence of ESG Ratings" found that the correlations of ratings between the providers averaged just 0.61, where 1.0 is perfect correlation and 0.0 is no correlation at all.[1] Thus, the information that decision makers receive from rating agencies is ambiguous. The divergence of ratings poses a real challenge for empirical research. It is difficult to determine the performance of high- versus low-rated ESG stocks when we cannot agree which stocks are rated high and which are low. A researcher's choice of one ESG rater versus another may significantly alter a study's results and conclusions. Several studies besides "Aggregate Confusion" have confirmed the lack of consensus in ESG ratings, including "Inside the ESG Ratings: (Dis)agreement and Performance"[2] and "Going Green Means Being in the Black"[3] as well as this following paper.

"Divergent ESG Ratings." Elroy Dimson, Paul Marsh, Mike Staunton[4]

To demonstrate just how much a challenge the divergence in ratings presents for investors, we will review the findings of this 2020 study. The authors found that while data is essential for making investment decisions, and most institutions rely wholly or partly on external providers of ESG data, there is minimal correlation between ESG ratings from alternative agencies. As Figure 5 showing ratings from two of the leading raters demonstrates, there is a wide divergence in scores—companies with a high score from one rater often receive a middling or low score from another.

Figure 5: MSCI versus Sustainalytics Rankings at Start-2019

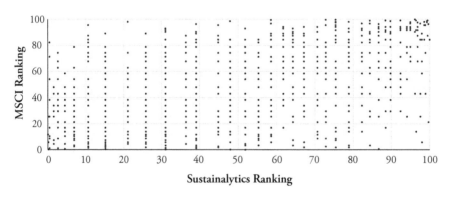

Source: Data from MSCI and Sustainalytics for 878 U.S. companies.

Figure 6 shows the rankings of six companies by three ratings providers and demonstrate that companies can receive dramatically divergent rankings on any one factor. For example, on the environmental factor, Facebook has a 1st percentile ranking by Sustainalytics and a 96th percentile ranking by MSCI.

Figure 6: Company Rankings by Different Providers

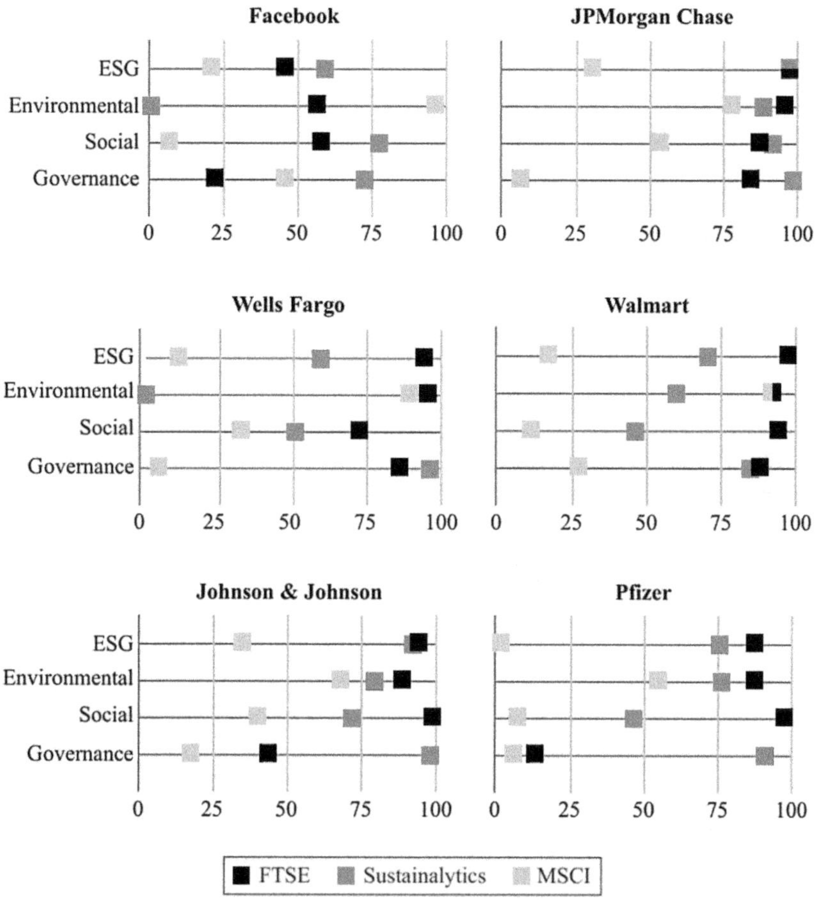

Source: Data from MSCI, FTSE Russell, and Sustainalytics.

Figure 7 shows that the pairwise correlations of rankings are also quite low. This is especially true for the individual components—for governance, they are virtually uncorrelated.

Figure 7: Correlations of Rankings

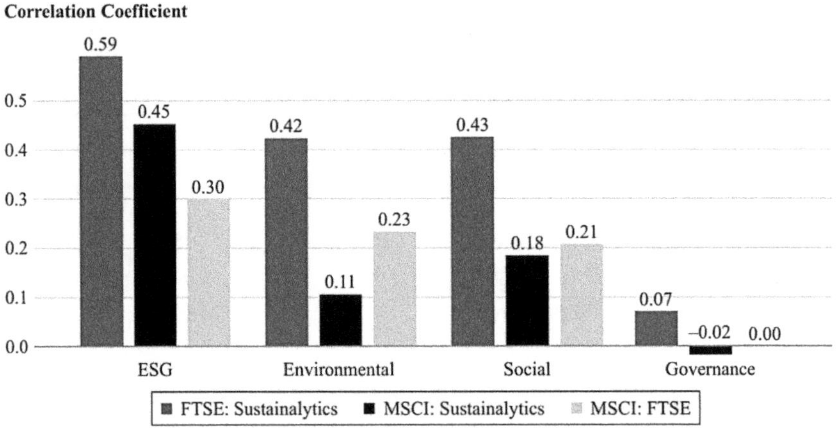

Source: Data from MSCI, FTSE Russell, and Sustainalytics.

Dimson, Marsh, and Staunton explained that the divergences are caused by five main factors:

1. There is a variety and inconsistency of the metrics that purport to measure much the same thing. The diversity of measure gives rise to considerable dissimilarity in ratings, reflecting firm-specific attributes, differing terminologies, and units of measurement.
2. There are differences in how raters define the benchmark for comparisons. For example, Sustainalytics compares companies to constituents of a broad market index, whereas S&P compares companies to industry peers.
3. At the company level, ESG ratings are plagued by missing data. When a company does not reveal metrics, some raters assume the worst and assign a score of zero. Others impute a score that reflects peers that do report the data. More sophisticated approaches use statistical models to estimate missing metrics but are often unclear about why a company gets a low or high rating.
4. Reflecting the expansion in the volume of public information and the lack of consensus on metrics, there is greater scope for raters to disagree about the scores for particular companies.
5. As Figure 8 demonstrates, weighting schemes, i.e., the relative importance raters put on different metrics, vary greatly:

Figure 8: Variation in Weighting Schemes

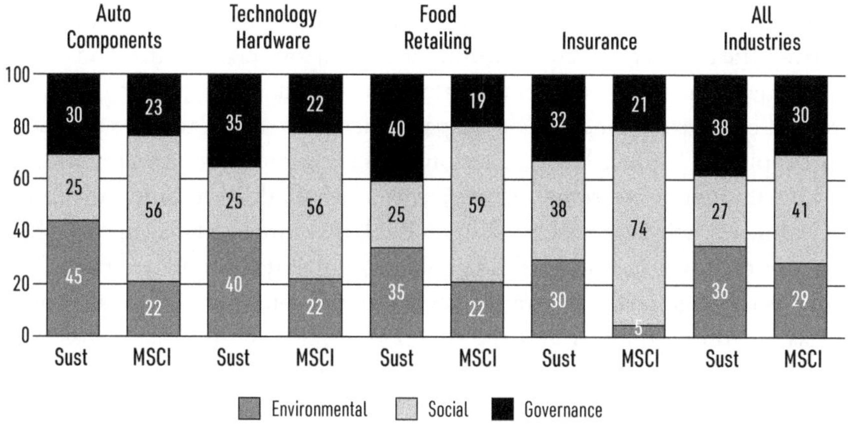

Source: Data from MSCI and Sustainalytics.

Summarizing, ESG investors face considerable challenges in allocating assets because the data used to construct ESG portfolios differs widely among providers, and there are large divergences in materiality assessments. This should not be a surprise, because there are no regulated, or even generally accepted, standards for what good ESG is (or is not). The result is that funds may not be aligned with investor objectives and beliefs. In addition, the return and risk of ESG funds can differ significantly and are driven by fund-specific criteria rather than by a homogeneous ESG factor. With that challenge in mind, we advise users of ESG ratings and rankings to study the relevant definitions and methodologies before using them. With that said, a lack of transparency about the data sources, weightings, and methodologies can make it difficult to ensure that companies' true ESG performance is accounted for when making portfolio selection and investment decisions. We recommend that instead of attempting to compare and contrast ratings and rankings of different agencies, investors should determine the ESG constructs that are material to their own investment strategies and then match them with an ESG rating or ranking product that closely resembles those constructs.

With the challenges created by ratings divergences in mind, we begin our review by examining evidence from one of the largest sovereign wealth funds.

Sovereign Wealth Funds: The Evidence

One of the largest SRI investors is the $1 trillion Government Pension Fund of Norway, the country's sovereign wealth fund. The sovereign wealth fund divests companies from its investment portfolio based on two types of exclusions. Product-based exclusions include weapons, thermal coal, and tobacco producers and suppliers. Conduct-based exclusions concern companies with a track record of human rights violations, severe environmental damage, and corruption. According to their 2017 analysis, Norges Bank Investment Management, which manages the sovereign wealth fund's assets, found that the fund had missed out on 1.1 percentage points of cumulative additional gain due to the exclusion of stocks on ethical grounds over the past 11 years. Specifically, the exclusions of tobacco companies and weapons manufacturers reduced returns by 1.2 and 0.8 percentage points, respectively.[5]

Findings such as these have led to the development of an investment strategy that focuses on the violation of social norms: vice investing, or sin investing.

Sin Investing: The Evidence

This strategy creates a portfolio of firms from industries that are typically screened out by sustainable mutual funds and ETFs, pension funds, and investment managers. Vice investors focus primarily on the so-called *sin stocks*: alcohol, tobacco, gambling, pornography, and weapons. The historical evidence on the performance of these stocks supports the theory.

"Fewer Reasons to Sin: A Five-Factor Investigation of Vice Stocks." Greg Richey[6]

In his 2017 study, covering the period October 1996 to October 2016, Richey employed several factor models to determine whether a portfolio of vice stocks (specifically firms that manufacture and sell products such as alcohol, tobacco, gaming services, and national defense) outperforms the S&P 500 (a benchmark to approximate the market portfolio) on a risk-adjusted basis. Factors are traits or characteristics of stocks, such as whether they are large or small stocks and value or growth stocks. Factor models have been found to explain the large majority of the variation in returns to diversified portfolios. Richey measured the performance of vice stocks using the single-factor capital asset pricing model (market beta), the original Fama-French three-factor model (adding size and value), the Carhart four-factor model (adding momentum), and the newer Fama-French five-factor model (market beta, size, value, profitability, and investment). His dataset included 61 corporations from vice-related industries.

Following is a summary of his findings:

- For the period October 1996 through October 2016, the S&P 500 returned 7.8 percent per annum. The Vice Fund returned 11.5 percent.
- All models found that the Vice Fund portfolio beta was between 0.59 and 0.74, indicating that the vice portfolio exhibited less market risk or volatility than the S&P 500 Index, which had a beta of 1 over the sample period. This reinforces the defensive nature of sin portfolios.
- The annual alphas (return above the risk-adjusted benchmark) on the CAPM, three-factor, and four-factor models were 2.9 percent, 2.8 percent, and 2.5 percent, respectively. All were significant at the 1 percent level. These findings suggest that vice stocks outperform on a risk-adjusted basis. However, in the five-factor model, which adds the investment and profitability factors, the alpha virtually disappeared, falling to just 0.1 percent per year. This result helps explain the performance of vice stocks relative to the market portfolio that previous models fail to capture. Richey concluded that the higher returns to vice stocks occurred because they are more profitable and less wasteful with investments than the average corporation.

Richey's findings are consistent with other studies on sin stocks.

"The Price of Sin: The Effects of Social Norms on Markets." Harrison Hong and Marcin Kacperczyk[7]

The authors of this 2009 study found that for the period 1965 through 2006, a U.S. portfolio long sin stocks and short their comparables had a return of 0.29 percent per month after adjusting for the four-factor model. As out-of-sample support, sin stocks in seven large European markets and Canada outperformed similar stocks by about 2.5 percent a year. They concluded that the abnormal risk-adjusted returns of vice stocks were due to neglect by institutional investors.

"Exclusionary Screening." Elroy Dimson, Paul Marsh, and Mike Staunton[8]

As further evidence that avoiding sin stocks comes at a price, this 2020 study found that for industry indices that covered the 120-year period 1900 through 2019, the highest returning industries in the U.S. were tobacco and alcohol. One dollar invested in the U.S. stock market in 1900 through 2019 would have provided an annualized return of 9.6 percent; that same dollar invested in the tobacco sector returned 14.2 percent. The second-best performing industry was alcohol. The U.K. produced similar findings. From 1900 through 2019, the U.K. stock market provided an annualized return of 9.3 percent. The best performing industry was alcohol, returning 11.5 percent, and tobacco was the next best performer.

They also examined the impact of screening out countries based on their degree of corruption (a measure of the quality of governance). Countries were evaluated using the Worldwide Governance Indicators from a 2010 World Bank policy research working paper by Daniel Kaufmann, Aart Kraay, and Massimo Mastruzzi, "The Worldwide Governance Indicators: Methodology and Analytical Issues."[9] The indicators comprised annual scores on six broad dimensions of governance. Economic theory would suggest that corruption is a risk factor. Therefore, investors in countries with greater degrees of corruption will demand a premium as compensation for the risk.

Dimson, Marsh, and Staunton found 14 countries that posted a poor score, 12 that were acceptable, 12 that were good, and 11 with excellent scores. Post-2000 returns for the last three groups were between 5.3 percent and 7.7 percent. In contrast, the markets with poor control of corruption had an average return of 11.0 percent. Interestingly, realized returns were higher for equity investments in jurisdictions that were more likely to be characterized by corrupt behaviors. As the authors noted, the time period is short and the result might just be a lucky outcome. On the other hand, it is also logical to consider that investors will demand a premium for taking corruption risk. However, the premium may also be a result of the same exclusionary factors found with sin stocks (investors boycott countries with high corruption scores, driving prices down, raising expected returns).

The Price of Taste for Sustainable Investment

"The Price of Taste for Socially Responsible Investment." Rocco Ciciretti, Ambrogio Dalò, Lammertjan Dam[10]

Ciciretti, Dalò, and Dam began their 2017 paper by observing that the demand for SRI can be explained by two different effects: the favorable risk characteristics of responsible assets, and investors' taste for such assets.

They wrote: "The risk effect arises when responsible assets exhibit financial risk characteristics that appeal to investors. For example, SRI might reduce exposure to stakeholder risk, such as potential consumer boycotts or environmental scandals, that have an impact on stock returns." Their explanation for the taste effect "is that certain investors do not want to facilitate 'irresponsible' corporate conduct and construct their portfolios accordingly."

The authors then focused their paper on the taste effect's contribution in risk-adjusted returns—in other words, "the price of taste."

To determine the price of taste, Ciciretti, Dalò, and Dam built a model that accounted for exposure to the market beta, size, value, and momentum factors, and incorporated an SRI score based on six dimensions: business behavior, corporate governance, community involvement, environment, human resources, and human rights. Their study covered the period July 2005 through June 2014 and 1,000 firms (295 in the United States, 512 in Europe, and 193 in the Asia-Pacific region).

Following is a summary of their findings:

- Overall, the average monthly excess return declines, moving from the worst to the best SRI portfolio.
- A strategy that buys the worst portfolio and sells the best portfolio yielded an additional excess return of 7.2 percentage points on an annual basis and was statistically significant (t-statistic = 4.0).
- Composing portfolios with firms that have higher responsibility does not increase the overall portfolio market beta, value, or momentum exposures. However, the size and corporate social responsibility (CSR) risk factor betas decrease, moving from the worst to the best SRI portfolios—companies become larger and SRI scores become better (decreasing stakeholder risk exposure for firms with higher social responsibility scores).
- There is a significant and negative relationship between social responsibility scores and risk-adjusted returns, with price of taste amounting to 4.8 percent annually for the representative responsible firm.

The authors concluded: "Both risk and taste play a role in explaining differences in returns between more and less responsible companies." They added that investors pay a price in terms of lower returns due to their preference for SRI and that the premium related to the responsibility score, the price of taste, is negative and significant. These findings are consistent with both theory and prior research.

Ciciretti, Dalò, and Dam provided further evidence of a sustainability premium in their 2019 study, "The Contributions of Betas versus Characteristics to the ESG Premium."[11] They found that firms with lower ESG scores exhibit higher expected returns. In other words, the research demonstrates that investors recognize increased risk and demand a premium for accepting it. Companies pay a price in the form of a higher cost of capital. The negative premium is driven mainly by ESG characteristics, not ESG risk factor betas (which are insignificant). They found that a one-standard-deviation decrease in ESG characteristic is associated with an increase in expected returns of 13 basis points (bps) on a monthly basis.

Based on an equilibrium model, Ciciretti, Dalò, and Dam concluded that their results indicate that the cross-sectional variation of expected returns related to the ESG premium is mainly driven by investor preferences for ESG-related issues rather than that systematic risk components are captured by ESG scores. In other words, asset flows to ESG stocks have driven down expected returns. They added: "Irrespective of risk considerations, investors are willing to forgo potential returns if a firm scores well on ESG items (or alternatively, investors are only willing to hold firms that score low on ESG items if they are compensated with higher returns)."

"Sustainable Investing in Equilibrium." Lubos Pastor, Robert Stambaugh, and Lucian Taylor[12]

Pastor, Stambaugh, and Taylor, authors of this 2019 paper, reached the same conclusion as Ciciretti, Dalò, and Dam. Both sets of authors noted that with the increased demand toward ESG funds, the expected equilibrium has likely shifted. Firms with high ESG scores have rising portfolio weights, leading to short-term capital gains for their stocks—realized returns may rise temporarily, though expected long-run returns fall. Ciciretti, Dalò, and Dam investigated how the long-run ESG premium evolves over time by calculating regressions of dividend-price ratios on the ESG characteristics, confirming this hypothesis.

Pastor, Stambaugh, and Taylor also found that:

- Investors differ in their preferences for sustainability, or ESG preferences. These preferences have two dimensions. First, agents derive utility from holdings of green firms and disutility from holdings of brown firms. Second, though they care about firms' aggregate social impact, they also care about financial wealth. However, they are willing to sacrifice some expected return in exchange for the utility benefits provided by green investing.
- Investors' taste for green holdings affects asset prices—the greener the asset, the lower its CAPM alpha in equilibrium. Green assets have negative alphas and brown assets have positive alphas. Consequently, agents with stronger ESG preferences, whose portfolios tilt more toward green assets and away from brown assets, earn lower expected returns.
- If ESG concerns strengthen unexpectedly, green assets can outperform brown assets despite having lower expected returns. The higher short-term returns are a result of the increased demand for the stocks of green firms

on valuations. "Exposure to ESG risk is why green assets may outperform brown assets over a period of time." Investor tastes/preferences can drive short-term returns through changes in valuations. Thus, the premium induced by exposure to the ESG risk factor can be large enough to overcome green stocks' negative alphas.

- The authors claim there is an ESG risk factor, as the strength of ESG concerns can change over time, both for investors in firms' shares and for the customers who buy the firms' goods and services. If ESG concerns strengthen, customers may shift their demand for goods and services to greener providers (the customer channel), and investors may derive more utility from holding the stocks of greener firms (the investor channel). Greener stocks are more exposed to the ESG risk factor.

"A Sustainable Capital Asset Pricing Model (S-CAPM): Evidence from Green Investing and Sin Stock Exclusion." Olivier Zerbib[13]

The previous findings are consistent with those reached by Olivier Zerbib, whose goal was to determine how sustainable investing through exclusionary screening and ESG integration affects asset returns. He developed an asset pricing model with a premium on neglected stocks (limited investor participation in financial markets entails an additional risk premium on the expected returns on neglected stocks) and a taste premium (induced by sustainable investors' tastes for assets related to the cost of externalities that they internalize). Both exclusion premia result from the reduction of the investor base. He then applied the model to green investing and sin stock exclusion using U.S. data between 2000 and 2018. His data sample included 348 green funds worldwide investing in U.S. equities as of December 2018.

Following is a summary of his findings:

- The S-CAPM model outperformed the Carhart four-factor model (market beta, size, value, and momentum). Consistent with economic theory, the model yielded a taste and an exclusion effect of 1.5 percent and 2.5 percent per annum (statistically significant), respectively.
- Premia increase when a group of investors are pessimistic about this asset and vice versa.
- Sustainable investors make a suboptimal choice when they construct portfolios with lower Sharpe ratios (a measure of risk-adjusted returns) than that of the mean-variance portfolio.

The knowledge that shunning investment leads to higher costs of capital suggests a way to improve the returns of sustainable investment strategies.

Enhancing Sustainable Investing Returns

Jason Hsu, Xiaoyang Liu, Keren Shen, Vivek Viswanathan, and Yanxiang Zhao, authors of the 2018 study "Outperformance through Investing in ESG in Need," examined whether screening for ESG firms with a high cost of capital would improve returns.[14] For each top ESG universe, they sorted the stocks into quintile portfolios according to their cost of equity. The characteristics chosen to estimate cost of equity were book-to-market, gross profitability, net operating assets, accruals, volatility, asset growth, and market beta.

Consistent with economic theory, they found that firms with a higher cost of equity tended to outperform firms with a lower cost of equity. Using Bloomberg scores, the firms with high costs of capital outperformed the firms with low costs of capital by 7.3 percentage points (t-statistic = 1.9). Using Thomson Reuters scores, the outperformance was 6.9 percentage points (t-statistic = 2.2). Using the S&P 500 as the benchmark, the authors found that a high cost of capital ESG strategy outperformed by about 3 percentage points per annum, with an annual turnover of about 60 percent (trading costs should be very low given that the universe is the 500 largest stocks).

"Do Investors Care about Carbon Risk?" Patrick Bolton and Marcin Kacperczyk[15]

Thanks to Bolton and Kacperczyk, we can also review the impact of carbon risk on stock returns.

A large body of academic research attempts to explain the cross-sectional pattern of stock returns based on exposures to factors such as size and value, profitability/quality, and momentum. One variable that had been missing from the analysis was corporate carbon emissions. The evidence of rising temperatures and the renewed policy efforts to curb carbon dioxide (CO_2) emissions raises the question of whether carbon emissions represent a material risk today for investors that is reflected in the cross-section of stock returns and portfolio holdings.

Three hypotheses were cited in this study:

1. Investors seek compensation for holding the stocks of disproportionately high CO_2 emitters and the associated higher carbon risk they expose

themselves to, giving rise to a positive relation in the cross-section between a firm's own CO_2 emissions and its stock returns.

2. Markets are inefficient, underpricing carbon risks.

3. Stocks of firms with high emissions are like other sin stocks—they are shunned by socially responsible, or ethical, investors to such an extent that the spurned firms present higher stock returns.

Bolton and Kacperczyk explored whether carbon emissions affect the cross-section of U.S. stock returns. Their data sample covered about 1,000 listed companies since fiscal year 2005, and over 2,900 listed companies in the U.S. since fiscal year 2016. Returns span the relatively brief period 2005 to 2017, a period of increasing attention from ESG-conscious investors. Firm-level carbon emissions data were assembled by seven main providers: CDP, Trucost, MSCI, Sustainalytics, Thomson Reuters, Bloomberg, and ISS.

The authors follow the convention of categorizing carbon emissions from a company's operations and economic activity into three different scopes:

Scope 1 is direct emissions from production.

Scope 2 is indirect emissions from consumption of purchased electricity, heat, or steam.

Scope 3 is indirect emissions from the production of purchased materials, product use, waste disposal, outsourced activities, etc.

Following is a summary of their findings:

- Power, electric, and multi-utility industries produce the most scope 1 emissions, while consumer finance, thrifts and mortgages, and capital markets are the cleanest. Metals and mining, electric utilities, and construction materials are the three most scope 2 emission-intensive industries (the cleanest industries mimic those based on scope 1 classification). Food products, metals and mining, and construction materials are the three most scope 3 emission-intensive industries. Internet software and services, health care technologies, and software are the three least-intensive industries.

- Stocks of firms with higher total CO_2 emissions (and changes in emissions) earn higher returns after controlling for the common factors of size, book-to-market, and momentum, and other factors (such as low beta and liquidity) and anomalies (such as idiosyncratic volatility and net stock issuance) that predict returns.

- There is also a significant carbon premium associated with the year-to-year growth in emissions—companies that succeed in reducing their emissions can afford to offer lower stock returns, but companies that keep on burning more and more fossil fuel must resign themselves to offering higher returns.

- The carbon premium is economically significant: A one-standard-deviation (SD) increase in the level and change of scope 1 emissions leads to a 1.8 percent and 3.1 percent increase, respectively, in annualized stock returns. A one-SD increase in the level and change of scope 2 emissions leads to a 2.9 percent and 2.2 percent increase in annualized returns. And a one-SD increase in the level and change of scope 3 emissions increases stock returns 4.0 percent and 3.8 percent on an annualized basis.
- The carbon premium cannot be explained through differences in unexpected profitability or other known risk factors.
- Institutional investors implement exclusionary screening based on direct emission intensity in a few salient industries—divestment is only based on scope 1 emission intensity, and there is no significant effect of the level of emissions on institutional investor portfolios. Nor do institutional investors underweight scope 2 and scope 3 emission-intensive firms. This is true both in aggregate and for each institutional investor category. Essentially, institutional investors have been applying exclusionary screens (or not) solely on the basis of scope 1 emission intensity.

Their findings led Bolton and Kacperczyk to conclude: "Our results are consistent with an interpretation that investors are already demanding compensation for their exposure to carbon emission risk." They noted that the carbon premium has only materialized recently: "We show that if we look back to the 1990s by imputing the 2005 cross-sectional distribution of total emissions to the 1990s, there is no significant carbon premium, consistent with the view that investors at that time likely did not pay as much attention to carbon emissions."

Bolton and Kacperczyk's findings of a carbon risk premium are consistent with economic theory (risk and expected return being related) and efficient markets. We now turn to reviewing the findings that appear to conflict with those of Bolton and Kacperczyk—a conflict which creates difficulty in interpreting the results of ESG research.

"Carbon Risk." Maximilian Görgen, Andrea Jacob, Martin Nerlinger, Ryan Riordan, Martin Rohleder, Marco Wilkens[16]

The impact of carbon risk on asset pricing was also the subject of this 2020 study, the authors of which quantified carbon risk via a "Brown-Minus-Green factor" (BMG) derived from 1,600 firms with data from four major ESG databases. This factor allowed the estimation of carbon risk (carbon beta). Their Brown-Green Score (BGS) is a composite measure of three indicators designed to separately capture the sensitivity of firms' value chains (e.g., current emissions), of their public perception (e.g., response to perceived emissions), and of their adaptability (e.g., mitigation strategies) to carbon risk.

Due to limited data availability, a problem with all ESG-related research, their data sample covered the relatively short period 2010 to 2016.

Following is a summary of their findings:

- Firms are becoming greener—mostly driven by green firms becoming significantly greener than brown firms. For instance, green firms reduce their average carbon intensity by roughly 16 percent annually versus roughly 2 percent annually for brown firms.
- The BMG factor significantly increases the explanatory power of common asset pricing models, suggesting that it is important in explaining variation in global equity prices.
- Firms perform worse if they surprise markets by becoming browner (their BGS score rises) compared to the previous year.
- Firms investing in innovation and clean technology, proxied by R&D expenditures, have lower carbon betas, while firms with dirty or "stranded" assets, proxied by property, plant, and equipment assets, have higher carbon betas.
- There was a strong contrast in the performance of the brown and the green portfolios over time. While the cumulative return of BMG was slightly positive in the period 2010 to the end of 2012, the effect reversed in the following period. Over the full period, brown firms performed worse than green firms on average during the sample period.
- The cumulative difference in returns between brown and green firms was roughly 14 percent, with green firms outperforming. This is consistent with increased investor focus on tackling climate change, which has led to cash flows into green firms and away from brown firms—the increased demand for the stocks of green firms explains why green firms outperformed brown firms, which is inconsistent with economic theory.
- Investors can achieve comparable expected returns and Sharpe ratios for their portfolios with similar exposures to other systematic risk factors (such as beta, size, and value), or to specific industries, while reducing carbon beta via a best-in-class approach—demonstrating that investors can achieve their sustainable investing goals without sacrificing returns by tilting their portfolios to companies with good scores but with similar exposure to other common factors.
- Carbon betas are high and positive in countries like South Africa, Brazil, and Canada, which means they are likely negatively affected if the world speeds up the transition to a low-carbon economy. In contrast, average

carbon betas are negative in European countries and Japan. On an industry level, tech firms have carbon betas near zero on average, while basic material and energy firms have the highest positive carbon betas, as expected. There are, however, significant differences in carbon betas within industries, suggesting that carbon risk is not simply a proxy for certain industries.

Their findings led the authors to conclude that the transition from a high-carbon to a low-carbon economy is ongoing. As a result, capital markets may not yet agree upon new equilibrium equity prices: "Systematic return differences between brown and green firms may thus reflect ongoing re-evaluations of firm fundamentals rather than changing expectations regarding discount rates." They added: "While carbon risk explains systematic return variation well, we do not find evidence of a carbon risk premium. We show that this may be the case because of: (1) the opposing price movements of brown firms and firms becoming greener, and (2) that carbon risk is associated with unpriced cash-flow changes rather than priced discount-rate changes."

Conflicting Forces

The conflicting forces can create problems in interpreting research findings. It's important to keep in mind that investor preferences lead to different short- and long-term impacts on asset prices and returns. Firms with high sustainable investing scores earn rising portfolio weights, leading to short-term capital gains for their stocks—realized returns rise temporarily. However, the long-term effect is that higher valuations reduce expected long-term returns. The result can be an increase in green asset returns even though brown assets earn higher expected returns.

In other words, there can be an ambiguous relationship between carbon risk and returns in the short term. As the authors of "Carbon Risk" noted: "Over time as the markets develop a better understanding of carbon risk and the unexpected component falls relative to the expected component, we should expect a positive relationship between returns and carbon risk." Without this understanding, investors can misinterpret findings that appear to show a lack of a carbon premium.

The reality was there was an ex-ante carbon premium, but the ex-post results showed a negative premium because of cash flows raising valuations of green companies. Given the continued trend in sustainable investing, it seems likely that it will be a while before we reach a new equilibrium. In the meantime, despite investors requiring a risk premium for carbon risks, green stocks can outperform brown ones.

The difference in impact of ESG-related cash flows on short-term and long-term returns helps explain the conflicting findings of the "Carbon Risk" study and those of Patrick Bolton and Marcin Kacperczyk, which we previously reviewed. Recall that Bolton and Kacperczyk's data series spanned 2005 through 2017, while the Görgen, Jacob, Nerlinger, Riordan, Rohleder, and Wilkens study only covered the period 2010 through 2017. Bolton and Kacperczyk found an economically significant carbon premium and concluded: "Our results are consistent with an interpretation that investors are already demanding compensation for their exposure to carbon emission risk." The differences in findings can be explained by the dramatic increase in ESG-related cash flows in the latter half of the period studied by Bolton and Kacperczyk, the only period covered by Görgen, Jacob, Nerlinger, Riordan, Rohleder, and Wilkens. The effect of those cash flows on valuations swamped the carbon premium demanded by investors—the new equilibrium that Görgen, Jacob, Nerlinger, Riordan, Rohleder, and Wilkens predicted had not yet been reached.

"Get Green or Die Trying? Carbon Risk Integration into Portfolio Management." Maximilian Görgen, Andrea Jacob, Martin Nerlinger[17]

Building on their work in the "Carbon Risk" study, Görgen, Jacob, and Nerlinger examined how integrating carbon risk impacts portfolio risk, exposure to common factors (such as value), and performance. Their 2021 study used their BMG factor to analyze a global dataset consisting of all constituents of the MSCI ACWI Investable Market Index (IMI) for the period October 2010 to December 2019. Their sample included almost 9,000 constituents and approximately 99 percent of the global equity investment opportunity set. Among their findings was that differences in factor exposures drove part of the return pattern they found in their "Carbon Risk" study (Figure 9). Factors considered included: SMB (small minus big, the size factor); HML (high book-to-market minus low book-to-market, the value factor); WML (winners minus losers, the momentum factor); and BMG (brown minus green, the carbon factor).

Figure 9: "Get Green or Die Trying? Carbon Risk Integration into Portfolio Management"

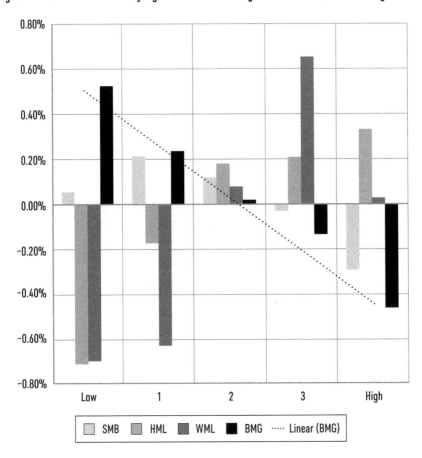

They also found that the carbon risk factor had low correlation to the size, value, and momentum factors, suggesting that it is a unique risk.

Görgen, Jacob, and Nerlinger repeated their portfolio construction, relying on "a more fundamentals-based measure, the carbon emissions score from MSCI." Their results were very different from those of their "Carbon Risk" study. In fact, they were reversed. They found that the brown portfolio with the worst carbon emissions score had the lowest mean return, at 13.7 percent. The green portfolio with the best carbon emissions score had a higher return but stood behind the middle portfolios (15.7 percent versus 16.3 percent for the second portfolio). Despite the different outcomes, they did find that once again the return pattern was explained by varying factor exposures, particularly the value factor. For example, there was a large change in the HML exposure, from -0.17 for the brown carbon beta portfolio to 0.36 for the brown carbon emissions score portfolio. In addition, the green portfolio changed its HML exposure significantly, from 0.37 to -0.01. These changes drove returns down for the brown portfolio and up for the green portfolio. They also found that the brown portfolio had a lower Sharpe ratio, greater market beta risk, and by far the largest negative alpha (-2.03 percent versus -0.65 percent for the green portfolio).

The Impact of Exclusionary Screens

Görgen, Jacob, and Nerlinger next examined portfolio construction strategies that use exclusionary screens (such as screening out the bottom 10 or 20 percent of the stocks with the worst sustainability scores). They found that the greenest portfolio had the worst underperformance, underperforming the benchmark by 3.3 percentage points annually, while the brownest portfolio outperformed the market by 2.4 percentage points annually. And the browner a portfolio, the higher the return. In addition, the total risk of the extreme screening portfolios was higher than that of the neutral portfolio—restricting the portfolio to stocks with the lowest carbon beta led on average to an increase of 2.9 percentage points in standard deviation. Thus, the stricter the exclusions, the more the Sharpe ratio of the portfolios deteriorated. They concluded: "Investors selecting the greenest or brownest stocks might lose risk-adjusted performance compared to the market. However, this loss comes with a more focused portfolio on a desired level of carbon risk exposure."

Best-in-Class Approach

Görgen, Jacob, and Nerlinger turned next to examining how a best-in-sector approach impacts portfolio performance. They constructed a portfolio that was equal weighted in each of the 11 Global Industry Classification Standard sectors and equal weighted the sectors, but included stocks with the 20 percent lowest carbon betas in each sector (see Figure 10).

Figure 10: Best-in-Sector Approach

Portfolio	Mean Return (p.a.)	SD	Sharpe Ratio	Alpha	Market Beta	BMG Beta
Low	12.55	16.97	1.00	−1.11	0.89	−0.51
2	13.81	15.15	1.16	−1.46	0.96	−0.20
3	14.12	13.74	1.32	−0.57	0.90	0.03
4	16.58	14.34	1.47	0.96	0.92	0.20
High	19.70	18.64	1.36	1.10	1.12	0.50

This figure reports risk and return measures for five best-in-class portfolios. Within each sector, stocks are sorted into quintiles based on their carbon beta. For the quintile portfolios shown, the sector quintile portfolios are aggregated on an equal-weighted basis. The mean annualized return, BMG alpha, and the standard deviation are shown in percent. For all other statistics, the absolute values are given.

The greenest (low) portfolio had a mean annualized return of 12.55 percent, a Sharpe ratio of 1.00, and a Carhart alpha of -1.11. Returns increased monotonically, with the brownest portfolio returning 19.70 percent with a Sharpe ratio of 1.36 and an alpha of 1.10.

Görgen, Jacob, and Nerlinger next applied their best-in-class approach to country portfolios. They found that brown portfolios across European countries had by far the lowest mean annualized return, at 5.25 percent. The green portfolio had the second lowest mean return, at 10.39 percent; this was, however, almost double the return of the brown portfolio. This performance is perhaps explained by the greater emphasis on sustainability in Europe, which in turn has led to greater cash flows into sustainable strategies—ESG investing now accounts for one of three dollars under professional management in the U.S. but one out of every two dollars in Europe. In the U.S. the performance of the green and brown portfolios was much more similar, though the greenest portfolio had the highest return and the highest Sharpe ratio (see Figure 11).

Figure 11: Best-in-Sector Approach: EU and U.S.

Portfolio	Mean Return (p.a.)	SD	Sharpe Ratio	Alpha	Market Beta	BMG Beta
Panel A: EU						
Low	10.39	23.83	0.46	−9.34	1.50	−0.73
2	13.03	19.55	0.66	−5.57	1.27	−0.49
3	12.61	17.58	0.69	−5.44	1.18	−0.34
4	14.24	16.95	0.82	−3.33	1.13	−0.23
High	5.25	21.47	0.29	−9.18	1.28	0.19
Panel B: North America						
Low	20.91	14.64	1.35	5.40	0.96	−0.21
2	17.72	13.54	1.25	1.54	0.96	−0.02
3	19.55	14.46	1.29	1.62	1.02	0.11
4	19.54	16.43	1.16	0.71	1.15	0.28
High	19.90	20.30	0.96	0.00	1.33	0.66

This figure reports risk and return measures for best-in-class country portfolios. Within each country, stocks are sorted into quintiles based on their carbon beta. For the quintile portfolios shown, the country quintile portfolios are aggregated on an equal-weighted basis. Panel A displays the results for European countries, Panel B for North American countries. The mean annualized return, BMG alpha, and the standard deviation are shown in percent. For all other statistics, the absolute values are given.

Their findings led Görgen, Jacob, and Nerlinger to conclude that "both brown and green stocks exhibit risks stemming from the uncertain transition process from a carbon-based to a low-carbon economy. Most sustainable ratings do not mirror this twofold character of carbon risk. Our measure of carbon risk, the carbon beta, can reflect both brown and green risk."

Most investors only consider that if the transition toward a low-carbon economy develops faster or more extensively than anticipated, brown stocks are more exposed to risk. However, if the transition develops slower or less extensively, green firms are the ones more at risk. It is extremely important to understand that known BMG risks are already incorporated into prices. Thus, only the unexpected should impact returns.

Görgen, Jacob, and Nerlinger also found that much of the returns of green and brown portfolios are explained by exposure to common equity factors, and that the return patterns vary as factor exposures change from low- to high-scoring portfolios.

Their findings also led the authors to conclude that "screening strategies allow investors to reach a certain threshold value of carbon beta; however, this comes with less risk-adjusted performance." They were also able to conclude that best-in-class approaches on sector levels allow investors to gain a certain degree of greenness or brownness without sacrificing sector exposure.

Summarizing their findings, they stated: "For the integration of carbon risk (either in the green or brown direction), we advise that investors carefully analyze all available information. In particular, the measure for greenness and brownness, respectively, influences risk and return profiles remarkably."

We would add that their findings of very different return results depending on which green versus brown metric was used (the carbon risk measure, BMG, or the MSCI carbon emissions measure) help explain the wide dispersion of findings from academic research on sustainable investing. You will find more evidence of this problem when we discuss the findings of the 2020 study "Have Investors Paid a Performance Price? Examining the Behavior of ESG Equity Funds."

We now turn to examining further research on the impact of the conflicting forces we have been discussing—investor preferences lead to different short- and long-term impacts on asset prices and returns. To review, firms with high sustainable investing scores earn rising portfolio weights, leading to short-term capital gains for their stocks—realized returns rise temporarily. However, the long-term effect is that higher valuations reduce expected long-term returns. The result can be an increase in green asset returns even though brown assets earn higher *expected* returns. In other words, there can be an ambiguous relationship between carbon risk and returns in the short term.

"Decarbonization Factors." Alexander Cheema-Fox, Bridget Realmuto LaPerla, George Serafeim, David Turkington, Hui (Stacie) Wang[18]

This ambiguous relationship was demonstrated by the 2021 study "Decarbonization Factors," covering the period June 2009 to 2018. They found that decarbonization factor returns (strategies associated with lowered carbon emissions) were associated with contemporaneous institutional flows into the factors—buying decarbonization factors when coincident flows were positive, while selling the factors when flows were negative, yielded significant alphas of between 1.5 percent and 4.4 percent in the United States and 2.5 percent and 8.5 percent in Europe. In addition, combining decarbonization factors without accounting for flows had little effect on portfolio performance. Their results led the authors to conclude:

"Institutional investor flows contain information about anticipated fundamentals related to climate change developments." Their findings are consistent with the economic theory that brown stocks have higher expected returns, though green stocks can outperform in the short term due to cash flows.

"Valuing ESG: Doing Good or Sounding Good?" Bradford Cornell and Aswath Damodaran[19]

With the mixed results in mind, Cornell and Damodaran investigated the interaction between ESG-related investment criteria and value in their 2020 study.

These were among their key findings:

- The evidence that socially responsible firms have lower discount rates, and thereby investors have lower expected returns, is stronger than the evidence that socially responsible firms deliver higher profits or growth.
- The evidence is stronger that bad firms get punished, either with higher discount rates or a greater incidence of disasters and shocks—ESG advocates are on much stronger ground telling companies not to be bad than telling them to be good.
- While the evidence is weak that being good improves a company's operating performance (increases cash flows), there is more solid backing for the proposition that being bad can make funding more expensive (higher costs of equity and debt).
- Investing in companies that are recognized by the market as good companies is likely to decrease rather than increase investor returns, but investing in companies that are good, before the market recognizes and prices in the goodness, has a much better chance of success.
- There is little consistent evidence that socially responsible funds that invest in these companies deliver excess returns.
- There is no evidence that active ESG investing does any better than passive ESG investing, echoing a finding in much of active investing literature.

"'Honey, I Shrunk the ESG Alpha': Risk-Adjusting ESG Portfolio Returns." Giovanni Bruno, Mikheil Esakia, and Felix Goltz[20]

The next study we review also focused on the conflicting evidence issue. The authors of this 2021 study sought to determine whether evidence supporting recent claims that ESG strategies generate outperformance was accurate. To make that determination, they constructed 12 ESG strategies that had been shown to outperform in popular papers. They then assessed the performance benefits to investors after accounting for sector and factor exposures, downside risk, and attention shifts. They used monthly ESG ratings data from MSCI (also known as Intangible Value Assessment, or IVA) from January 2007 to June 2020. ESG ratings range from 0.0 to 10.0, with a high score indicating strong performance on ESG issues. They used the component scores for the environmental, social, and governance components of the overall rating. They used the scores, as published by MSCI, to design strategies that focused on one component. In addition, they used aggregate ESG scores. They then constructed the aggregate ESG score of a firm as the weighted average of the component scores.

They then designed long/short strategies that captured performance differences between ESG leaders and ESG laggards. At each monthly rebalancing date, they selected 30 percent of the stocks with the highest ESG score in the long leg, and 30 percent of stocks with the lowest score in the short leg. The rebalancing date was the third Friday of the calendar month. Stocks within the long and the short legs were equally weighted. They then evaluated strategy returns from January 2008 to June 2020. They constructed three types of strategies, following popular industry papers:

- *Overall ESG Score and Component Scores (E, S, and G)*: selecting stocks based on their overall ESG score, or the score for one of the three components, leading to four different strategies.
- *ESG Momentum Score*: selecting stocks based on their ESG Momentum, defined as the change of their ESG score over 12 months.
- *Combined Score (ESG and ESG Momentum)*: selecting 30 percent of stocks in the long leg by selecting 40 percent of stocks with the highest ESG score and then excluding 10 percent of stocks with the lowest ESG Momentum. Similarly, the short leg selected 40 percent of stocks with the lowest ESG score and then excluded 10 percent of stocks with the highest ESG Momentum.

They then measured the level of returns of ESG strategies that did not come from exposure to standard factors, employing a standard time-series regression. Their multifactor model included seven factors: the market, value, size, momentum, low volatility, high profitability, and low investment factors.

Following is a summary of their conclusions:

- When accounting for exposure to standard factors, none of the 12 different strategies constructed to tilt to ESG leaders added significant outperformance, whether in the U.S. or in developed markets outside the

U.S. Across the different ways of using ESG ratings to build the strategies and across the two universes, none of the estimates of multifactor alpha were significantly different from zero—implying that an investor cannot improve their Sharpe ratio by using these ESG strategies.

- Seventy-five percent of CAPM alpha outperformance was due to quality factors that were mechanically constructed from balance sheet information.
- ESG strategies have pronounced sector biases, except in the case of the ESG Momentum strategy. For example, in the U.S., ESG strategies overweight technology stocks. And sector neutrality weakens the performance of the ESG strategies.
- ESG strategies do not offer significant downside risk protection—accounting for exposure of the strategies to a downside risk factor does not alter the conclusion that there is no value added beyond implicit exposure to standard factors such as quality (quality companies tend to be large, profitable, and invest conservatively). In other words, ESG strategies tend to be large-cap quality strategies. Over the sample period, an investor who tilted to quality factors with the same intensity as the U.S. ESG strategy would have outperformed the ESG strategy.
- Recent strong performance of ESG strategies can be linked to an increase in investor attention—flows into sustainable mutual funds showed that attention to ESG rose remarkably over the later period of their sample, from about 2013. Alpha estimated during low attention periods was up to four times lower than alpha during high attention periods, and at times even turned negative. Therefore, studies that focus on the recent period tend to overestimate ESG returns.

Their findings led Bruno, Esakia, and Goltz to conclude: "Claims of positive alpha in popular industry publications are not valid because the analysis underlying these claims is flawed. Omitting necessary risk adjustments and selecting a recent period with upward attention shifts enables the documenting of outperformance where in reality there is none." Their conclusion is consistent with the observation by Cornell and Damodaran, who stated:

"There is one possible scenario where being good benefits both the company (by increasing its value) and investors in the company (by delivering higher returns), but it requires an adjustment period, where being good increases value, but investors are slow to price in this reality. After all, concern over ESG is a relatively new phenomenon coming to the fore during the past 10 years or so; it is possible that market prices have been adjusting to a new equilibrium that reflects ESG considerations. As the market adjusts to incorporate ESG information, and assuming that the information is material to investors, the discount rate for highly rated ESG companies will fall and the discount rate for low-rated ESG companies will rise. Due to the changes in the discount rates, the relative prices of highly rated ESG stocks will increase and the relative prices of low-ESG stocks will fall. Consequently, during the adjustment period the highly rated ESG stocks will outperform the low-ESG stocks, but that is a one-time adjustment effect. Once prices reach equilibrium, the value of high-ESG stocks will be greater and the expected returns they offer will be less. In equilibrium, highly rated ESG stocks will have greater values, but investors will have to be satisfied with lower expected returns."

"Environmental, Social, and Governance (ESG) Investing: An Evaluation of the Evidence." Wayne Winegarden[21]

We now turn our attention to a study on the performance of the relatively few sustainable mutual funds with long track records.

Wayne Winegarden, author of this 2019 study, analyzed the performance of 30 ESG funds that had either existed for more than 10 years or had outperformed the S&P 500 Index over a short-term time frame.

The following is a summary of his findings:

- Of the 18 ESG funds examined that had a full 10-year track record, a $10,000 ESG portfolio (equally divided across the funds, including the impact from management fees) would be 43.9 percent smaller after 10 years compared to a similar investment in an S&P 500 Index fund.
- Only one of the 18 funds exceeded the return of an S&P 500 benchmark investment over a five-year investment horizon, and only two were able to beat the S&P 500 benchmark over a 10-year investment horizon.
- ESG funds were more expensive, with an average expense ratio of 0.69 percent versus the much lower (single-digit) expense of an S&P 500 Index fund. The average expense ratio of the subcategory of ESG funds that focused on social goals was an even higher 0.89 percent. Over long investment horizons, these much higher expenses create a significant drag on returns, assuming returns are similar otherwise.
- ESG funds were also riskier as measured by concentration. On average, their top 10 holdings constituted 37 percent of the portfolio compared to 21 percent for a broad-based S&P 500 Index fund, significantly reducing diversification benefits. In one fund, the VanEck Vectors Environmental

Services ETF, the top 10 holdings represented 64 percent of the portfolio. Concentration at these levels imposes large risks on investors.

Winegarden concluded: "Judged against past performance, ESG funds have not yet shown the ability to match the returns from simply investing in a broad-based index fund. Explicitly recognizing this tradeoff is essential to enable investors to better pursue their financial goals in the manner that reflects their values and the costs they are willing to bear."

"Have Investors Paid a Performance Price? Examining the Behavior of ESG Equity Funds." Jan-Carl Plagge and Douglas Grim[22]

Jan-Carl Plagge and Douglas Grim, of the research team at Vanguard, provide further evidence on ESG equity funds in their 2020 study. They investigated the performance characteristics of investable ESG equity funds in order to assess whether support for a particular direction in performance impact can be found. The dataset comprised both index and active equity mutual funds and exchange traded funds with a U.S. investment focus that indicates the use of ESG factors in their investment process. Their data sample covered the 15-year period 2004–2018.

Their selection of ESG funds followed Morningstar's Sustainability Rating strategies. They removed from their sample all funds with an industry-specific investment focus—they assumed the characteristics of these funds are mainly driven by industry-specific (rather than ESG) characteristics. As evidence of the increasing popularity of ESG investing, their empirical dataset began with a total of 98 funds and gradually increased over time to a total of 267 funds by the end of 2018.

Following is a summary of their findings:

- After controlling for style factor exposures, the majority of funds in any of the tested ESG categories did not produce statistically significant positive or negative gross alpha.
- An industry-based performance contribution analysis revealed that while systematic difference in allocations relative to the broad market exist, their median contribution to performance is close to zero over time.
- Return and risk differences of ESG funds can be significant and appear to be mainly driven by fund-specific criteria rather than by a homogeneous ESG factor. For example, some funds have a large-cap focus, others a growth focus, and even one with a midcap focus. In addition, there are differences in industry concentrations (which lead to dispersion in returns).

- Across all four categories (index, active, exclusion based, and non-exclusion based), the majority of observations display higher volatility than the broad market. This should not be a surprise because, by definition, ESG funds are less diversified than the market.
- The average expense ratio of active ESG funds was 1.1 percent per annum, more than twice as high as the average expense ratio of index ESG funds, at about 0.5 percent per annum.
- ESG funds with higher average expense ratios generally produce lower net alpha, an inverse relationship that holds true for both active and index ESG funds.
- Across all fund categories and all time periods (including three five-year subperiods), the majority of gross alphas were negative in median terms, though not on a statistically significant basis.
- There was a modest decline in gross alphas over time for the categories of active funds and exclusionary-based and non-exclusionary-based funds—evidence of increasing market efficiency.
- A Fama-French five-factor (market beta, size, value, investment, and profitability) analysis revealed negative loadings on the size factor (ESG companies tend to be larger). The other factor loadings tended to cluster around zero. The alphas also tended to cluster around zero. However, for active funds, the share with positive alphas declined over time.

Plagge and Grim concluded that due to the wide dispersion of outcomes caused by systematic differences in portfolio holdings, investors are best served by assessing investment implications on a fund-by-fund basis. They added:

> "Our mixed and dispersed performance results suggest that it is difficult to make generalizations on the investment risk and return impact when replacing a conventional U.S. equity fund with an ESG fund. Carefully assessing the important and unique attributes of both funds seems to be an essential step in determining the potential direction and magnitude of any differences."

We can also examine the performance of socially responsible hedge funds. The research uncovers some important, and disturbing, findings.

"Socially Responsible Hedge Funds." Hao Liang, Lin Sun, Melvyn Teo[23]

The authors of this May 2020 study, covering the period 1994–April 2019, examined the performance of hedge funds whose management companies endorse the United Nations Principles for Responsible Investment (PRI). Their fund universe had a total of 18,440 hedge funds, of which 3,896 were live funds and 14,544 were dead funds—demonstrating the importance of taking into account survivorship bias. Their dataset included 2,321 PRI signatories. By the end of the sample period in April 2019, there were 174 PRI signatory hedge fund firms managing 489 hedge funds with $316 billion under management, an elevenfold increase in the hedge fund assets managed by PRI signatories. In addition, during this period the assets managed by hedge fund firms that endorsed the PRI increased from a modest 3 percent to 30 percent of all hedge fund assets.

The authors calculated firm ESG performance primarily using Thomson Reuters data. The Thomson Reuters ESG ratings measure a company's relative ESG performance, commitment, and effectiveness across 10 main themes: environmental resource use, environmental emissions, environmental product innovation, workforce, human rights, community, product responsibility, management, shareholders, and corporate social responsibility (CSR) strategy. The ratings are derived from more than 400 company-level ESG metrics, which are based on information from annual reports, company websites, nonprofit organization websites, stock exchange filings, CSR reports, and news sources. They complemented the Thomson Reuters ESG data with data from MSCI ESG Research (STATS) and Sustainalytics.

The MSCI ESG score is based on strength and concern ratings for seven qualitative issue areas: community, corporate governance, diversity, employee relations, environment, human rights, and products, as well as concern ratings for six controversial business issue areas: alcohol, gambling, firearms, military, nuclear power, and tobacco.

The Sustainalytics ESG ratings gauge how well companies manage ESG issues related to their businesses and provide an assessment of firms' ability to mitigate risks and capitalize on opportunities. Sustainalytics assesses a company's ESG engagement along four dimensions:

1. *Preparedness*: assessments of company management systems and policies designed to manage material ESG risks.
2. *Disclosure*: assessments of whether company reporting meets international best practice standards and is transparent with respect to the most material ESG issues.
3. *Quantitative Performance*: assessments of company ESG performance based on quantitative metrics such as carbon intensity.
4. *Qualitative Performance*: assessments of company ESG performance based on the controversial incidents that the company is involved in.

Following is a summary of their findings:

- Signatories exhibit better ESG performance than do nonsignatories. However, 21 percent of signatory ESG scores fell below the median ESG score—a significant number of signatories do not walk the talk.
- ESG scores are highly persistent—ESG performance is a durable characteristic of investment firms.
- Hedge funds managed by investment management firms that endorse the PRI underperformed those managed by other investment management firms by 2.5 percent per annum (t-statistic = 3.93) after adjusting for covariation with the Fung and Hsieh seven factors (bond, commodity, and currency trend-following factors, equity and bond market factors, and equity- and bond-size spread factors). The spread in raw returns was 1.44 percent (t-statistic = 2.06).
- The underperformance of signatory hedge funds is substantially stronger in signatories with low ESG scores—low-ESG signatory hedge funds underperformed low-ESG nonsignatory hedge funds by 7.72 percent per annum (t-statistic = 3.18) after adjusting for risk. In contrast, the difference in risk-adjusted performance between high-ESG signatory and nonsignatory hedge funds was a modest 0.54 percent per annum (t-statistic = 0.74).
- Signatories that do not walk the talk exhibit greater operational risk.
- While hedge funds that endorsed the PRI underperformed other hedge funds after adjusting for risk, they attracted larger flows and harvested greater fee revenues—signatories attracted an economically and statistically meaningful 16 percent more flows per annum than did nonsignatories.

Liang, Sun, and Teo concluded: "The results suggest that some signatories strategically embrace responsible investment to pander to investor preferences." They added: "The findings suggest that the underperformance of signatory hedge funds cannot be traced to high ESG stocks and, therefore, support the agency [risk, misalignment of interests] view." They also noted: "Low-ESG signatories are more likely to disclose new regulatory actions as well as investment and severe violations on their Form ADVs, suggesting that they deviate from expected standards of business conduct or cut corners when it comes to compliance and record keeping." Unfortunately, they also noted: "Investors appear unaware of the agency and operational issues percolating at such signatories. Low-ESG signatories attract as much fund flows as do high-ESG signatories." The bottom line is that some firms appear to strategically endorse responsible investing but don't practice what they preach.

Their findings were consistent with those of Soohun Kim and Aaron Yoon, authors of the 2020 study "Analyzing Active Managers' Commitment to ESG:

Evidence from United Nations Principles for Responsible Investment."[24] They found "a significant increase in fund flow to signatory funds regardless of their prior fund-level ESG score. However, signatories do not improve fund-level ESG score while exhibiting a decrease in return. Overall, only a small number of funds improve ESG while many others use the PRI status to attract capital without making notable changes to ESG." And finally, they shockingly found that "signatories vote less on environmental issues and their stock holdings experience increased environment related controversies." It is a shock, they added, because "environmental controversies have been documented to be tail risks that have significant negative implications to stock prices."

In a related study, Rajna Gibson, Simon Glossner, Philipp Krueger, Pedro Matos, and Tom Steffen, authors of the 2020 paper "Responsible Institutional Investing Around the World," found similar results for U.S. domiciled institutional funds: U.S. institutions that publicly commit to responsible investing do not exhibit better ESG scores.[25] However, non-U.S. institutions that publicly commit to PRI principles do exhibit higher ESG scores. Consistent with other research, they also found "weak evidence of lower equity portfolio returns when comparing them to non-PRI signatories." However, they also found "evidence that negative screening, integration, and engagement lower portfolio risk."

Unfortunately, the evidence demonstrates that at least a significant portion of hedge funds use PRI as a marketing ploy and a way for companies to get free money. And there is evidence that responsible investing has negatively impacted their returns. The same is true for institutional funds in general, though the evidence of a negative impact on returns is weaker.

Development of a Socially Responsible Factor

"Classifying and Measuring the Performance of Socially Responsible Mutual Funds." Meir Statman and Denys Glushkov[26]

Meir Statman and Denys Glushkov added two social responsibility factors to the commonly used Carhart four-factor model (beta, size, value, and momentum).

The first social responsibility factor they proposed is the top-minus-bottom factor (TMB), consisting of relations, environmental protection, diversity, and products. The second factor is the accepted-minus-shunned factor (AMS), consisting of the difference between the returns of stocks of companies commonly accepted by socially responsible investors and the returns of stocks of companies they commonly shun. Shunned stocks included those of companies in the alcohol, tobacco, gambling, firearms, military, and nuclear industries.

Statman and Glushkov built their social responsibility factors with data from the MSCI ESG KLD STATS database and noted: "The two social responsibility factor betas capture well the social responsibility features of indices and mutual funds. For example, TMB and AMS betas are higher in the socially responsible KLD 400 Index than in the conventional S&P 500 Index." Their study covered the period January 1992 (when data first became available) through June 2012. To construct their two social responsibility factors, they calculated each company's TMB-related score (total strengths minus total concerns) at the end of each year based on their set of five social responsibility criteria (employee relations, community relations, environmental protection, diversity, and products) and its AMS-related score, based on whether it is "shunned" or accepted. They then matched the year-end scores with returns in the subsequent 12 months.

The long side of the TMB factor is a value-weighted portfolio of stocks from firms that rank in the top third of companies sorted by industry-adjusted net scores in at least two of their five social responsibility criteria and not in the bottom third by any criterion. The short side of the TMB factor is a value-weighted portfolio of stocks from firms ranked in the bottom third of companies sorted by industry-adjusted net scores in at least two of the five social responsibility criteria and not in the top third by any criterion.

Similarly, the long side of the AMS factor is a value-weighted portfolio of the accepted companies' stocks, and its short side is a value-weighted portfolio of shunned companies' stocks. Statman and Glushkov constructed the TMB and AMS portfolios as of the end of each year.

Following is a summary of their findings:

- On average, the returns of the top social responsibility stocks exceeded those of the bottom social responsibility stocks. The TMB factor's mean annualized return was 2.8 percent.
- On average, the returns of accepted stocks were lower than the returns of shunned stocks. The AMS factor's mean annualized return was -1.7 percent.
- There was virtually no correlation of returns between the two factors.
- The six-factor alpha for the TMB factor was 0.55 percent, implying that social responsibility improves performance when it is in the form of high TMB. The incremental alpha due to high TMB was generally statistically significant.
- The six-factor alpha for the AMS factor was -0.36 percent, implying that social responsibility detracts from performance when it is in the form of high AMS. The negative alpha could be viewed as the price of avoiding sin stocks. However, the AMS score was not statistically significant.
- The difference in alpha was most pronounced when comparing funds with high TMB and low AMS betas to funds with low TMB and high AMS

betas. The first group had high alpha and the second had low alpha. The difference in annualized alphas was a statistically significant 0.91 percent.

Statman and Glushkov concluded: "A lack of statistically significant differences between the performances of socially responsible and conventional mutual funds is likely the outcome of socially responsible investors' preference for stocks of companies with high TMB and high AMS. The first preference adds to their performance, whereas the second detracts from it, such that the sum of the two is small. A proper analysis of socially responsible mutual funds' performance requires separate accounting for the effects of TMB and AMS on performance."

Their finding that the AMS factor produces negative alpha is consistent with both the previously discussed theory and prior research. The finding of positive alpha for the TMB factor, however, is a puzzle for the same reason that the negative alpha for AMS should be expected. If enough sustainable investors shun stocks with low TMB scores, the cost of capital of such companies will rise, and so will their expected returns. Hence the apparent anomaly. Perhaps the alpha could be explained by exposure to another factor (such as quality or low beta) not included in the four-factor model (beta, size, value, and momentum).

The research provides us with other possible explanations:

- The 2011 study from Alex Edmans, "Does the Stock Market Fully Value Intangibles? Employee Satisfaction and Equity Prices," found that stocks of companies with highly satisfied employees earned higher returns than other stocks.[27]
- The 2005 study "The Eco-Efficiency Premium Puzzle," by Jeroen Derwall, Nadja Guenster, Rob Bauer, and Kees Koedijk, found that stocks of companies with good environmental records earned higher returns than other stocks.[28]
- The 2007 study by Alexander Kempf and Peer Osthoff, "The Effect of Socially Responsible Investing on Portfolio Performance," found that stocks of companies that ranked high overall on community, diversity, employee relations, environment, human rights, and products did better than stocks that ranked low on those measures.[29] In each case, higher returns could result from investor myopia—they tend to focus on possible negative short-term costs (such as higher wages) and underestimate long-term benefits.

We have another important issue to consider. The evidence demonstrates that with sustainable investing there are two conflicting forces at work. The evidence does suggest that the exclusionary issue leads to a reduction in returns.

However, the sustainability issue also leads to a reduction in risks. Perhaps the two might offset each other in terms of *risk-adjusted* returns.

"Is ESG an Equity Factor or Just an Investment Guide?" André Breedt, Stefano Ciliberti, Stanislao Gualdi, Philip Seager[30]

In this 2019 study, its authors sought to determine the impact that ESG investing has on risk-adjusted returns, employing asset-pricing models for benchmarks. They used the MSCI ESG database, which contained monthly ratings for 16,799 worldwide companies. Their study covered the period January 2007 through October 2017.

Following is a summary of their findings:

- ESG scores might have a developed-region bias; emerging markets have lower ESG scores than developed markets.
- ESG score is negatively correlated to the size (SMB) factor and slightly positively correlated to the low-volatility (LV)/low-beta (LB) factors. Large-cap stocks and low-volatility/low-beta stocks have higher ESG scores.
- An equity-market-neutral portfolio constructed with ESG ratings as a predictor showed flat worldwide performance. (Performance was marginally positive in Europe but negative in the United States. None of the results, however, was statistically significant.)
- The portfolio's total performance could be explained by negative SMB exposure, negative momentum (UMD) factor exposure, and positive LB exposure.
- The portfolio's remaining unexplained performance was flat.
- The environmental and social scores do not contribute to performance, and the positive benefit of the governance score is explained well by its correlation to the profitability factor.

The authors concluded that their results indicate that "any benefit from incorporating ESG credentials into a portfolio is already captured by other well-defined and known equity factors. An ESG-tilted process does not deliver higher risk-adjusted returns."

While this evidence demonstrates that ESG information yields no additional benefit, it also indicates—importantly—that ESG information does not negatively affect risk-adjusted returns. This information does, however, allow investors to express their social views through their investments without any penalty, at least in terms of risk-adjusted returns.

The research provides us with another perspective on sustainable investing, one that is inconsistent with traditional economic theory (specifically efficient markets).

Do Markets Efficiently Price Sustainable Risks?

"ESG Risks and the Cross-Section of Stock Returns." Simon Glossner[31]

An interesting approach to analyzing the performance of ESG investing was taken by the author of this 2017 study. He used data on ESG risks provided by RepRisk, which since 2007 has screened thousands of information sources (e.g., print and online media, NGOs [nongovernmental organizations], government bodies) on 28 predefined ESG issues, such as environmental pollution, human rights violations, and fraud:

> "This collection of ESG issues is then used to calculate an ESG-related reputational risk exposure score, the RepRisk Index, for each firm in the sample. In this process, RepRisk distinguishes major from minor issues based on the severity, reach, and novelty of an issue. The RepRisk Index ranges from 0 to 100. A higher number denotes a higher ESG risk: An index value between 0–25 indicates a low risk, 26–50 a medium risk, 51–75 a high risk, and 76–100 a very high risk. ... A firm has a high ESG risk exposure when its RepRisk Index reached values of larger than 50 over the past two years, indicating that the firm had many and severe ESG issues."

Glossner created a portfolio of the stocks with RepRisk scores with a two-year peak RepRisk Index of larger than 50. In other words, instead of analyzing whether firms do well by doing good, his study asked whether doing bad destroys shareholder value. Unfortunately, his dataset is only available for the short period 2009 through 2016. There were 38 firms with high ESG risks in December 2010, and 95 firms (mostly large cap, with median market cap of $49 billion) with high ESG risks in December 2014.

Following is a summary of his findings:

- In December 2014, the most common industries of the 95 firms with high ESG risks were banking (9 firms), pharmaceutical products (8), retail (8), business services (7), and petroleum and natural gas (7). Note the absence of the three sin industries of tobacco, alcohol, and gaming.

- Negative ESG events are associated with significant negative abnormal returns over the short term (21 days). For example, an increase in the RepRisk Index of larger than 10 points has a significant negative abnormal return of 0.40 percent. If the RepRisk Index increases at least by 30 points (indicating more severe ESG issues), the negative abnormal return exceeds 2 percent.
- Firms with high ESG risks have more ESG issues in the next year than firms with low or medium ESG risks—there is persistence in ESG scores.
- Firms with high ESG risks have significantly weaker operating performances (based on four different ratios: return on equity, one-year sales growth, net profit margin, and return on assets), more negative earnings surprises, and more negative earnings announcement returns than peers. The abnormal returns of the earnings announcements explain about half of the negative alpha of the U.S. portfolio with high ESG risks.
- A value-weighted U.S. portfolio of firms with the worst histories of ESG issues is associated with negative abnormal stock of about 3.5 percent, statistically significant at the 1 percent confidence level.
- A similar European portfolio (44 firms) exhibits significant abnormal returns of between 2 percent and 4 percent. The negative alphas are significant at the 5 percent level with the Carhart four-factor European model, and at the 1 percent level with an eight-factor world model. This provides out-of-sample support for the U.S. findings.
- Robustness checks confirm that the abnormal returns of these firms are not the result of common risk factors: The underperformance stems from underperforming industries, negative outliers, weak profitability, weak corporate governance, or many other firm or stock characteristics.

Glossner's findings led him to conclude that investors underestimate the negative consequences of high ESG risks, underreacting to prior negative ESG events. Thus, high ESG risks destroy shareholder value. He provided two explanations for the negative alphas:

First, despite the evidence demonstrating persistence in ESG scores, "Investors are negatively surprised when firms with high ESG risks have new ESG issues." This indicates that investors underestimate the persistence of weak ESG scores.

Second, "Firms with high ESG risks have significantly weaker operating performances, more negative earnings surprises, and more negative earnings announcement returns than peers."

He added that because the stock markets do not fully capitalize the negative consequences of intangible risks, his findings provide "a socially responsible investment strategy that is also profitable—short U.S. or European firms with a notable history of ESG issues." Alternatively, investors could screen them out of eligible universes—the negative/exclusionary screening performed currently by many, if not the majority, of ESG funds today.

While Glossner's finding that investors underreact to negative past ESG events conflicts with the efficient market hypothesis, it is consistent with the literature from the field of behavioral finance. The basic hypothesis of behavioral finance—the study of human behavior and how that behavior leads to investment errors, including the mispricing of assets—is that due to behavioral biases, investors/markets make persistent mistakes in pricing securities. An example of a persistent mistake is that investors underreact to news—both good and bad news are only slowly incorporated into prices, resulting in the momentum anomaly. The explanations for underreaction include optimism, anchoring, and confirmation biases, each of which can cause investors to underweight or ignore contrarian information. The literature also demonstrates that anomalies often occur in intangibles (such as accruals, R&D research, and patents)—and ESG risks are intangible risks.

Note that the publication of his findings could eliminate the anomaly, as the evidence clearly shows that there are persistent risks when investing in firms with the worst ESG histories. However, there are limits to arbitrage that can prevent sophisticated investors from correcting mispricings, allowing anomalies such as those Glossner found to persist. It's also possible that at least some of the negative alphas he found were due to cash flows away from stocks with high negative ESG scores, leading to their short-term underperformance. However, the cash flows could not explain the negative surprises in earnings.

Glossner's findings provide some interesting insights and some valuable information for constructing portfolios. They also provide another example of how markets are not perfectly efficient, and how anomalies can persist due to behavioral errors investors persistently make, and the presence of limits to arbitrage.

Glossner followed up on his work with the 2021 study "ESG Incidents and Shareholder Value."[32] He used a dataset of negative incident news to examine poor ESG practices and answer the following questions: Is a firm's incident history predictive of future ESG incidents? How do high incident rates impact firm value over time? Do stock markets properly price incident-based ESG information? If not, what friction prevents investors from doing so? He measured a firm's past incident rate in order to quantify the frequency and severity of past incident news (e.g., environmental pollution, poor employment conditions, or anticompetitive practices). The incident news came from RepRisk. His sample included news of over 80,000 incidents of about 2,900 unique firms traded on U.S. stock markets between 2007 and 2017. Glossner created portfolios with low (0–25), medium (26–50), and high (51–100) incident scores.

Glossner began by noting that incident-based ESG measures have two main advantages over conventional ESG ratings used in previous research:

"First and conceptually, an incident measure captures poor ESG practices in a direct way, through past realizations of ESG-related business risks and criticism raised by stakeholders themselves. An incident measure could therefore be a better predictor of future incidents than conventional ESG ratings. The problem with conventional ESG ratings is that it is unclear what they measure. Conventional ratings aggregate hundreds of ESG criteria into one company score using very different approaches. As a result, these ratings often disagree with each other because the news character of incidents allows conducting event studies. Second, and empirically, with an incident measure, it is easier to identify its value implications."

Following is a summary of his findings:

- Firms' past ESG incident rates predict more incidents, weaker profits, and lower risk-adjusted stock returns—suggesting that poor ESG practices negatively impact firm performance through a higher probability of new incidents.
- Conventional ESG ratings show less predictive power for future incident news than past ESG incident rates.
- A value-weighted U.S. portfolio with high ESG incident rates is associated with a statistically significant negative alpha of about -3.5 percent per year, translating into a yearly shareholder value loss of about $186 billion. The pattern is robust to risk factors, industries, outliers, and other robustness checks, including his European market finding of a statistically significant -2.5 percent a year return for the value-weighted portfolio.
- Lower risk-adjusted returns are caused by analyst forecast errors as well as lower returns around earnings announcements and subsequent incidents— past ESG incident rates predict negative sell-side earnings surprises, suggesting that analysts overestimate the earnings of firms with high incident rates. This result was robust to analyst-year and industry-year fixed effects and thus cannot be explained by analyst or industry characteristics. When firms with past high ESG incident rates announce their quarterly earnings, abnormal returns are about -1.4 percent per year.
- High ESG incident rates are associated with a significantly higher disagreement among conventional ESG ratings. The finding that more incidents correlate with more rating disagreement could be the result of greenwashing activities—the process of conveying a false impression or providing misleading information about how a company's products are more environmentally sound—which can lead to mispricing.

- Firms with high incident rates experience incidents in all ESG dimensions (environmental, social, and governance).
- Limits to arbitrage cannot explain the lower returns to high ESG incident rates.
- In December 2014, the most common industries of the 95 firms with a high incident score were banking (9 firms), pharmaceutical products (8), retail (8), business services (7), and petroleum and natural gas (7).

Glossner concluded: "Overall, these findings suggest that poor ESG practices negatively impact long-term value, which is not fully reflected in stock prices." He added: "A responsible investor may therefore improve her investment performance by screening out firms with high incident rates, assuming that a sufficient fraction of investors continues to neglect incident-based ESG information."

Glossner's findings provide some interesting insights and some valuable information for constructing portfolios. They also provide another example of how markets are not perfectly efficient, of how anomalies can persist due to behavioral errors investors persistently make, and of the presence of limits to arbitrage. And, as noted earlier, it is also possible that the publication of his findings could eliminate the anomaly.

"Stock Price Overreaction to ESG Controversies." Bei Cui and Paul Docherty[33]

Glossner's finding of underreaction to negative ESG news is consistent with those of Bei Cui and Paul Docherty. They investigated the possible downside of the trend toward ESG investing by examining how this approach might affect market efficiency. They hypothesized that with ESG now a highly salient aspect of an investor's information set, given cognitive limitations investors might devote substantial resources to examining ESG characteristics to the detriment of other firm fundamentals—ESG investors might overweight information related to social performance relative to a firm's financial fundamentals, potentially resulting in the market becoming less efficient. In support, they cited research showing evidence of inflows to funds that have good fund-level social responsibility ratings, and outflows from funds with poor ratings. This relationship is likely to encourage institutional investors to focus on the ESG characteristics of stocks and pay less attention to fundamentals—consistent with evidence that shows institutional investment constraints can affect stock prices.

The authors began by noting that the literature demonstrates that stocks that have higher ESG ratings have lower crash risk and are less likely to hoard bad information. Since crash risk is priced, lower average returns of socially responsible mutual funds documented by many studies within the literature may be associated with investor aversion to crash risk. They also noted that the research shows that the stock market reacts to ESG news in an asymmetric manner; there is a significant negative reaction to the bad ESG news but little reaction to the good news. The relationship is likely to encourage institutional investors to focus on the ESG characteristics of stocks and pay less attention to fundamentals. They examined ESG news that was released between 2000 and 2018. The news about ESG events was obtained from RavenPack.

Following is a summary of their findings:

- Consistent with salience theory, an overemphasis on ESG results in the market overreacting to news about ESG controversies—there was a negative announcement effect when news about ESG controversies was released, but these returns mean reverted over the subsequent 90 days.
- Across all firms, at the 1 percent confidence level, there was a cumulative abnormal return over the 20-day event window (-10 to 10) of -0.773 percent around bad news, while the average abnormal return of -0.004 percent around good news was insignificant.
- The overreaction was more pronounced within smaller firms and stocks that were held by more transient investors before the announcement.
- The price reaction to ESG news events was more pronounced for firms with a higher institutional holding before the news release, and there was a statistically significant decrease in institutional holdings following the release of bad ESG news compared with the equivalent change following good news.
- Indicating the potential leakage of information, there was a clear increase in abnormal trading volume for bad ESG news announcements and only a small increase in abnormal trading volume when there were good ESG news announcements.

The authors concluded: "Contrarian investors are likely able to profit from the unpopular strategy of buying stocks after bad ESG news is released."

The Impact of Sustainable Investing on Investment Strategies

"ESG Investing: From Sin Stocks to Smart Beta." Fabio Alessandrini and Eric Jondeau[34]

We now turn to the impact of sustainable investing on investment strategies. Fabio Alessandrini and Eric Jondeau examined whether improving the ESG of a portfolio impacted performance, tracking error relative to a benchmark, and the efficiency of factor-based strategies. The study covered the period 2007–2017. They considered two types of screening: the negative exclusion of firms based on their ESG scores and the positive (or best-in-class) screening based on the industry-adjusted average score:

- ESG exclusion does not lead to a reduction in risk-adjusted returns.
- ESG exclusion does lead to regional and sectoral tilts as well as (possibly undesirable) risk exposures of the portfolios.
- Almost all passive portfolios considered are negatively exposed to the size factor because large firms usually have higher scores than small firms. In addition, the exclusion process leads to an increased allocation to more expensive stocks (lower value exposure). Factor analysis also showed that ESG screening leads to greater exposure to profitable companies.
- ESG screening sometimes leads to a less intensive use of the targeted factor. For instance, for the smart beta strategy based on size, in the world portfolio the loading on the SMB factor decreases from 1.48 (0 percent exclusion) to 1.23 (50 percent exclusion) in the four-factor model, although it remains highly significant. Similarly, for the momentum strategy, the momentum factor loading decreases from 0.81 to 0.58. For the value strategy, the factor loading on HML (high minus low) in the U.S. decreases from 0.72 to 0.37.
- There are large discrepancies between regions: Europe is the region with the highest average score (6.8), the Pacific is close to the world average (5.8), and the U.S. and emerging countries are below the average (5.0 and 4.2, respectively). Therefore, everything else equal, investors willing to increase the score of their portfolio will tend to overweight firms in Europe and the Pacific. One explanation of why European firms had higher grades than U.S. firms arises from the more stringent regulation in Europe.
- ESG portfolios have a relatively lower weight in the financial and energy sectors, and relatively higher weights in information technology and industrials. Industry biases are more pronounced when E, S, and G criteria are used for screening compared to the industry-adjusted average ESG score.
- Environmental risk is not rewarded with a corresponding positive premium, while the governance risk is indeed rewarded, as the exclusion of the worst companies leads to a lower alpha.

Alessandrini and Jondeau concluded: "The (possibly undesirable) exposure of ESG portfolios to some regional or sectoral tilts or to some risk factors may be mitigated by building algorithms that optimize the ESG profile while keeping the exposures to various risk factors under control."

"Primary Corporate Bond Markets and Social Responsibility." Michael Halling, Jin Yu, Josef Zechner[35]

To this point we have examined the impact of sustainable investment strategies on equity risk and returns. Do we see the same effects in the bond market? The authors of this study examined the impact of ESG scores on bond markets. They began by noting that:

> "Primary bond markets represent a setting in which expected risk premia can be quantified via observed spreads over a riskless reference rate. Primary markets have the additional advantage that offering prices are usually intermediated by investment banks, which should ensure that corporate bonds can be issued at a fair spread which is less likely to be influenced by temporary market (il)liquidity levels, which seems to be the case in secondary bond markets. At the issue stage, bonds generally also have a recent credit risk rating, which effectively controls for many issuer and bond characteristics."

Their data sample covered 5,261 U.S. bond issues from 2002 to 2020. Their analysis focused on the first two ESG components—E and S.

Following is a summary of their findings:

- There is a robust negative relation between E and S ratings and issue spreads in the corporate bond primary market—even when controlling for bond ratings and various firm characteristics, such as net book leverage, size, industry, and profitability, good ES performance is rewarded in primary bond markets by lower credit spreads.
- The effect is strongest for low-rated bonds—for highly rated issuers (i.e., AAA or AA), the aggregate E and S score is insignificant. However, the employee-related score significantly reduces corporate bonds spreads even for highly rated issues.
- The ES score effect is strongest for firms in manufacturing, agriculture, mining, and construction.
- Slightly more than 60 percent of the sample observations come from ES-good firms. Those bond issues pay significantly lower spreads (difference of 45 bps).
- Not all ES dimensions are equally important, as the above results are driven mostly by the product-related dimension and to a lesser extent by the employee-related dimension—other dimensions such as environment, community, or human rights, which get more attention in the media and by policymakers, do not seem to matter for the pricing of corporate bonds.

- Environment-related aspects only seem to matter for those industries with largest exposure to environmental risks.
- During expansions, a high score on employee relations has a significantly negative effect on spreads in the primary market—firms with high scores on employee relations seem to have a comparative advantage in expansions, which are usually characterized by tighter labor markets. During recessions, the coefficient on employee relations loses its significance.

An interesting observation is that the authors found some evidence that the explanatory power for spreads had decreased in recent years. They hypothesized that a potential explanation for such a pattern is that in late 2015 Moody's and S&P announced that they would take ESG dimensions more explicitly into consideration when determining credit ratings, thereby reducing the information content in the respective E and S scores. Fitch, the third leading rating agency, joined Moody's and S&P in taking ESG dimensions into account in 2017. Halling, Yu, and Zechner added that their "results suggest that ratings do not fully subsume all the effects of ESG scores on credit spreads." They concluded: "Our evidence suggests that some ES-dimensions capture information that is relevant for default risk."

The evidence shows that high ESG scores lead to both higher equity valuations and lower corporate bond spreads. Thus, we can conclude that a focus on sustainable investment principles leads to lower costs of capital, providing companies with a competitive advantage. It also provides companies with the incentive to improve their ESG scores. In other words, through the focus on sustainable investment principles, investors are causing companies to change behavior in a positive manner.

"Carbon Emissions, Institutional Trading, and the Liquidity of Corporate Bonds." Jie Cao, Yi Li, Xintong Zhan, Weiming Zhang, Linyu Zhou[36]

Support for the aforementioned findings comes from a 2021 study that investigated how firms' carbon emission levels affect institutional investors' trading behaviors and liquidity conditions of corporate bonds. Its authors began by noting that relative to the equity market, the corporate bond market is less liquid, has higher transactions costs, and is more dominated by institutional investors. In addition, "The over-the-counter nature of the corporate bond market renders it heavily reliant on dealer intermediation…and institutional investors are much more likely to trade in herds in the corporate bond market. Should institutional investors of corporate bonds react to concerns for carbon emissions, the impact would be reflected in both their trading patterns and market liquidity."

Their data sample covered 28,701 unique corporate bonds from 1,274 unique U.S. public firms over the period 2007–2019 and represented 57 percent of the corporate bond market. Causality was further established by exploiting two shocks: the Paris Agreement (December 2015) and the election of U.S. President Trump (November 2016). Firms' carbon emission scores were from their MSCI ESG rating. They focused on mutual funds and insurance companies, as they are the major participants in the corporate bond market.

Following is a summary of their findings:

- Both mutual funds and insurance companies are more likely to sell corporate bonds in herds if the bonds' issuing firms have higher carbon emissions.
- Mutual fund flows negatively respond to the fund's carbon exposures.
- Bond mutual fund managers have the incentive to dump the high-carbon bonds to attract flows and avoid redemptions, leading to potentially higher selling pressure on the high-carbon bonds.
- Mutual funds are more likely to sell high-carbon bonds in the face of investor redemptions.
- Bonds issued by high-emission firms experience worse liquidity conditions.
- Institutional investors' sell-herding levels toward bonds with high-emission issuers greatly intensified after the Paris Agreement and lessened following the Trump election.

Their findings led the authors to conclude that end investors of corporate bond mutual funds are sophisticated enough to take into account exposures to carbon emissions. The result is that carbon emissions affect mutual funds' trading decisions. They added that:

"Constraints faced by institutional investors can amplify shocks for underlying markets. For mutual funds, we find that when facing investor redemptions, funds tend to sell more high-emission bonds. For insurance companies, we find that they are more likely to sell high-emission bonds with higher risks of becoming 'fallen angels', likely driven by their capital constraints."

These effects become amplified during times of market stress.

Our next study examines the impact sustainable investors are having on the high-yield market.

"ESG Impact on High-Yield Returns." Martin Fridson, Lu Jiang, Zhiyuan Mei, Daniel Navaei[37]

The authors of this 2021 study opened their contribution to the sustainable investing literature by examining the ESG indexes' composition for confounding factors (also known as *lurking variables*), such as differences in weighted average credit ratings and maturity/duration that might affect their analysis. As you consider their findings, keep in mind that in late 2015 Moody's and S&P announced that they would take ESG dimensions more explicitly into consideration when determining credit ratings. Thus, all else equal, companies with lower ESG scores will have lower credit ratings.

Following is a summary of their findings:

- Like the rating agencies, the market rates the ESG portfolios more highly than the standard All HY index—option-adjusted spreads (OAS) are lower (see Figure 12).

Figure 12: Maturity, Duration, and Option-Adjusted Spreads

Index	Ave. Maturity (years)	Effective Duration	OAS (bps)
Conventional			
All HY	6.35	4.20	644
BB	8.08	4.64	469
ESG			
ESG Tilt	6.43	4.19	560
Duration-Matched ESG Tily	6.34	4.20	550
Best-in-Class	6.01	4.01	620

SOURCE: ICE Indices, LLC. Data as of June 30, 2020

- ESG-based high-yield indexes produced higher historical returns, lower volatility, and thus a higher Sharpe ratio than a standard high-yield index. However, the differences were not statistically significant. Also note that the BB Index similarly outperformed the All HY Index as well, and the ratings of the three ESG indexes were higher than for the All HY Index but lower than the ratings of the BB Index (see Figure 13).

Figure 13: Portfolio Performance by Month

	Mean (%)	Std. Dev (%)	Sharpe Ratio (x)
All months (42)			
All HY	0.351	2.354	0.09
BB	0.442	2.006	0.15
ESG Tilt	0.391	1.934	0.13
Duration-Matched ESG Tily	0.377	1.908	0.13
ESG Best-in-Class	0.366	2.220	0.12
Up price months (22)			
All HY	1.663	1.250	1.22
ESG Tilt	1.480	1.094	1.23
Duration-Matched ESG Tily	1.431	1.069	1.22
ESG Best-in-Class	1.619	1.155	1.29
Down price months (20)			
All HY	−0.842	2.558	−0.38
ESG Tilt	−0.599	2.059	−0.36
Duration-Matched ESG Tily	−0.580	2.057	−0.35
ESG Best-in-Class	−0.732	2.428	−0.36

SOURCE: ICE Indices, LLC. Data as of June 30, 2020

- The apparently superior downside protection provided by ESG-oriented funds in down markets is explained by two major confounding factors: ESG-based high-yield indexes are underweighted in energy bonds and lowest-rated issues. Thus, the ESG indexes' superior downside protection derives largely from compositional features that are merely side effects of selecting issues on the basis of favorable ESG scores.
- The ESG indexes achieved their total return edge over the ICE BofA US High Yield Index—statistically insignificant though it was—in the months in which the ICE BofA US High Yield Index posted negative price returns.
- There was no evidence that high-yield investors can obtain superior downside protection by concentrating in bonds of companies that lack significant involvement in controversial weapons—bonds of issuers that

had significant involvement in controversial weapons had higher returns than those that did not.

- Energy companies with good ESG scores showed no tendency to either provide or not provide superior downside protection in a high-yield bear market.

Their findings led the authors to conclude: "In the case of high-yield bonds, our findings do not support the contention of some ESG proponents that concentrating on issues with favorable ESG scores improves investment performance." On the other hand, ESG investors did not pay a penalty in the form of lower risk-adjusted returns for expressing their values in their investments.

"Where's the Greenium?"[38] David Larcker and Edward Watts

Our next study examines whether the same effect is found in the municipal bond market. Larcker and Watts focused on the U.S. municipal bond market because green bonds offer the same credit protections as their non-green counterparts. The only difference between the two is that the proceeds from the sale of green bonds are allocated to fund environmentally friendly projects (such as sustainable water management and energy production). Thus, any differences in security pricing can be attributed to investor preferences for sustainability features rather than differences in expectations about future cash flows or risk.

Another benefit of using municipal bonds is that the average issuance size of municipal bonds is only about $5 million versus about $400 million for U.S. corporate bonds. The authors noted:

> "Since the size of green issues is small, there is ample opportunity for green investors to be the marginal trader, which would not be the case for very large green issues in a market setting where green investors do not have the capacity to buy most of the offering. This means that investors with utility for green investments and the willingness to trade off bond yield for green use of funds are likely to be the marginal trader setting the price of the bond. Thus, there are strong reasons to believe that our setting is one where we are most likely to find a greenium (if it actually exists)."

Their data sample consisted of 640 matched pairs of green and non-green issues, issued on the same day, with identical maturity and rating, and issued by the same municipality over the period June 2013 through July 2018.

Following is a summary of their findings:

- There was an economically trivial difference in yield (and spread) between green and non-green bonds of approximately 0.45 bps (indicating a slight green bond discount).
- In approximately 85 percent of matched cases, the differential yield was exactly zero. In addition, among the remaining 15 percent of securities, approximately 40 percent implied a negative differential (or a green bond premium), while the other 60 percent implied a positive differential (a green bond discount). And there is no theory suggesting green bonds should trade at a discount.
- There was no relationship between issuance size and estimated premiums.
- There was no meaningful association between green and non-green bonds and market liquidity.
- Greenwashing—the process of conveying a false impression or providing misleading information about the environmental soundness of a company's products—was found not to be a cause of the lack of a meaningful association between greenness of bonds and market liquidity.
- The underwriting cost charged for issuing green bonds was about 10 percent higher than for almost identical non-green bonds. However, in 70 percent of cases, the differentials were precisely zero, indicating that in most situations underwriters tend to view these securities as identical.
- Green issuances did help to somewhat broaden the issuers' investors base—green issues had 12 to 20 percent less ownership concentration.
- Green bonds are, on average, approximately one notch higher in credit quality, which may reflect wealthier municipalities' preferences toward environmental sustainability.

Their findings led Larcker and Watts to conclude that their results "provide strong evidence that investors are unwilling to sacrifice returns to support environmentally friendly projects, and thus the greenium is equal to zero." They added that, at least in the municipal bond market, the evidence suggests that investor sustainability preferences are unlikely to drive the asset pricing differentials found in some of the prior literature. However, they did add that while "a greenium does not currently exist, as the market matures and gains momentum a greenium may emerge."

"Greenhouse Gas Emissions and Expected Returns." Wei Dai and Philipp Meyer-Brauns[39]

We now turn to examining the impact on greenhouse gas emissions on expected stock and bond returns. In their 2020 study Wei Dai and Philipp Meyer-Brauns examined how company-level greenhouse gas emissions have been related to company financials as well as the expected returns of U.S. companies' stocks and bonds from 2009 to 2018. They began by noting: "As investors seek to incorporate such environmental considerations into their investment decisions, it is important to understand the potential impact of environmental characteristics on firm performance and security returns." They added: "A stock's current market value reflects expectations about future cash flows discounted by the expected return. It is plausible that the environmental profile of a firm could impact its expected cash flows."

Dai and Meyer-Brauns examined the impact of company emissions on stock returns not only on a standalone basis but also controlling for price variables such as market capitalization and relative price combined with cash flow variables such as profitability, which, consistent with valuation theory, are known to contain reliable information about the cross-section of expected stock returns.

Following is a summary of their findings:

- Neither emission intensity, emission level, nor change in emission level provide additional information about future profitability beyond what is contained in current profitability.
- There is little evidence that these emission metrics are reliably associated with the cross-sectional expected returns of stocks after controlling for known drivers of expected stock returns such as market capitalization, relative price, and profitability.
- There is no compelling evidence supporting the issuers' emission metrics as additional drivers of expected bond returns.

Dai and Meyer-Brauns concluded: "Our results provide further evidence that prices quickly incorporate information and reflect the aggregate expectations of market participants, including information about a company's environment-related risks and opportunities." They added: "Our results suggest that investors can pursue environmental goals without compromising sound investment principles."

Returns to Private Impact Investing

"Impact Investing." Brad M. Barber, Adair Morse, Ayako Yasuda[40]

Having completed our review of the research on ESG and SRI investment strategies, we conclude this chapter with a review of the evidence on private impact investing.

Brad M. Barber, Adair Morse, and Ayako Yasuda focused their research on venture capital (VC) and growth equity funds that are structured as traditional private equity funds but with the intentionality that is the hallmark of impact investing—to generate both positive social or environmental returns and positive financial returns.

Using data from Preqin (a provider of data on alternative investments), they constructed a sample of 24,000 investments by about 3,500 investors over the period 1995–2014. These investments reflected 4,659 funds—the combination of traditional VC and impact VC funds. From this sample they isolated 159 as being impact funds using a strict criterion that the fund must state dual objectives in its motivation. They then constructed six impact categories: environmental impact (28 percent), minority and women funding (11 percent), poverty alleviation (43 percent), social infrastructure development (e.g., health, education and mainstream infrastructure) (16 percent), small and medium enterprises (SMEs) funding (42 percent), and focused regional development (jobs creation and economic development funds in a specific region) (33 percent).

Following is a summary of their findings:

- Traditional funds had mean and median internal rates of return (IRR) of 11.6 percent and 7.4 percent respectively, while impact funds had mean and median IRR of 3.7 percent and 6.4 percent respectively. The same pattern emerged for value multiples and imputed public market equivalents. After controlling for fund characteristics, the ex-post financial returns earned by impact funds were 4.7 percentage points lower than those earned by traditional VC funds.
- From 2000 onward, the standard deviation of IRRs for traditional and impact funds was 16.8 percent versus 14.7 percent.
- In random utility/willingness-to-pay (WTP) models, investors accepted 2.5–3.7 percentage points lower IRRs ex-ante for impact funds.
- Development organizations, public pensions (which may be subject to political pressures), Europeans, and United Nations Principles of Responsible Investment signatories had high WTP.
- Financial institutions—banks and insurance companies—had high WTP, likely reflecting their incentives to invest in local communities, either to

comply with the Community Reinvestment Act (CRA) and/or to garner goodwill from the community or politicians/regulators.

- Mission focus (i.e., development organizations and foundations) was associated with a positive WTP of 3.4–6.2 percentage points in expected excess IRR.
- Political or regulatory pressure was associated with a positive WTP of 2.3–3.3 percentage points in expected excess IRR.
- Those subject to legal restrictions (e.g., Employee Retirement Income Security Act) exhibited low WTP.
- Impact funds focused on environmental impact, poverty alleviation, and women or minorities generated the highest WTP estimates. In contrast, impact funds focused on small- and medium-sized enterprises and social infrastructure (e.g., health, education, and mainstream infrastructure) funds did not generate investment rates that reliably differed from those of traditional VC funds.

Summarizing their findings, Barber, Morse, and Yasuda concluded: "Our results provide compelling evidence that investors are willing to pay for nonpecuniary characteristics of investments." They noted that this is consistent with research findings that SRI mutual fund flows are less sensitive to performance than non-SRI flows. They added: "This result indicates that the capital allocation decisions, though certainly governed by the linchpin risk-return tradeoff of wealth maximization in standard utility models, are also shaped by the real-world consequences of the investments that people make."

Summary

While sustainable investing continues to gain in popularity, economic theory suggests that if a large enough proportion of investors choose to avoid the stocks of companies with low sustainability ratings, the share prices of such companies will be depressed. Thus, they would offer higher expected returns (which some investors may view as compensation for the emotional cost of exposure to what they consider offensive companies). With this knowledge, investors are positioned to pursue their financial goals in the manner that reflects their values and the costs they are willing to bear to achieve those values. On balance, the evidence does suggest that investors who desire to express their views through socially responsible investing may be paying a price in the form of lower expected returns. The reason is that some screens, like those that eliminate sin stocks, lead to lower returns.

On the other hand, there are other screens that provide exposure to factors that have led to higher returns (such as profitability), or reduced tail risks. And there is some evidence that investors are underestimating the risks of companies with the worst sustainability scores. The latter two issues suggest that it is possible that intelligent design of a sustainable investment strategy can allow investors to create an efficient portfolio—while accepting lower raw returns yet gaining the benefit of risk reduction.

The reduction in risk, especially tail risk, is important and covers a wide spectrum of risks: reputation risk (e.g., the Volkswagen Dieselgate scandal), human capital risk, litigation risk (PG&E's legal claims of more than $10 billion for California wildfires and BP's $18 billion in claims for the Deepwater Horizon disaster), regulatory risk, corruption risk, and climate risk (including the risk of stranded assets).[41] Each of these risks can impact a company's stock price, its cost of capital, and thus its ability to compete.

Emirhan Ilhan, Zacharias Sautner, and Grigory Vilkov confirmed this in their study "Carbon Tail Risk," finding "strong evidence that climate policy uncertainty is priced in the option market" and that the cost of option protection against downside tail risk is greater for firms with more carbon-intensive business models.[42]

Tinghua Duan, Frank Li, and Quan Wen, authors of the 2020 study, "Is Carbon Risk Priced in the Cross Section of Corporate Bond Returns?" also found that bonds of high-carbon emission (CE) firms were riskier on average than those of low CE as indicated by a higher bond market beta, downside risk, higher illiquidity, and lower credit ratings. They also had more negative cash flow surprises and deteriorating creditworthiness in the future.[43]

The gains in reduced risk offset the lower raw returns, producing similar risk-adjusted returns. In addition, the evidence shows that if ESG investors are willing to tilt their portfolios to those sustainable firms with higher costs of capital, they can have their cake (earn higher expected returns) and eat it too (express their social views).

Peter Diep, Lukasz Pomorski, and Scott Richardson, authors of the 2021 study "Sustainable Systematic Credit," provided evidence that this was true in the corporate bond market as well as in equity markets.[44] They found that there were only modest distortions (in terms of expected returns and possibly higher tracking error from reduced investment opportunity set) from incorporating such ESG objectives. Their findings led them to conclude: "It is currently possible to have significant improvements in the ESG and carbon emission profile without meaningfully changing portfolio attractiveness."

It is also important to note that the ESG premium is time varying. The heightened demand for ESG investments has led to rising valuations of stocks with high ESG scores relative to stocks with low ESG scores, producing short-term capital gains and blurring the expected negative premium. However, the short-term benefit comes at the expense of lower long-term expected returns. Since it is likely that the trend favoring ESG investing will continue, the price ESG investors pay for expressing their social views through their investments, in the form of lower expected returns, might be offset (at least to some degree) by continued rising valuations. However, what cannot continue forever eventually ceases.

With this in mind, investors should be aware of the findings of Ravi Bansal, Di Wu, and Amir Yaron, authors of the 2019 study "Is Socially Responsible Investing a Luxury Good?"[45] They concluded that green stocks outperform brown stocks in good times but underperform in bad times. They argued that "green stocks are similar to luxury goods in that they are in higher demand when the economy does well and thus financial concerns matter less." This is consistent with a wealth-dependent investor preference that is more favorable toward ESG during good times (when risk aversion is low), resulting in higher temporary demand for ESG. This is similar to the time-varying shifts exhibited in the demand for luxury goods. Thus, we can see how time-varying preferences can cause green stocks to outperform over some periods even though they have lower expected returns. It also demonstrates that the risks to ESG investors might show up at the worst possible time, during a bear market when labor capital is also at risk. If you have high risk aversion, like most investors, the risk that ESG investments will perform poorly in bad times should be considered when deciding on your investment strategy.

For investors, the takeaway is that if you are going to make ESG investing a core of your investment philosophy, thorough due diligence is required before committing assets. That due diligence should not only include the screening methodologies but also a careful examination of factor loadings, industry concentrations, country exposures, and expenses. And it may even be difficult to find a fund that exactly meets your own personal criteria. For those investors with sufficiently large investable assets, there are separately managed account providers that will build individually tailored portfolios (which provide the added benefit of tax efficiency).

We close this chapter with an important reminder. A firm's ESG score plays two important roles: It provides important information about the firm's fundamentals (both its risk and return characteristics) and it can also affect investor preferences. As Lasse Heje Pedersen, Shaun Fitzgibbons, and Lukasz Pomorski explain in the study "Responsible Investing: The ESG-Efficient Frontier," each investor should determine their own efficient ESG frontier (the highest Sharpe ratio for their preferred ESG level), evaluating the costs and benefits of sustainable investing, and then construct a portfolio based on that frontier.[46] Their paper also provided important insights into when ESG scores should predict returns positively (for example, if the market has not yet fully incorporated information provided by positive governance ratings, which indicate reduced risks) or negatively in equilibrium (for example, through screening out of assets with high expected returns). In addition, it is also possible that sustainable investors could benefit if an unexpected increase in ESG demand were to reinforce demand for green products, boosting the profits of green firms at the expense of brown firms.

CHAPTER 7

The Impact of Sustainable Investing–How Sustainable Investors Are Changing the World

T HE POPULARITY OF sustainable investing has led to a dramatic increase in the attention it receives from the academic community. In the prior chapter we reviewed the research findings on how sustainable investing impacts the risk and expected returns of portfolios. In this chapter we will review the research on how sustainable investing has affected companies, their employees, and the wider world.

Sustainable Investing Is Making Companies Better

The academic research has found that companies that adhere to positive ESG principles have lower costs of capital, higher valuations, and are less vulnerable to systemic risks. In Chapter 1 we explained that ESG investing covers many different investment approaches, addressing three main areas, each with its own main objective:

1. *ESG*: Improve the risk-return characteristics of a portfolio.
2. *SRI*: Align the portfolio with the investor's beliefs.
3. *Impact Investing*: Use capital to trigger change for social or environmental purposes.

In the prior chapter you learned that the research has produced some mixed results, finding positive, negative, and nonexistent correlations between ESG and financial performance. The inconclusive results may stem from the three different approaches, from the differences in the underlying ESG data used, the varying methodologies applied (especially insofar as they control for common factor exposures), and the fact that the heightened demand for ESG investments has led to rising valuations of stocks with high ESG scores relative to stocks with low ESG scores. Increased cash flows have two effects: First, they lead to short-term capital gains, but ultimately, the higher valuations mean that investors should expect lower future returns over the long term.

"Foundations of ESG Investing: How ESG Affects Equity Valuation, Risk, and Performance." Guido Giese, Linda-Eling Lee, Dimitris Melas, Zoltán Nagy, and Laura Nishikawa[1]

In an effort to address these issues, the authors of this 2019 study began by noting that one limitation of prior research was that it failed to differentiate between correlation and causality: "Often, a correlation between ESG and financial variables is implicitly interpreted to mean that ESG is the cause and financial value the effect, although the transmission easily could also be reversed." Therefore, they took a different approach: "Instead of simply looking for correlations between ESG characteristics and financial performance in historical data, we first analyze the transmission channels from ESG to financial performance and develop a fundamental understanding of how ESG characteristics affect corporations' valuations and risk profiles. Afterwards, we verify these transmission mechanisms using empirical analysis." Their approach provides three benefits:

1. It mitigates the risk of correlation mining between ESG data and financial performance data.
2. It reduces the risk of finding correlations that are caused by unintentional exposures to common factors.
3. It better differentiates between correlation and causality by studying transmission channels.

The authors explained that their analysis was designed to help explain how ESG affects the financial profile of companies in a fundamental way—deriving an understanding of the causal relationship of ESG by examining the transmission channels found in discounted cash flow models, specifically between cash flow, risk and valuation channels, and ESG scores—producing more convincing evidence than simple correlation studies.

They sought to answer the following five questions:

1. Is there convincing evidence based on cash flow?

The study found that firms with strong ESG profiles are more competitive because they use resources more efficiently, are better at developing human capital and managing innovation, have better long-term planning, and have better incentives for senior management. This leads to the ability to generate excess returns, higher profitability, and *ultimately* higher dividends. The highest ESG scoring firms were more profitable and had higher dividends than the lowest ESG scoring firms. These findings explain the economic rationale of the cash flow channel.

2. How well do high-ESG-scoring firms manage business and operational risks (idiosyncratic tail risk)?

The results demonstrated that firms with high ESG scores have better risk management and better compliance standards, leading to fewer extreme events such as fraud, corruption, and litigation (and their negative consequences). The result is a reduction in tail risk in high ESG scoring firms relative to the lowest ESG scoring firms. The highest scoring ESG firms also had lower idiosyncratic risk. And research shows that firms with high idiosyncratic risk have produced lower returns. The results provide the economic rationale for the risk channel.

3. Does a strong ESG profile lead to higher valuations?

The valuation channel is governed by a firm's exposure to systematic risk. High ESG scoring firms have less exposure to market shocks and exhibited lower recent five-year volatility of earnings when compared to low scoring firms.

Thus, they have lower betas. The lower betas result in higher valuations (such as lower book-to-market and higher price-to-earnings ratios), producing lower costs of capital and *ultimately* lower expected returns. Their results explain the economic rationale for the valuation channel.

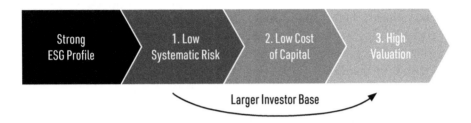

The transmission channel from lower systematic risk to higher valuations can also be explained through the relative size of the investor base. Companies with low ESG ratings have a relatively small investor base because of investor preferences (many risk-averse investors and socially conscious investors avoid exposure to companies with low ESG ratings) and information asymmetry (the problem of asymmetric information between companies and their investors is less severe for companies with high ESG ratings because these companies are typically more transparent, in particular with respect to their risk exposures and their risk management and governance standards).

4. What about causality?

Do higher ESG ratings lead to higher valuations, or do higher valuations lead to higher ESG ratings? It's the chicken-and-egg problem. The authors explained:

"Higher ESG ratings can—through lower systematic risk and lower cost of capital—lead to higher valuations. Alternatively, higher valuations can indicate successful companies that have more money to invest in sustainability-related areas, leading to a higher ESG rating."

They explain the economic rationale:

- An improving ESG profile means a company is becoming less susceptible to systematic risks.
- Lower systematic risk leads to a reduction in a company's cost of capital. The reduction in cost of capital leads to an increase in valuation.

They conducted three tests of causality—for changes in the volatility of common factor risk, changes in beta, and changes in valuation—relative to three categories: decreases in ESG scores, increases in ESG scores, and no change. The changes in financial variables were observed over a three-year period after the change in ESG rating occurred. Upgrades in ESG ratings were associated with *declines* in a firm's systematic risk profile and declines in beta compared to neutral or downgraded companies. Upgrades in ESG ratings were associated with *increases* in valuation as measured by relative increases in price-to-earnings ratios. Importantly, rating upgrades had a lower incident frequency than rating downgrades. Thus, rating changes are a leading indicator for idiosyncratic risks.

5. Given the results of causality tests, is there a link between changes in ESG ratings and future return performance between highest and lowest ESG scoring firms?

The database used was the MSCI ESG Rating for the MSCI World Index universe covering the period January 2007 to May 2017. The universe contained more than 1,600 stocks. All risk and factor calculations were performed using the Barra Long-Term Global Equity Model (GEM LT). Their results were neutralized for industry exposure (through the use of industry-adjusted ESG scores) and size.

Improvement in ESG scores (ESG momentum) results in improved valuation (lower costs of capital) and reduction in specific risk (reduced incidence of tail risk) profiles, thus indicating that ESG momentum can be a source of alpha. They cited research demonstrating that "companies that show a positive ESG rating trend significantly outperformed both the benchmark and a comparable strategy that tilted the portfolio weights toward companies with high ESG ratings." The authors concluded: "ESG momentum can be a useful financial indicator in its own right and may be used in addition to the actual ESG rating in index or portfolio construction methodologies."

By creating transmission channels, Giese, Lee, Melas, Nagy, and Nishikawa provide us with clear and intuitive explanations for how ESG affects the valuation and performance of companies, both through their systematic risk profile (lower costs of capital and higher valuations) and their idiosyncratic risk profile (higher profitability and lower exposures to tail risk).

Such evidence, combined with the powerful trend toward sustainable investing, has caused companies and investment firms to take notice.

Corporations Take Notice

In August 2019 the Business Roundtable, which represents nearly 200 CEOs of the biggest U.S. companies, announced the end of shareholder primacy and called for the role of a corporation to be redefined, suggesting that a large number of firms view sustainability issues as strategically important. In addition, BlackRock CEO Larry Fink sent a letter to investors in January 2020 detailing his plans to incorporate ESG as a new standard for investing. His announcement surely was influenced by the fact that ESG investing now accounts for one out of every three dollars under professional management in the United States and one out of every two dollars in Europe.

What is important to recognize is that the popularity of ESG investing has impacted the costs of capital of companies. Because ESG investors favor companies with high ESG scores and avoid those with low ESG scores, those with low ESG scores will tend to have higher costs of capital, putting them at a competitive disadvantage. Thus, one positive result of the popularity of ESG investing is that it is causing companies to focus on improving their ESG scores in order to lower their costs of capital.

As you will see, improving ESG scores also improves employee satisfaction.

Corporate Sustainability, Stock Returns, and Employee Satisfaction

"Do High Ability Managers Choose ESG Projects that Create Shareholder Value? Evidence from Employee Opinions." Kyle Welch and Aaron Yoon[2]

In their 2021 study, Welch and Yoon examined whether ESG coupled with employee satisfaction can enhance firm value. They began by noting that prior research, including the 2018 study "Crowdsourced Employer Reviews and Stock Returns,"[3] has found that firms experiencing improvements in crowdsourced employer ratings significantly outperform firms with declines. Thus, they are an important determinant of firm value.

Welch and Yoon hypothesized that "firm engagements in ESG may instill a sense of purpose to employees and motivate them. In addition, motivated employees will be more productive, which may lead to enhanced firm value. In such a case, it is possible that ESG coupled with employee satisfaction may enhance firm value over and beyond the effect from employee satisfaction."

Their data is from MSCI ESG Ratings and Glassdoor (for employee satisfaction) and covered the period between 2011 and 2018. Returns were benchmarked against the Fama-French five-factor model (beta, size, investment, profitability, and value).

Following is a summary of their findings:

- Firms with high ratings on both ESG and employee satisfaction significantly outperform those with low ratings on both and with high employee satisfaction alone.
- When the ESG rating is the only signal, there was no meaningful alpha in the long/short portfolio.
- Using employee satisfaction as the only signal to create portfolios, the long/short portfolio generated annual equal-weighted and value-weighted alphas of 2.4 percent.
- Ranking by quartiles, the equal-weighted and value-weighted portfolios of firms with high ESG performance and employee satisfaction significantly outperformed the portfolio of firms with low ratings on both topics by 5.6 percentage points and 5.8 percentage points, respectively.
- The equal-weighted (and value-weighted) portfolio of firms with high ESG performance and employee satisfaction outperformed the firms with low ESG performance and high employee satisfaction by 2.8 percentage points, and the firms with high ESG performance and low employee satisfaction by 5.6 percentage points.
- The equal-weighted and value-weighted long portfolios (firms with high ESG performance and employee satisfaction) outperformed the portfolio of firms with high ESG alone by 3.5 percentage points and 3.3 percentage points, respectively.
- The equal-weighted (and value-weighted) long portfolio of firms outperformed the portfolio of firms with high employee satisfaction alone by 1.6 percentage points.
- Their results were robust to alternative factor models, different subsamples or subperiods, and alternative portfolio construction rules.
- Across all horizons, firms performing better on ESG and employee satisfaction produce superior future sales growth and return on equity.

Welch and Yoon noted that "our results are driven by the firm social investments rather than environmental and governance related investments." They also offered the important caution that while "firm social investments drive our results, readers should be cautious and note that we are not claiming that ESG causes employee satisfaction and that this leads to firm value. Rather, we document that portfolio of firms that score high on ESG and employee satisfaction significantly outperforms those firms with high employee satisfaction alone, indicating that employee satisfaction is an important condition for ESG to enhance shareholder value."

Their results led Welch and Yoon to conclude that "ESG's role on shareholder value is incremental to that from employee satisfaction." They added: "Overall, results suggest that ESG coupled with employee satisfaction enhance shareholder value and these findings have implications not only for asset managers who integrate ESG factors into their portfolios but also for firm managers who implement ESG practices."

Welch and Yoon demonstrated that employee satisfaction may be a condition that better enables ESG to enhance value. Their results demonstrated that ESG coupled with employee satisfaction is a valuable signal to predict stock returns. These findings have implications for asset managers who integrate ESG factors into their portfolios.

We have further evidence that ESG investors are providing societal benefits. Lubos Pastor, Robert Stambaugh, and Lucian Taylor, authors of the 2019 study "Sustainable Investing in Equilibrium,"[4] found that sustainable investing leads to positive social impact through its impact on asset prices. By pushing green asset prices up (lowering the cost of capital) and brown ones down (raising the cost of capital), investors' tastes for green holdings induce more investment by green firms and less investment by brown firms. The more investors care about ESG, the greater the positive social impact.

Momentum in ESG Ratings and Performance

"Sustainable Investment–Exploring the Linkage Between Alpha, ESG, and SDG's." Madelyn Antoncic, Geert Bekaert, Richard Rothenberg, Miquel Noguer[5]

This 2020 study provides further evidence of how sustainable investors impact firms' actions, rewarding those that show improved sustainability ratings with even higher valuations.

They began by noting: "SDGs [sustainable development goals] are much broader than the ESGs and focus on good health and well-being, the elimination of poverty, zero hunger, quality education, clean water and sanitation, reduced inequity, as well as the environment and other issues encapsulated in ESGs. Most importantly, the SDGs call for leaving no one behind." They added: "Leveraging their role as allocators, asset owners can ensure more long-term centric practices among corporations through the lens of an SDG investment strategy and thus support the goals of all facets of sustainable growth."

The authors explored "the possibility of creating an active portfolio that achieves the goals associated with ESG investing but still generates alpha, consistent with fiduciary duties." They did note that by incorporating ESG into the investment process, it is conceivable that ESG becomes a risk factor itself, but it is unlikely that such a factor would be associated with a positive risk premium: "If ESG firms manage to lower their cost of capital by their ESG actions and/or increase their future cash flows by avoiding certain risks, firms with good ESG performance would be valued more highly than similar firms with less exemplary ESG performance. ... It is conceivable that such a valuation premium should be associated with lower returns going forward and can clash with the fiduciary duty of institutional investors."

Antoncic, Bekaert, Rothenberg, and Noguer also examined the SDG impact of the resulting active portfolio relative to the benchmark—the MSCI USA Index. From the roughly 640 stocks in the index, they created an active portfolio of about 50 stocks using the MSCI ESG ratings that showed positive ESG momentum to measure ESG performance and tracked its performance relative to the index. The idea is similar to the concept of fundamental momentum in equities. For example, in his 2015 study, "Fundamentally, Momentum is Fundamental Momentum,"[6] Robert Novy-Marx demonstrated that stocks that have recently announced strong earnings tend to outperform going forward.

The data sample for their study was the period 2013–2018. At the end of each year, stocks in each of 11 GICS (Global Industry Classification Standard) sectors were ranked on their absolute and relative ESG momentum, and the GICS 10 percent highest-ranking stocks were selected. These stocks were held for a full year, after which the portfolio was rebalanced. The stocks within each industry, and the industry portfolios themselves, were market-value weighted. They found that ESG momentum portfolios (both relative and absolute) outperformed the index. Specifically, the relative momentum portfolio generated a highly significant Fama-French three-factor (beta, size, and value) alpha of 5.6 percent per year. Adding the two additional factors of investment and profitability did not change this conclusion.

In terms of factor loadings, the authors found that size and value loadings were not statistically significantly different from zero. In the five-factor model, the conservative minus aggressive (CMA) exposure was borderline statistically significant and negative. The negative CMA exposure suggests the ESG portfolio included firms with aggressive investment strategies, which are typically associated with low future returns. While the alphas for the relative momentum portfolio were significantly different from zero, the alphas for the absolute ESG momentum portfolios were positive but no longer statistically significant. The factor exposures of the absolute ESG momentum portfolio were very similar to those of the relative ESG momentum portfolio.

Relying on data from Global AI, the authors then measured the SDG impact of the active portfolio relative to the benchmark:

"Global AI Co. uses state-of-the-art Big Data techniques to examine a comprehensive set of unstructured data, including news articles, self-reported company data, blogs, NGO [nongovernmental organizations] reports and social media and then creates daily SDG scores at the company level. The scores are available at the individual SDG level, (i.e., company scores are available for each of the 17 SDGs as well as its SDG rating at the overall company level), and can be interpreted as z-scores reflecting sentiment regarding a particular SDG in recent information releases involving the company."

The authors noted:

"The SDG footprint can show how companies have an either positive or negative net influence on SDGs and potentially reveal hidden risks. This creates incentives for corporations to quantify and increase their net SDG contributions and SDG score in order to become more attractive to investors concerned with sustainable investments, which control trillions in assets under management."

They found that "the ESG portfolio shows better sustainability footprint than the benchmark, and persists for at least a year."

Antoncic, Bekaert, Rothenberg, and Noguer demonstrated that—at least over the relatively short period studied—the active ESG relative momentum portfolio significantly outperformed the benchmark index and that the outperformance persisted when controlling for the Fama-French three- and five-factor models, providing hope that ESG investors don't necessarily have to pay a price for expressing their values in their portfolios. They also showed that companies have an incentive to improve their ESG ratings, making themselves more attractive to investors, thereby reducing their cost of capital.

As you consider the findings, keep in mind that the trend toward incorporating ESG is impacting valuations. The cash flows are creating an ESG valuation premium, which should be associated with lower returns going forward. That said, in the short term the cash flows are creating momentum in valuations favoring companies with higher ESG ratings.

The Environmental Impact of ESG Investors

From 2014 to 2018, sustainable investments grew from 18 percent to 26 percent of assets under management in the U.S., reaching a total of $12 trillion. Over the same period, the average carbon intensity of Nasdaq, AMEX, and NYSE companies decreased about 30 percent. The downward trend in corporate greenhouse gas emissions may be partly due to the pressure exerted by green investors who underweight, or exclude from their investments, the most carbon-intensive companies, thereby increasing their cost of capital.

"Environmental Impact Investing." Tiziano De Angelis, Peter Tankov, David Zerbib[7]

This 2020 study examined whether green investing pushes companies to reduce their greenhouse gas emissions and, if so, what factors lead companies to adjust their emissions. Their database covered 348 green funds investing in U.S. equities as of December 2018 and their holdings over the period 2007–2018.

Following is a summary of their findings:

- Environmental stringency of green investors pushes companies to reduce their greenhouse gas emissions by raising their cost of capital. They are more inclined to do so if their abatement costs are low and the proportion and stringency of green investors is high. For example, because they internalize large negative externalities for the coal industry, green investors induce a 1.7 percent annual increase in return on the coal industry compared to utilities. This finding is consistent with prior research showing that the stock returns of the most polluting companies are increased by a positive premium.
- By internalizing the negative impact of green investors on their financial valuations, companies are incentivized to pay a cost to mitigate their emissions by adopting less carbon-intensive technologies to lower their cost of capital. For example, when the proportion of green investments doubles from 25 percent to 50 percent, the carbon intensity falls by 5 percent over a one-year horizon.

These findings are good news for ESG investors, as they demonstrate that their actions are reducing emissions, one of their goals. Here's more good news.

Investors Respond to Fund Climate Responsibility Rankings

The 2015 Paris Agreement recognized finance as an important element to successfully transition to a low-carbon economy. Policymakers hoped to achieve this objective, to a large extent, by mandating an increase in the level of climate-relevant information available to investors. For instance, the European Commission's action plan on sustainable finance, adopted in March 2018, proposed the introduction of an EU-wide eco-label aimed at helping retail investors express their investment preferences on sustainable activities.

In April 2018 Morningstar introduced an eco-label for mutual funds, the Low Carbon Designation (LCD). To receive the LCD, a mutual fund has to comply with two criteria:

- A 12-month trailing average Portfolio Carbon Risk Score below 10 (out of 100).
- A 12-month trailing average Fossil Fuel Involvement below 7 percent.

The Portfolio Carbon Risk Score is calculated only for funds with more than 67 percent of their portfolio assets with a carbon risk rating from the ESG research provider Sustainalytics. As of April 2018, having a Portfolio Carbon Risk Score below 10 represented inclusion among the 29 percent of funds with the best performance in this dimension, and having a 12-month trailing average fossil fuel involvement below 7 percent represented a 33 percent underweighting of fossil fuel-related companies relative to the global equity universe.

"When Investors Call for Climate Responsibility, How Do Mutual Funds Respond?" Marco Ceccarelli, Stefano Ramelli, Alexander Wagner[8]

This 2019 study provides evidence on the behavior of sustainable investors. The authors began by noting that prior research had established that those who invest according to nonpecuniary motives have a smaller flow-to-performance sensitivity. Thus, fund managers, especially those with poor past performance, will be keen to attract climate-conscious investors. Their study examined the behavior of both investors and fund managers. Their database, from Morningstar Direct, included all open-end mutual funds domiciled in Europe (about 11,000) and the U.S. (about 7,000), both equity and fixed income, and covered the one-year period January through December 2018.

Following is a summary of their findings:

- About 25 percent of European funds and about 15 percent of U.S. funds were designated LCD.
- Eight percent of funds self-classify as socially conscious, yet only a third of those received the LCD.
- From May through the end of December 2018, funds that were awarded the LCD enjoyed significantly higher (3.1 percent) monthly flows than conventional funds. The effect was stronger for European funds (3.7 percent).

- Funds that received, or lost, the LCD in the quarterly updates that followed the initial publication also experienced similarly sized flow effects.
- Fund managers adjust their portfolios because they expect the LCD to have a positive effect on flows—funds that barely missed receiving the label rebalanced their portfolios toward more climate-friendly companies compared to fund managers that barely got the LCD.

Ceccarelli, Ramelli, and Wagner concluded:

"Our findings suggest that, as investors call for climate-conscious investment products, financial intermediaries use the vehicles at their disposal to respond to this increase in demand. These results have important practical implications: First, they alert mutual fund managers to the importance of sustainability—and especially climate responsibility—as a key competitive edge. Second, they inform policy-makers of the potential effects of eco-labelling schemes to re-orient capital flows towards the transition to a low-carbon economy."

The evidence clearly demonstrates that investors do express their social preferences through fund selection. In addition, their actions can impact the costs of capital of firms—firms with positive attributes receive more investor flows, lowering their cost of capital. The reverse effect holds as well—firms with negative attributes receive fewer flows, thus raising their cost of capital. The result is that stocks with positive attributes may see their valuations rise in the short term.

The Impact of Environmental Regulation on Companies

"Exporting Pollution: Where Do Multinational Firms Emit CO2?" Itzhak Ben-David, Yeejin Jang, Stefanie Kleimeier, Michael Viehs[9]

This 2020 study demonstrates that by expressing their values through their investments, sustainable investors are influencing the behavior of multinational corporations. It examined the impact of environmental policies on multinational firms' polluting activities both at home and in foreign countries during the 2010s. Combining firm-level data about multinational firms' CO_2 emissions in each country and information about the country-level environmental regulations and enforcement, the authors assessed the impact of home versus foreign environmental policies on firms' pollution allocations.

Their dataset included 1,970 large multinational public firms headquartered in 48 countries and their CO2 emissions in 218 countries during the 2008–2015 period. They began by noting:

> "As signs of climate change accumulate, countries around the globe are taking action, yet the strictness of their environmental policies vary significantly. Diversity and lack of coordination in regulations across countries can lead to 'carbon leakage,' meaning that firms decide strategically where to locate their production based on existing environmental policies."

Following is a summary of their findings:

- There has been a general improvement in environmental regulation over time. However, it remains weak in several large regions, especially in developing countries in Africa, South America, and Asia.
- Firms headquartered in countries with strict environmental policies perform more of their polluting activities abroad in countries with relatively weaker policies.
- These effects are largely driven by tightened environmental policies in home countries that incentivize firms to pollute abroad (they are pushed) rather than lenient foreign policies that attract those firms (versus pulled).
- A one-standard-deviation increase in the strictness of environmental policies in the home country was associated with a 29 percent reduction of CO2 emissions at home, but it was also associated with up to a 43 percent increase in emissions abroad. These results lend support to the concern that strict environmental policies may lead to carbon leakage.
- Although firms headquartered in countries with strict domestic environmental policies are more likely to export pollution to foreign countries, they nevertheless emit less overall CO2 globally. Thus, stricter environmental policies at home are associated with a partial, but positive, impact on reducing overall pollution.
- For firms that have strong governance, the positive effect of strict regulations on pollution is more pronounced—when the home country sets strict environmental policies, well-governed firms produce fewer emissions domestically and export fewer emissions to foreign countries.

Their findings led Ben-David, Jang, Kleimeier, and Viehs to conclude: "Multinational firms pollute abroad because of the tightening of policies in the home countries, not because of pollution opportunities abroad." The findings on multinational firms' CO2 emissions patterns in response to the stringency of countries' environmental policies highlight the need for global coordination of regulations on carbon dioxide emissions—without collective action, multinational firms with production facilities around the globe may continue to benefit from regulatory arbitrage opportunities by exporting pollution. On the other hand, these findings suggest that stringent national environmental standards can have a positive impact on curbing firms' global pollution.

Their finding that firms with strong governance reduce emissions at home while keeping foreign emissions unchanged suggests that "good corporate governance *could* be a proxy for a strong shareholder base that pushes an agenda of corporate social responsibility." It is also possible that the relationship was caused by the fact that Western countries tend to have stronger governance and also lower emissions, making it appear there is a causal relationship when there is not. With that said, firms with good corporate governance and lower emissions are positively recognized by shareholders with higher valuations (resulting in lower costs of capital, which provide a competitive advantage). In this way sustainable investors are able to influence corporate behavior by expressing their values through their investments.

"Social Preferences of Investors and Sustainable Investing." Harshini Shanker[10]

Harshini Shanker explored several issues around supply and demand for sustainable investing:

- Are sustainable investments the exclusive territory of a small set of so-called socially responsible mutual funds, or do conventional funds also prioritize sustainability?
- Are socially responsible fund portfolios more sustainable than conventional fund portfolios?
- Does the conventional investor in the market have social preferences?
- Are their preferences of a different nature than those of their socially responsible counterparts?

To answer these questions Shanker used Morningstar Sustainability Ratings, which are available on more than 20,000 mutual funds. Morningstar assigns each fund a *globe* rating ranging from 1 to 5, with 5 being the most sustainable. The worst 10 percent and best 10 percent of funds receive 1 and 5 globes, respectively. Morningstar categorizes a fund as socially conscious if the fund declares a noneconomic investment objective in its prospectus—

Shanker deems these funds to be *SR* (socially responsible) funds. Following is a summary of her findings, some of which seem quite surprising:

- A large fraction of conventional funds systematically prioritizes sustainable investments even without an explicit ESG mandate.
- The sustainability ratings of conventional funds are highly persistent over time, suggesting they did not end up with a high globe rating by accident—they consciously choose sustainability for its own sake.
- Conventional funds with above-average globe ratings outnumber the entire population of sustainable funds and manage assets roughly 3.5 times the collective value of sustainable fund assets—sustainable investing is therefore not restricted to ESG funds.
- Only 27 percent of 5-globe funds have a self-declared SR mandate. Thus, almost three-fourths of 5-globe funds deliver sustainability even without an explicit SR objective.
- Conventional funds with 4- or 5-globe ratings collectively manage 3.5 times the assets under management (AUM) of the whole universe of SR funds.
- Half the ESG fund universe are rated 3 globes or fewer, making their portfolios no better than an average conventional fund portfolio. And only one-fourth of them manage a 5-globe Morningstar rating. (This could be explained by the fact that many funds use ESG ratings other than Morningstar's, and there are often wide dispersions in ratings.)
- The average globe rating of a conventional fund is 2.8, while that of an SR fund is 3.5. Thus, the one-fourth of conventional funds that are rated 4 or 5 globes are more sustainable than the average SR fund.
- There is no evidence that 5-globe funds outperform 1-globe funds. The result is consistent across conventional and SR fund categories.

Because Shanker found that the poor globe ratings are highly persistent over time, she ruled out that ratings are temporary and accidental. She concluded that "these poorly rated SR funds are only pretending to be SR but systematically making unsustainable investments, i.e., they are greenwashing." Evidently, in a large percentage of cases, SR investors were not receiving what they signed up for.

On the other hand, Shanker noted that "conventional funds with high globe ratings are giving investors more than they signed up for." She also found: "Conventional investors have strong social preferences. A low-globe conventional fund would need to offer roughly twice the excess return of a high-globe fund to enjoy the same level of capital flow." She added: "While conventional investors reward high-globe funds handsomely for their social attribute, they do not proportionately penalize low-globe funds."

Turning now to how SR investors react to the financial performance, Shanker noted:

> "In the category of SR funds whose financial performance is below the peer median, SR investors reward high-globe funds, indicating a willingness to sacrifice financial return for social good. However, when SR funds perform well financially, the globe rating appears to lose its relevance. The evidence is consistent with a propensity to trust an SR fund to deliver on its promise, causing the investor to fail to monitor globe ratings in general until the fund performs poorly financially. Poor financial performance elicits scrutiny and accords a salience to the globe rating, consequently allowing high-globe funds to be rewarded. However, irrespective of financial performance, low-globe funds are not punished to the same extent that high-globe funds are rewarded, and greenwashing behavior remains largely unpunished."

These findings led Shanker to argue that "both types of investors value sustainability, and both react to good and bad social performance asymmetrically"—weak social performance is not punished to the same extent that strong social performance is rewarded. Her finding that there is no evidence that 5-globe funds outperform 1-globe funds led her to rule out that investors value sustainability due to a rational belief that sustainability predicts financial performance. They invest, she found, for "non-economic reasons (warm glow, reputation, etc.,)." She concluded: "The demand for sustainability among investors drives even conventional funds to systematically and persistently invest sustainably, with the number and size of such 'sustainable' conventional funds dominating the entire population of SR funds."

Does Sustainable Investing Deprive Unsustainable Firms from Fresh Capital?

"Does Sustainable Investing Deprive Unsustainable Firms from Fresh Capital?" David Blitz, Laurens Swinkels, Jan Anton van Zanten[11]

While there is a substantial body of research on sustainable investing's impact on investor returns, there had been no research on its impact on the ability of firms to raise capital prior to this 2020 study. The authors chose to study the primary market (new stock and bond issuance) because the secondary market doesn't reflect the raising of new capital, only the exchange of ownership of existing shares. Their hypothesis was: "If sustainable investing is effective at significantly increasing the cost of capital of unsustainable firms, or even blocking their access to capital markets entirely, then one would expect to see this reflected in capital flows in the primary market." Thus, they examined whether fresh capital is flowing more toward sustainable as opposed to unsustainable firms.

They began by noting that an objective of sustainable investing is to support sustainable companies and hurt unsustainable firms (we would add that an objective of sustainable investing is to transform companies), thereby giving the latter an incentive to improve their corporate behavior:

> "It may sound obvious that divestment negatively affects the target firm, but this mechanism is actually not so clear-cut. The issue here is that divesting comes down to selling one's position in a stock or bond to another investor, who ends up holding the position instead. Thus, divestment is merely a transfer of ownership from one investor to another, which has no direct impact on the firm. However, divestment may hurt firms indirectly, by increasing their cost of capital. As a result, new projects will have a lower net present value, making it less attractive for a firm to expand its business operations. Divestment on a sufficiently large scale may even come down to a boycott that effectively blocks a firm's access to capital markets, thereby severely limiting its funding opportunities and hence future growth."

Their study covered the period 2010–2019 and all stocks in the MSCI All World Index. To assess which companies raise fresh capital, they classified a firm as an equity issuer if its number of shares outstanding increased by at least 10 percent over the year. Similarly, they classified a firm as a debt issuer if the book value of its debt increased by at least 10 percent over the year. The typical number of equity issuers was between 100 and 150 per annum, while the typical number of debt issuers was in the 200 to 300 range. They excluded IPOs (because there can be many reasons for a firm to go public other than raising money for new business activities, such as enhancing firm visibility and publicity, motivating management and employees, exploiting mispricing, tax avoidance in some jurisdictions, and cashing in by owners of the private firm) and debt refinancings (because it doesn't raise new capital). They used a broad range of metrics from multiple providers to capture the various styles of sustainable investing because the correlation between the scores of different providers is low.

Following is a summary of their findings:

- There is no evidence that fresh capital is flowing more toward sustainable than toward unsustainable firms, as the sustainability profile as well as the carbon footprint of equity issuers was similar to that of the broad universe, and the sustainability scores of debt issuers were lower than the average scores of the universe.
- Unsustainable firms appear to have no problems obtaining funding in public markets.
- Their results were stable over time—they did not observe that sustainable firms had started to dominate issuance in recent years or since the signing of the Paris climate agreement in 2015.

Their findings led Blitz, Swinkels, and van Zanten to conclude:

"Our results suggest that sustainable investing has not been able to deprive unsustainable firms from fresh capital. However, they do not disprove that sustainable investing may have prevented such firms from raising even more capital, nor that further mainstreaming of sustainable investing may lead to more noticeable impact on capital flows."

We have discussed the now-significant body of research that demonstrates that by expressing their values through their investments, sustainable investors are impacting corporate behaviors in a positive way as companies try to gain a competitive advantage by reducing their cost of capital. We conclude this chapter with a review of the research on whether the mutual fund industry is walking the talk—are ESG-oriented funds' claims of picking portfolio firms that exhibit superior treatment of all stakeholders (as opposed to shareholder primacy) borne out by the evidence?

Do Sustainable Funds Walk the Talk?

We now move on to examining the findings from two studies seeking to answer the question: Do sustainable funds walk the talk?

"Do ESG Funds Make Stakeholder-Friendly Investments?" Aneesh Raghunandan and Shivaram Rajgopal[12]

The authors of this 2021 paper focused on whether self-labeled ESG-oriented mutual funds invest in firms that have better track records with consumers, employees, the environment, taxpayers, and shareholders. They assessed firms' track records with respect to these groups of stakeholders based on fundamental measures of behavior, or misbehavior, toward each group. Their primary measure of stakeholder-centric behavior was compliance with social (e.g., labor or consumer protection) and environmental laws. They also considered a host of other measures of stakeholder-centric behavior related to E, S, and G distinctively: carbon emissions, reliance on taxpayer-funded corporate subsidies, CEO compensation, board composition, and the balance of power between management and the shareholder.

Their tests centered around four primary types of stakeholder treatment measures:

1. Comprehensive federal enforcement records pertaining to firms' (mis)treatment of the environment, employees, and consumers.
2. The extent to which they are actually green, measured using data on carbon emissions.
3. Key features of their corporate governance structure.
4. The extent to which firms impose costs on local taxpayers via their reliance on subsidies and other forms of regulatory support.

They also addressed fund-level issues, including management fees and financial performance.

Raghunandan and Rajgopal limited their study to funds issued by financial institutions that also issued at least one non-ESG fund in the same year, and compared ESG funds to non-ESG funds managed by the same financial institutions in the same year. They identified 147 distinct mutual funds over the period 2010–2018 that claimed to be ESG-oriented. They then tracked the stakeholder-related behavior of stocks included in (and added to) these funds relative to stocks held by 2,428 non-ESG funds run by the same financial institutions during the same years.

Following is a summary of their findings:

• ESG funds held portfolio firms with worse track records for compliance with labor and environmental laws relative to portfolio firms held by non-ESG funds managed by the same financial institutions in the same years—ESG funds' portfolio firms have significantly more violations of labor and environmental laws and pay more in fines for these violations relative to non-ESG funds issued by the same financial institutions in the same years.

- Relative to other funds offered by the same asset managers in the same years, ESG funds hold stocks that are more likely to voluntarily disclose carbon emissions performance but also stocks with higher carbon emissions per unit of revenue—ESG funds' portfolio firms, on average, exhibit worse performance with respect to carbon emissions in terms of both raw emissions output and emissions intensity (i.e., CO_2 emissions per unit of revenue), and average penalties for environmental violations are higher.

- ESG funds are more likely to pick stocks that voluntarily disclose emissions—companies with good ESG data are more likely to disclose these data in order to appeal to the small subset of investors who demand ESG data; at the same time, however, firms with poor or no ESG data are likely to be shunned by those investors who are motivated by ESG considerations.

- There is no observable difference in scope 1 emissions between ESG funds' and non-ESG funds' portfolio firms, and ESG funds select portfolio firms with higher levels of scope 2 and 3 emissions (firms with a greater indirect carbon footprint).

- ESG funds' portfolio firms spend more money on lobbying politicians and obtain more frequent and higher-value government subsidies, suggesting that ESG funds' portfolio firms rely on higher levels of taxpayer-funded regulatory support relative to non-ESG funds. In the context of prior evidence that such subsidies typically crowd out rather than foster private investment, this suggests that ESG funds choose firms that are more likely to shift their costs of investment onto taxpayers.

- There is no evidence that ESG funds are buying firms based on expectations of future improvement—increased monitoring by ESG funds does not correlate with any improvement in portfolio firms' future compliance with stakeholder-centric regulations.

- ESG funds appear to underperform financially relative to other funds within the same asset manager and year and charge higher fees (the motivation for the offerings).

- ESG funds' portfolio firms have lower levels of board independence (the G in ESG).

Another interesting finding was that consistent with prior research ("The Influence of Firm Size on the ESG Score: Corporate Sustainability Ratings Under Review"[13] and "ESG Performance and Disclosure: A Cross-Country Analysis"[14]), ESG scores, which appear to be based on news-driven coverage of ESG, do not appear to correlate well with the actual contents of the firms' voluntary disclosures.

Raghunandan and Rajgopal concluded: "Our findings suggest that socially responsible funds do not appear to follow through on proclamations of concerns for stakeholders." They noted: "Our results raise questions about what exactly the purchasers of shares in self-labelled ESG or 'socially responsible' mutual funds are getting in exchange for this higher management fee." They added: "A key takeaway of our study is that asset managers do not necessarily 'walk the talk.'"

Their findings are supported by the SEC's April 2021 ESG Risk Alert, which specifically highlighted "overreliance on composite ESG scores as a sign of inadequate due diligence and of poor fund-level compliance more generally."[15] The SEC's bulletin emphasizes the need to understand whether ESG funds that claim to incorporate specific environmental or social factors into portfolio allocation decisions actually pick stocks that obtain superior performance with respect to these stated factors.

The takeaway for investors is that before investing in an ESG fund, a high level of due diligence is required in order to verify claims of picking stakeholder-friendly stocks. Another takeaway, one regulators should consider, is that sufficient demand for the securities of high-quality ESG companies by a large number of institutional investors could create a situation in which companies are forced to disclose ESG information regardless of its quality. Consequently, average ESG quality would improve over time as companies vie to attract widespread investor interest in their securities (to minimize their cost of capital).

We next examine the findings of research on the narrower group of SRI funds (versus the broader ESG category) to determine if SRI funds walk the talk and examine if their investments impact corporate behavior.

"Does Socially Responsible Investing Change Firm Behavior?" Davidson Heath, Daniele Macciocchi, Roni Michaely, Matthew Ringgenberg[16]

This 2021 study's authors assembled a novel set of outcome variables designed to measure whether socially responsible investing affects different firm stakeholders. Their outcome variables assessed the relation between SRI and firm customers, employees, and society in general. They examined nine different measures of employee satisfaction using data from Glassdoor, three measures of customer satisfaction using data from the Consumer Financial Protection Bureau, two measures of workplace safety using data from the Occupational Safety and Health Administration (OSHA), two measures of diversity on boards of directors using data from BoardEx and Institutional Shareholder Services, and eight different measures of pollution using data from the Environmental Protection Agency. Their data sample covered U.S. open-end mutual funds for the period 2011–2018.

Following is a summary of their findings:

- SRI funds choose to invest in stocks with better environmental and social responsibility. For example, SRI fund ownership is strongly related to lower pollution and an increase in investments in pollution-abatement technologies at the firm level.
- Employees at firms with more ownership by SRI funds rated their firm better in nearly every category, including career opportunities, compensation benefits, corporate culture, and overall job satisfaction. Using OSHA data, SRI fund ownership was associated with fewer workplace injuries as measured by hospitalizations and amputations.
- Firms with greater SRI ownership have significantly more women on their boards of directors and slightly more non-Caucasian board members.
- Greater SRI fund ownership is associated with fewer customer complaints and better relief for complaints, and relief that occurs in a timelier manner.
- SRI fund ownership does not lead to further improvements in environmental or social responsibility—following an exogenous increase in SRI capital allocated to a stock, there was no change in air, land, or water pollution, nor any change in workplace safety, employee satisfaction, or gender or racial diversity on corporate boards.

Their findings led Heath, Macciocchi, Michaely, and Ringgenberg to conclude that while SRI funds are not engaged in greenwashing (conveying a false impression or providing misleading information about how a company's products are more environmentally sound), "our results suggest there is a relation between SRI fund ownership and firm behavior, but it is largely driven by selection effects, not treatment effects."

The findings are inconsistent with SRI funds improving the environmental behavior of their portfolio firms. They added: "It is possible that SRI is successful at changing corporate behavior at longer horizons; our results show it is not successful in changing corporate behavior at short- and medium-term horizons measured in months and years."

Finally, they added this caveat: "It is also possible that SRI funds indirectly cause firms to behave differently via the threat of entry or exit. For example, a firm could dramatically reduce its pollution in order to attract capital from SRI funds."

This is a statement of importance, because the academic research, as we have discussed, has demonstrated that companies that adhere to positive environmental, social, and governance principles have lower costs of capital, higher valuations, are less vulnerable to systemic risks, and are more profitable. The evidence that a focus on sustainable investment principles leads to lower costs of capital provides companies with the incentive to improve their ESG scores—or they will be at a competitive disadvantage.

Research has demonstrated that improving ESG scores has also been found to improve employee satisfaction and that environmental stringency of green investors pushes companies to reduce their greenhouse gas emissions by raising their cost of capital.

IPO Pricing: Does Sustainability Matter?

A large body of academic literature has found underpricing of IPOs—there is a positive return from the offer price to the closing price of the first trading day. The literature has also documented that IPOs with both high and low underpricing significantly underperform mature firms over the first year after going public and that the underperformance existed whether or not the IPO occurred in a period of *hot* issuance.

"ESG and the Pricing of IPOs: Does Sustainability Matter." Alessandro Fenili and Carlo Raimondo[17]

Fenili and Raimondo contribute to both the IPO and the sustainable investing literature with their hypothesis: "Information frictions may be what causes most of the underpricing." They argued that disclosing more ESG information in the S-1 prospectus (mandatory communication occurring before the IPO date) diminishes the information asymmetry between the company and the investors, positively benefiting the companies' financial performance in terms of less underpricing and evaluation.

Their second hypothesis was that the most negative relationship with underpricing, in order of magnitude, should be found with the governance disclosure, the environmental, the social, and the ESG disclosure as a whole.

Their third hypothesis was that there is a negative correlation between the amount of ESG disclosure in the S-1 and the firm evaluation. Based on a sample of 783 U.S. IPOs over the period 2012 through June 2019, they computed a text-based measure of ESG disclosure in IPOs.

Following is a summary of their findings:

- The amount of ESG disclosure in S-1s was negatively associated with IPOs' underpricing. For example, IPOs in the first environmental quartile had average first-day returns of 29.82 percent compared to 14.87 percent for the fourth environmental quartile, a difference of 14.95 percentage points. The differences between the other extreme quartiles of social, governance, and ESG were 7.3 percentage points, 9.3 percentage points, and 12.0 percentage points, respectively.
- A large increase in the number of environmental, social, governance, and ESG words in the S-1 form leads to reduced information asymmetry, a decrease in underpricing, and a positive effect for the company.
- The most negative relationship with underpricing, in order of magnitude, was found with the ESG topic as a whole, the governance topic, the social topic, and then the environmental topic—this result may be due to the retail investors finding the disclosure of all three ESG variables as a whole more useful rather than examining them individually.
- Not only has there been a trend that S-1 forms become more prolonged and detailed on average, but the same is happening for the ESG disclosure as a whole. Such a trend is likely a result of companies seeing that it is critical to disclose more, and possibly be more detailed, on such topics.
- Their findings were robust to various tests.

Fenili and Raimondo concluded: "More and more investors use the ESG criteria to evaluate investment opportunities and IPOs, also because they might want to avoid investing in companies associated with insufficient and inefficient environmental, social, and governance practices." They added: "Disclosing ESG information diminishes the information asymmetry, thus bringing a positive benefit to the companies' financial performance (translated into a negative correlation with underpricing, since it is bad for the firm). Also, disclosing more ESG information improves the investors' ability to better evaluate the firm in the future."

We conclude this chapter with a review of the impact of active ownership—active engagement by shareholders on ESG issues—on corporate behavior and profitability. While traditional shareholder activism and hedge fund activism typically focus on issues related to the interests of shareholders only, ESG activism focuses on a broader range of issues.

Does Shareholder Activism Improve Companies?

"Active Ownership." Elroy Dimson, Oğuzhan Karakaş, Xi Li[18]

This 2015 study sought to determine whether one can infer a causal link between engagements and subsequent corporate performance. To find the answer, the authors analyzed an extensive proprietary database of corporate social responsibility engagements regarding environmental, social, and governance concerns with U.S. public companies covering the period 1999–2009. They identified 382 successful and 1,770 failed engagement processes where an institutional investor had warned the company of its key ESG-related problems or demanded changes to them.

Following is a summary of their findings:

- On average, engagement on ESG activities gave rise to a positive size-adjusted abnormal return of 2.3 percent over the year after initial engagement.
- The average one-year size-adjusted abnormal return after initial engagement was 7.1 percent for successful engagements, but there was no adverse reaction to unsuccessful ones.
- The positive abnormal returns were most pronounced for engagements on the themes of corporate governance and climate change.
- Compared to matched firms, companies with poorer performance, inferior governance structure, greater reputational concerns, and higher shareholding from the asset manager were more likely to be targeted.
- Engagements were more likely to be successful in achieving activist objectives if the target firm was more concerned about its reputation and had higher capacity to implement change and larger headroom for improvement, especially for those on environmental and social issues.
- Collaboration between the asset manager and other activist investors and stakeholders significantly increased the success rate of environmental and social engagements. This was not found to be the case with corporate governance engagements.
- Consistent with arguments that ESG activities attract socially conscious customers and investors, after successful engagements, particularly for those on environmental and social issues, engaged companies experienced .improvements in their operating performance, profitability, efficiency, shareholding, and governance.

Their findings led Dimson, Karakaş, and Li to conclude that successful engagement has a positive impact on ESG factors and a company's finances.

Conclusion

There is a mounting body of evidence that the sustainable investing preferences of investors are having a favorable impact on the behavior of companies, providing them with the incentive to improve their sustainability ratings lest they be at a competitive disadvantage in terms of their cost of capital and ability to attract and retain talent. These findings provide further support for the trend toward increasing shareholder activism related to sustainable investing objectives.

With that said, there is also disturbing evidence, as presented by Raghunandan and Rajgopal, that some SRI and ESG funds do not appear to walk the talk by investing in more sustainable companies. This raises questions about what exactly buyers of self-labeled ESG or socially responsible mutual funds are getting in exchange for higher management fees. The bottom line is that investors should perform thorough due diligence on a fund before they consider investing. In the next chapter, we provide some guidance on how to research whether a fund is greenwashing or is actually walking the talk.

CHAPTER 8

How to Invest Sustainably

W E NOW TURN our attention to the practical aspects of building a sustainable investment portfolio. The science behind portfolio construction goes well beyond the scope of this book. For those interested in an in-depth discussion on this topic, including such issues as asset allocation, asset location (which assets to hold in taxable versus tax-advantaged accounts), the use of Monte Carlo simulations, the creation of an investment policy statement, and the need for ongoing care and maintenance of the portfolio, we recommend Larry's book, co-authored with Kevin Grogan, *Your Complete Guide to a Successful and Secure Retirement.*[1] With that said, in this chapter we will discuss general principles and provide guidelines to follow.

The good news is that for those already comfortable with their knowledge in these areas, the process of investing sustainably is not so different from conventional investing. However, it does require some additional research and analysis. Thankfully, today there exists a plethora of tools and investment products from which to choose. While complicating the task of choosing the right providers, it is preferable to not having enough good options, which was the case until quite recently.

Principles All Investors Should Consider

Nothing about sustainable investing changes the fundamental principles of investing. You should keep these in mind when building your sustainable investment program:

- *Markets are Highly Efficient*: Stock prices quickly adjust to publicly available information. The takeaway is that attempts to outsmart the market through security selection and/or market timing are unlikely to be successful.

- *Diversify*: The only free lunch in investing is diversification. The takeaway is to avoid concentration through individual security selection. Instead, invest in all the companies that meet the criteria you establish. The result should be a portfolio that owns hundreds (if not thousands) of companies, in dozens of countries, across multiple asset classes.
- *Invest for the Long Term*: Investing for the next quarter or next year has more to do with speculating than investing. The takeaway is that the investment horizon should be decades.
- *Control Expenses*: Whatever you pay in fees, trading costs, and taxes is subtracted from your overall return. However, this does not mean that one should necessarily choose funds with the lowest expense ratios, as funds can add significant value through intelligent design.

Choosing Whether to Do It Yourself or to Hire a Professional Advisor

The choice of whether to hire a professional advisor or to invest on your own is a personal one. A good rule of thumb is to seriously consider professional help when your portfolio reaches $100,000. A good advisor can help you make better decisions at any portfolio size—at larger amounts, they can add more value and keep you from making costly mistakes. Advisors who have expertise in sustainable investing are still in the minority. Those who are experts will usually highlight their sustainable offerings on their website or in their communications.

Appendix B provides an in-depth discussion to help you with this decision.

Maintain Your Investment Process

The best way to achieve both your financial and sustainability goals is by integrating your portfolio's design with your sustainability objectives in a holistic manner. It should begin with defining your ability (including considering the stability of your labor capital and how it correlates with the risk of equities), willingness, and need to take risk. This will allow you to determine your asset allocation. Having accomplished that objective, you can focus on identifying the investment vehicles that come closest to incorporating your sustainable values.

Following are our recommended five steps to achieving this goal:

1. *Set your financial goals and your risk budget*: Give consideration to your ability, willingness, and need to take risk.
2. *Set your asset allocation*: Select the asset classes that give you the best chance of achieving your financial goals and the percentage to invest in each.
3. *Select your investments*: Choose for each asset class the funds or ETFs that align your sustainable values with your financial goals.
4. *Monitor, rebalance, and tax manage*: Monitor regularly to determine if there is the need to rebalance and tax manage the portfolio. This is not just an end of year task.
5. *Review the plan*: Review whenever your underlying assumptions have changed. We recommend an annual review or whenever significant life events occur.

The process is largely the same for sustainable investors and conventional investors. The only step to change significantly is Step 3—the selection of the sustainable investments for each asset class. We will cover each step to raise some considerations that you might consider when shifting to sustainability.

Step 1: Set Your Financial Goals and Your Risk Budget

With the ESG investment options available today, you can build portfolios with similar risk and return profiles to conventional portfolios. There may not be a need to adjust your overall expectations for your public market investments. One reason for the rising popularity of ESG investing is the ability to shift stock and bond investments to sustainability without altering your expected financial outcomes.

Investors looking to do more in terms of aligning their portfolio to their specific individual values might adopt an SRI approach. Whether you need to adjust your expectations comes down to the degree to which you exclude companies you take issue with, or overweight firms you like. If your requirements are too exacting, you will alter the risk and return characteristics of your portfolio.

Investors might also have an opportunity to look beyond their stock and bond investment portfolio. They might consider impact investing.

Impact investing, as defined in Chapter 1, is effectively a for-profit approach to solving social and environmental problems. Because it usually involves the use of private placements, impact investing sits outside the public investment portfolio. Some investors find impact investing attractive and will adjust the amount of capital they allocate to their investment and philanthropy buckets accordingly. Perhaps they will shift some of their philanthropic capital to impact investing, often taking advantage of various tax-planning opportunities.

The takeaway is that with an ESG approach you can probably maintain your financial goals without changing your risk budget. If you tune your investments to your individual values with SRI or impact investing, you may be altering the risk and return characteristics of the portfolio. There may be increased variation in potential outcomes. This is suitable as long as you build this into your plan and are prepared for it.

Step 2: Set Your Asset Allocation

A straightforward approach to shifting to sustainable investing is to simply search for ESG funds to replace the conventional ones you use currently. For example, if you use a low-cost index fund for your core equity market exposure, look for an ESG index strategy with the same core equity market approach. Constructing your sustainable portfolio this way will likely maintain the risk and return profile of your existing plan (see Figure 14).

Figure 14: Sustainable Asset Allocation

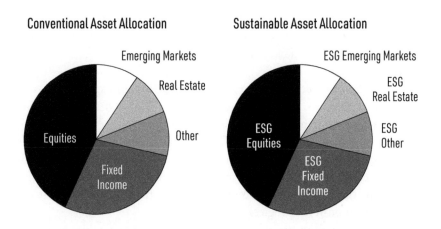

Some investors might choose to alter their asset allocation, though doing so only around the edges rather than making wholesale changes. You might be tempted to exclude an asset class for which you cannot find a suitable sustainable vehicle—it is hard to find ESG funds in some areas, such as international small value. We suggest you take a patient approach and stay invested in the existing conventional fund until a sustainable alternative becomes available. We recommend investors strive to keep their allocations the same and to minimize any changes so that overall risk and return characteristics remain intact.

Investors seeking to add more sustainability to their portfolio can often do so by simply adding an allocation to a particular theme that is important to them. For example, you could add a renewable energy fund, a sustainable agriculture fund, or a clean tech investment. With this approach you can tune your portfolio more to your preferences without having to make a wholesale shift to an SRI approach or to a separately managed account. However, keep in mind that these specialized investments often have uncertain risk and return attributes. Thus, you would be wise to limit the exposure to these alternative categories to 10 or 20 percent.

Step 3: Select Your Investments

When you begin searching for sustainable investments, you need to perform due diligence on the same financial criteria you would normally use for your conventional investments. The sustainable research should be seen as an additional layer rather than a replacement of an existing process. Do not change the investment principles you adhere to nor the investment philosophy you believe in.

Sustainable investors may, however, want to adjust a few of their financial criteria in order to expand the options available to them. Three criteria in particular may warrant adjustment:

1. *Expenses*: Sustainable funds often have higher overall expense ratios than conventional funds. This need not be a deal breaker. Investors might be happy to pay more for several reasons:
   - For the manager to use those fees for shareholder engagement whereby they encourage companies in the fund to do better on sustainability issues. If investors want companies to be more sustainable, they might want their managers to use the power of their voice and their proxy votes to push for progress.
   - For the manager to buy or create additional sustainable research and data. Expanding the quantity and quality of sustainable data helps all investors and companies get better at sustainability over time.
2. *Track Record*: Investors sometimes wait for a fund to be three years or even five years old before they commit. The rationale here is to be able to examine the managers' performance over time. This prudent approach makes sense in many cases. With sustainable investing there are caveats because sustainable

investing is still relatively new and is evolving rapidly. Many funds have only recently been launched. And the newer ones often have better data, better processes, and even lower expenses than their older cousins. In some asset classes, younger funds are all that are available. Sustainable investors might find more, and better, options if they are willing to consider younger funds.

3. *Investment Vehicle*: There are more sustainable investment options to choose from than ever before, and those options are no longer limited to just mutual funds. There are now hundreds of ETFs with sustainable mandates. And dozens of providers will now custom build and manage an individual portfolio according to your specific tastes in a separately managed account (SMA). Which vehicle is most suitable for your investments comes down to your needs and desires.

Mutual funds and ETFs are comingled vehicles. This means hundreds or even thousands of investors are invested into the same portfolio. Each has their pro-rata share of the overall fund. Each investor gets the same holdings, the same experience, the same returns, etc. An SMA, on the other hand, has only one investor. There are significant differences in expenses (SMAs generally are more expensive), in taxes (SMAs can be more tax efficient), and in how you buy and sell these three vehicles, which are beyond the scope of this book. We will focus here only on the differences in the application of sustainability considerations.

Much has been made of the benefits of the flexibility of the SMA for the sustainable investor. Because the investor has decision-making power over the holdings in their account, they can choose to include or exclude any particular type of product, or company, sector, or country, and thus are able to express their values to a very specific level. This is certainly an advantage for the SRI investor, who has strongly held beliefs that they are not willing to compromise. For the ESG investor, however, the SMA might be unnecessary or even undesirable.

ESG investing, as we detailed in Chapter 1, is about the risks and opportunities that are most material to the company, not to the investor. The ESG investor wants to prioritize investing in the companies doing better on sustainability metrics. Few investors have more expertise in this area than professional investment managers. The analysis is complicated and ongoing. Issues change, new data becomes available, and companies change. It is difficult to keep up.

The ESG investor who wants shareholder engagement might also prefer a fund or ETF over a separately managed account. By joining a fund with more assets and more investors, they are effectively amplifying their voice and their potential impact.

Today, there is a wide range of choices in ESG funds with options ranging from light ESG tilts to strong ones. Some ESG funds place a higher emphasis on particular issues within ESG, such as climate change, or diversity, or risk management. Investors have ample opportunity to tailor a portfolio to their needs without an SMA. Many ESG funds also exclude controversial companies, such as tobacco firms and gun manufacturers. Thus, investors who find these firms objectionable will find common cause with many funds. The majority of sustainably minded investors will not require an SMA to meet their objectives.

Step 4: Monitor, Rebalance, and Tax Manage

All investors should regularly monitor their portfolio to determine if it needs to be rebalanced back to targeted asset allocations. They should also look for opportunities to reduce taxes by offsetting gains where possible. Sustainable investors have a bit more of a job to do on the monitoring side, as they are asking managers to deliver on sustainability in addition to financial performance. We recommend that on an annual basis you obtain from the fund sponsors not just financial reports but sustainability reports (sometimes called an impact report or stewardship report). These reports tell you a lot about the managers' commitment to sustainability. They are often the same reports you use to select managers in the first place.

Step 5: Review the Plan

It is important to review your plan on an annual basis to ensure that the fund sponsors are continuing to practice what they preach. In addition, the sustainable investment landscape is rapidly changing, with new vehicles that implement the latest academic research findings. And competition is driving fees lower. You want to make sure you have the best-in-class vehicles in your portfolio.

A Framework for Selecting ESG Managers

The challenge of investing for sustainability has changed. It used to be difficult to find any funds that met your financial and sustainability criteria. However, today there are dozens that might. The difficulty now is in sorting out all the options, not to mention figuring out what information is needed to do the sorting. To provide some structure to the research process, we use the following four-part framework to evaluate the sustainability of an investment option:

ESG Quality	ESG Tilt	Shareholder Engagement	Manager Commitment
The degree to which the manager uses state-of-the-art data and processes for research	The degree to which the fund prioritizes investments into more sustainable companies	The degree to which the manager tries to improve company sustainability performance	The degree to which the manager tries to build capacity for sustainability in markets

ESG Quality

As a relatively new discipline, ESG investing is evolving rapidly as data improves in terms of methods of research and selecting securities. As techniques evolve, how can investors determine the quality of the strategy a fund uses?

- *Intentionality*: Make sure the funds you are considering have a sustainability mandate. A quick look at the fund documents will tell you whether the fund is being intentional about ESG. If you skip this step and go right to looking at ESG scores, rankings, and ratings, you might find funds that happen to accidentally score well. This is a problem, because if the manager did not build the ESG tilt intentionally, there is a good chance it will disappear when new securities are selected.
- *Strategy*: The oldest, and still most common, form of sustainable investing is the simple exclusion of certain stocks. This is a valid strategy for investors who want market exposure minus a certain industry (e.g., fossil fuels). However, it is a blunt approach. For example, some oil and gas companies are trying to provide solutions by rapidly transitioning to renewables. You should consider whether to reward, rather than penalize, such behavior. Exclusionary strategies sometimes miss these nuances. You should not be willing to pay a fund much more than you would an index fund for such a simple strategy. Inclusionary and best-in-class strategies, in which managers find or overweight the companies that are leading on sustainability, require more insight, more effort, and better data.
- *Data*: We have covered the limitations of ESG data, and in particular the unreliability of ESG ratings You can get a better sense of the quality of a manager's approach by the type of data they use. It is still very common for managers to base their sustainability decisions on a researcher's ESG ratings of a company despite the obvious shortcomings. Better managers use individual data sources on the issues that are material and impactful to

the company in question. The highest quality managers strive to get that data from independent third-party sources rather than from the company's own reports, where possible.

ESG Tilt

Investors now have dozens of choices for ESG funds in most asset classes. Some of those funds are meant to closely mimic the characteristics of the market, similar to a traditional index fund. Others try to maximize sustainability by overweighting companies performing well on sustainability criteria and underweighting those not doing so well. Those with a higher emphasis on sustainability can be said to have more ESG tilt. Among the multitude of approaches, three basic categorizations emerge, listed here in ascending order of tilt:

- *ESG Consideration*: Managers in this category are, for the most part, relying on traditional financial or fundamental analysis to select companies in which to invest, and then may look to environmental, social, and governance issues as an additional consideration.
- *ESG Integration*: The fund manager is fully integrating environmental, social, and governance issues into their traditional security selection process.
- *ESG Focus*: The focused approach involves analyzing companies with environmental, social, and governance issues as a primary determinant of portfolio selection.

In general, the greater a portfolio is tilted to ESG, the greater its performance will vary from a conventional portfolio or benchmark over short time periods. Investors keen to prioritize sustainable companies in their portfolio will want more ESG tilt. These investors must be willing to accept that these deeper ESG portfolios look and perform differently from conventional portfolios or benchmarks. Even if long-term performance expectations are similar, a deep ESG portfolio's returns will vary more from the market in the short term. Investors who are not comfortable with this tracking variance should choose a portfolio with less tilt.

Shareholder Engagement

Engagement is the use of shareholder power to influence corporate behavior. Active shareholder engagement is important to many sustainable investors. They want their manager to use their voice and vote to encourage companies to make positive changes. Managers have a variety of ways to influence companies, with some making significantly more effort than others.

The main levers of influence, from least to most effort, are:

- *Proxy Voting*: It is a requirement for U.S. fund managers to vote their proxies. Most of the time these votes are for business-as-usual affairs, such as approving the appointment of an auditor, or electing board members. As more investors have shown interest in sustainability, managers are now submitting more shareholder resolutions for ESG issues. These shareholder resolutions are put to a vote at annual shareholder meetings. Some managers have strong ESG proxy voting policies and processes, and have strong voting records. Others tend to vote against these resolutions, and many managers fall somewhere in the middle. Thankfully, because managers are required to disclose all their proxy votes, it is not a mystery how managers are using them.
- *Direct Dialogue*: A straightforward approach managers can take is to simply write, call, or meet with company representatives. Managers can ask specific questions they have about the company and its operations to learn how they are dealing with ESG risks. They can raise issues the company might not yet have considered, such as the growing threat of wildfires or the potential impact of new regulations. And they can let the company know what investors now expect of them, what their peers are doing, and what it will take to remain, or become, an attractive investment.
- *Collaborations*: Managers can amplify their voice and influence by collaborating with other managers and advocacy groups. One way to do this is to submit, or sponsor, a shareholder resolution to try to garner enough votes by working with other shareholders. Another way is to find like-minded shareholders and engage in direct dialogue with a company in a united effort.

Manager Commitment

ESG investing is still a relative newcomer on the investing scene. While value investing has been practiced for more than 100 years and small-cap investing for more than 50 years, ESG has been around for less than 20. As a result, the tools, techniques, and strategies are still in development, and the information, the data, and the reporting are rapidly evolving. Some managers are actively involved in building this new infrastructure to support ESG, others less so. Investors who want to see system-level change, or just want their fees to go to those most committed, will want to use managers who are leaning into this effort.

Investment managers have ample opportunities to support and build capacity in ESG. You can evaluate their commitment by looking at what membership organizations they join, what advocacy initiatives they take on, and how responsibly they run their own firm—whether they walk the talk.

Memberships

In the early days, being a member of the PRI was a statement of leadership. With more than 3,000 managers being members now, it no longer serves as a strong differentiator. There are other non profit bodies that the more committed managers have joined, including:

- Ceres Investor Network brings together more than 200 institutional investors managing more than $47 trillion in assets with the aim of advancing sustainable investment practices.
- Global Sustainable Investment Alliance (GSIA) is an alliance of regional responsible investment associations:
  - US SIF: 190 members from the U.S. managing $5 trillion in assets.
  - Eurosif: A network of more than 400 European associations managing more than $8 trillion in assets.
  - UKSIF: 260 members from the U.K. managing more than £10 trillion in assets.
  - RIAA: More than 300 members across Australia and New Zealand managing more than $9 trillion in assets.
- Climate-focused bodies, including:
  - Climate Action 100+: 615 investors from around the world managing $60 trillion in assets.
  - The Institutional Investors Group on Climate Change: 350+ investors from 22 countries managing €42 trillion in assets.
  - Net Zero Asset Managers Initiative: 128 signatories managing $43 trillion in assets.

More details on these organizations and others are listed in Appendix D: ESG Resource Guide.

Advocacy

Investment managers who invest for sustainability are well aware that ESG data and reporting are not as consistent and standardized as financial information. Some choose to work with what is available and wait for improvements. Others commit to building capacity for ESG by sponsoring and advocating for various initiatives to integrate sustainability in capital markets. Improving corporate disclosures is an area in which there are many impactful initiatives underway. Some of these include the Task Force on Climate Related Financial Disclosures (TCFD), the Partnership for Carbon Accounting Financials (PCAF), and the Value Reporting Foundation (merger of the Sustainability Accounting Standards Board and the Integrated Reporting Council). You should ask what roles the manager takes on in these groups—are they just signing on as a signatory, or are they committing staff time to task forces, working groups, and educational committees?

Policy is another important lever that committed managers work on. As we write this book, both the European Union and the U.S. Securities and Exchange Commission are drafting regulations on ESG disclosures for both public companies and investment managers. Are the managers you are considering part of the effort? Managers can join *sign-on* letters as a fairly low commitment. Submitting comments on draft legislation takes significant time and resources. Meeting with federal and state legislators to educate policymakers is another level entirely, one that only the most passionate firms undertake.

Walking the Talk

Another way to measure a manager's commitment to sustainability is to what degree they practice it in their own business. Financial services firms have a reputation for having low emissions relative to other industries. However, since they are stewards of capital, they can affect many stakeholders in impactful ways. You can evaluate an investment manager on ESG performance just as you would any other company, with appropriate adjustments for materiality given their industry.

- *Environmental*: Financial services firms typically do not make physical goods or transport them from place to place. Their environmental impact is found elsewhere. Typical investment firms find that business travel is the largest source of their carbon emissions, followed by their offices' use of energy. Committed firms will have active policies in place to regularly measure and report their carbon footprint and to reduce it over time. Better firms will have a Paris-aligned, science-based, or net-zero target for their emissions. The most committed firms have stopped allocating capital to the dirtiest forms of energy and extraction, such as coal, tar sands oil, and exploration and drilling in sensitive areas.
- *Social*: Financial services firms employ many highly educated and highly compensated people. The industry's track record on diversity and inclusion is poor. There are indeed very few female and minority investment managers,

and a large gender pay gap remains. The caricature of the typical board of directors as pale, male, and stale is largely accurate. Look for firms that make strong efforts to redress inequality and offer transparent reporting on their progress. Another important stakeholder group for investment managers is their clients. Modern firms offer products with transparent (and low) fee structures. They are fiduciaries, always acting in the best interests of their clients. You might be surprised to find that many firms still cling to the old ways of seeing clients as profit centers. Warning flags include your advisor or manager charging a sales commission, frequently encouraging you to change investments, or having a complicated fee structure.

- *Governance*: Risk management is paramount in financial services. Firms committed to sustainability disclose their own risks as well as the risks in their products. They also work to reduce systemic risk in capital markets. Look for firms that disclose climate risks in their prospectuses and fund literature. Better firms have publicly available information about their company's exposure to the physical and transition risks from climate change in the form of a TCFD report.

Research Tools for Selecting ESG Managers

The rapid increase in the popularity of sustainable investing has led to the development of more reports, research tools, and databases on the sustainability of companies and investment products. These tools were once reserved for the investment managers willing to pay for them. However, today some of this information is made available free to any investor with an internet connection. While additional and accessible information is certainly good for the sustainably minded investor, we caution investors on how best to use it.

ESG Ratings and Research

The free ESG information available online often features a summary rating or ranking of the company or the fund. While these headline ratings are attractive for their simplicity, they are unlikely to be helpful in comparing one investment versus another. ESG ratings are notoriously unreliable. As we discussed in Chapter 6, ESG ratings on stocks from one researcher to another only agree about half the time. As you have seen, MSCI might give a high score to a company that Sustainalytics scores low. The ESG ratings on funds suffer the same problem. This is not an indictment of any particular rater's process. Instead, it is a recognition that these ratings are opinions and should be treated as such. The bottom line is that, for the purposes of comparing one fund to another, we would not recommend using ratings.

You should also be aware that ESG researchers publish more than just ESG ratings. You will often see a carbon or emissions figure, and perhaps a percentage of the portfolio invested in fossil fuels or brown energy firms. Some provide detail on whether the fund holds any controversial companies, such as those involved in alcohol, tobacco, gambling, pornography, weapons, etc. These more granular bits of data can be useful in determining what the portfolio is actually invested in and therefore are far more valuable than the ESG rating. A few caveats are in order:

- Do not compare a carbon or emissions figure from one researcher with another. The reason is that different researchers might be using different methodologies and/or different metrics. If you try to compare one company or fund versus another, make sure you get the data from the same researcher.
- Do not compare metrics across different asset classes, countries, or sectors. A data point for a broad equity fund will be substantially different from a bond fund or a real estate strategy.

The Prospectus

Suggestions to read the prospectus are usually met with a polite nod and dismissal, if not a full eye roll. This is because investors have learned that these documents are usually filled with overly broad descriptions and legalese. However, it is precisely this feature that makes them valuable for the sustainable investor. If you want to know exactly what a manager has committed to doing in a fund strategy, the prospectus will tell you what legal counsel has signed off on.

To get a sense of the degree of ESG tilt a manager is employing, compare prospectus language. If the only text in a prospectus related to sustainability is something like "may consider ESG issues," the fund's tilt to ESG is probably light. If the prospectus includes a detailed paragraph on the ESG strategy within the Principal Investment Strategies section, the manager is taking sustainability seriously and probably emphasizing investments into more sustainable companies.

The prospectus can also provide a quick test on how important shareholder engagement is to a manager. Managers truly committed to shareholder engagement will at least mention their efforts in the prospectus.

Fund Literature

You will not find a complete description of a manager's ESG strategy in the prospectus because the language is typically broad to afford the manager flexibility. To know what they are actually doing, you will need to consult their more detailed materials:

- The fact sheet, while short, provides a quick test on intentionality. If ESG is truly the main strategy, it will be the theme of this document.
- Brochures and websites can be helpful, but they rarely offer much insight. The main thing you learn is whether they are allocating resources to marketing their sustainability offering. If you do not perceive much effort, their commitment may be lacking.
- A strategy paper is a detailed description of how the manager runs the portfolio. The best ones include references to third-party research that backs up their approach. You may have to call or email the manager to obtain this information.
- The slide deck is what the fund manager uses to present their product to professional investors. You might find some that are reserved for professional investors only due to compliance reasons, but a few managers have a recorded presentation that you can find on their website.

Impact Reports

The impact report goes by many names, including stewardship, engagement, ESG, sustainability, or even the now somewhat antiquated corporate social responsibility, or CSR, report. We will use the term *impact report* to cover all of these publications. If you are looking for a manager who is serious about sustainability, they will have a report that details their investment, engagement, and advocacy efforts. If they do not have one, look for another manager.

The impact report is one of the most important tools the sustainable investor can use to evaluate a manager. The better ones will go in depth on all four parts of the ESG manager evaluation framework detailed above: ESG Quality, ESG Tilt, Shareholder Engagement, and Manager Commitment. These reports should detail all the efforts the manager is making and provide quantitative measures of their results. They are usually published annually. Comparing the latest report to earlier versions can tell you if the manager is leading, or just responding to, the rapid changes occurring in sustainable investing.

Manager Interview

Speaking with the investment manager or someone on their team is the best way to determine if their investment approach coincides with your objectives. You will learn a great deal about their process, their expertise, and their commitment. In addition, you will have an opportunity to have your questions answered. What should you ask? We have provided a list of the most relevant and illuminating questions in Appendix E: ESG Manager Interview Guide.

Summary

This chapter provided a framework for building your sustainable investment portfolio. We summarized the basic principles of investing because sustainable investing does not supersede them. We then outlined some issues that would lead you to maintain or adjust your asset allocation and your investment selection process.

The bulk of the work of building a sustainable investment portfolio lies with the investment manager selection process. We have outlined a framework for selecting ESG managers—evaluating the quality of their approach, the strength of their portfolio tilts, their shareholder engagement, and their commitment to ESG. We hope this framework is helpful and encourage investors to use it rather than relying on ESG ratings, which are not as robust and informative as we would like. More resources for manager selection are included in Appendices C, D, and E, including a manager interview guide and a list of mutual funds and ETFs to consider.

CONCLUSION

W E HAVE ALMOST reached the end of our journey through the world of sustainable investing—a journey designed to guide you through the complexities created by the investment industry. Our goal was to provide you with the information needed to develop an investment strategy that enables you to achieve your financial goals while also expressing your personal values rather than having to sacrifice them. With that in mind, we will review the most important lessons and the key takeaways.

In Chapter 1 we discussed that while the financial services industry has responded to demands for sustainable investment strategies with a dizzying array of product launches, fund sponsors are not using consistent terms to describe their products, using terms like ESG and SRI interchangeably, or calling the whole field *impact investing*. Others use terms such as *values-based investing*, *mission-driven investing, ethical investing,* or even just *responsible investing*.

The lack of a common nomenclature makes it difficult for investors to understand what products are available, what their purpose is, and what their performance might be. Thus, we provided in-depth explanations, and examples, of the commonly used terms. Investors who clearly define their own values and objectives are more likely to be sure the strategy they ultimately employ, be it ESG, SRI, or impact investing, is right for them.

In Chapter 2 we discussed how sustainable investors have an array of options when it comes to constructing and managing their portfolios. We then explored the most common methodologies used by fund managers.

Chapter 3 explored the types of investors that champion sustainability, a group that is large and diverse, including early pioneers as well as those working on the cutting edge today. These investors have developed different strategies and methodologies reflecting who they are, and who they invest for.

In Chapter 4 we explored the various motivations of sustainable investors and discussed the three types of returns to them: financial, societal (improved outcomes for people and the planet), and personal (emotional benefits). The key takeaway is that investors should make sure the investment strategies they employ align not only with their financial objectives but also with their societal goals and personal values.

Chapter 5 provided a historical review of the evolution of ESG investing. We discussed how early ESG investors were faced with real challenges, as they lacked the critical ingredients needed to invest in a more responsible manner—data and a consistent set of metrics to compare companies. Fortunately, ratings organizations were formed to address this problem. Unfortunately, there is no consistency in how the ratings are determined either in terms of the metrics used or their weighting schemes. The result is that for any one company there can be a wide dispersion of scores among the various providers.

One key takeaway is that instead of attempting to compare and contrast ratings and rankings of different agencies, investors should determine the ESG constructs that are material to their own investment strategies and then match them with an ESG rating or ranking product that closely resembles those constructs. We also discussed how climate risk is changing the narrative on sustainable investing. The key takeaway is that all investors should be incorporating ESG risks into their investment strategies, as ESG risks that affect future cash flows are already having an impact on stock prices.

Chapter 6 provided the important insight that economic theory posits that if a large enough proportion of investors favor companies with high sustainability ratings and avoid those with low sustainability ratings, the favored companies' share prices will be elevated and the sin stock shares will be depressed. Specifically, in equilibrium, the screening out of certain assets based on investors' taste should lead to a return premium on the screened assets.

The result is that the favored companies will have a lower cost of capital because they will trade at a higher P/E ratio. The flip side of a lower cost of capital is a lower expected return to shareholders. Conversely, the sin companies will have a higher cost of capital because they will trade at a lower P/E ratio. The flip side of a company's higher cost of capital is a higher expected return to shareholders.

The hypothesis is that the higher expected returns (above the market's required return) are required as compensation for the emotional cost of exposure to offensive companies. On the other hand, investors in companies with higher sustainability ratings are willing to accept the lower returns as the cost of expressing their values. To examine how much value investors placed on the non pecuniary benefits of sustainable investing, the authors of the 2021 study "Dynamic ESG Equilibrium" developed and applied an equilibrium model that accounts for ESG demand and supply dynamics.[1] They explained: "A dynamic model can naturally accommodate preference shocks for sustainable investing as well as supply shocks. Preference shocks reflect the unexpected component of the growing interest in sustainable investing over recent years." Their sample period was 1992–2020. They found that investors were willing to accept about 1 percent lower returns for aligning their investments with their values.

There is also a risk-based hypothesis for the sin premium. It is logical to hypothesize that companies neglecting to manage their ESG exposures could be subject to greater risk (that is, a wider range of potential outcomes) than their more ESG-focused counterparts. The hypothesis is that companies with high sustainability scores have better risk management and better compliance standards. Their stronger controls lead to fewer extreme events such as environmental disasters, fraud, corruption, and litigation (and their negative consequences). The result is a reduction in tail risk in high-scoring firms relative to the lowest-scoring firms. The greater tail risk creates the sin premium.

We then discussed how investor preferences can lead to different short- and long-term impacts on asset prices and returns. For example, if investor demand increases for firms with high sustainable investing scores, that could lead to short-term capital gains for their stocks—realized returns rise temporarily. For example, the authors of the aforementioned study "Dynamic ESG Equilibrium" found that despite investor preferences for sustainable investments creating a brown premium of about 1 percent per year, over the period 2018–2020 the increased demand for sustainable investments led to a green portfolio outperforming by about 7 percentage points a year (14 percent versus 7 percent).[2] However, the long-term effect is that the higher valuations reduce expected long-term returns. The result can be an increase in green asset returns even though brown assets earn higher expected returns. In other words, there can be an ambiguous relationship between sustainable risks and returns in the short term. These conflicting forces, along with the difficulties created by the dispersion in sustainability ratings by the various providers, can create challenges for investors in interpreting the findings from academic papers.

As an example, Philippe van der Beck, author of the 2021 study "Flow-Driven ESG Returns" found that the performance of ESG investments was strongly driven by price pressure arising from flows toward sustainable funds, causing high realized returns that do not reflect high expected returns.[3] In addition, he found that due to the inelastic demand (lack of sensitivity to valuations) from sustainable investors, withdrawing $1 from the market portfolio and investing it in ESG funds increases the aggregate value of high ESG-taste stocks by $2–2.50. He also found that the price pressure arising from quarterly flows of only $5 billion was sufficient to account for all the outperformance of ESG funds over the market portfolio in recent years.

Despite these difficulties, the literature does provide us with some key takeaways:

1. Sustainable investment strategies that do not take into account factor exposures should expect lower returns. However, sustainable strategies also reduce risk. Thus, there may not be a sacrifice in risk-adjusted returns.
2. In the short term, the increased demand from sustainable investors might even be sufficient to offset the ex-ante lower expected return as valuations of green stocks relative to brown stocks increase. However, once a new equilibrium is reached, lower returns, along with lower risk, should be the expectation. This is important, as the evidence from studies such as "Do Investors Value Sustainability? A Natural Experiment Examining Ranking and Fund Flows" has found that mutual fund investors, both individual and institutional, collectively treat sustainability as a positive fund attribute, allocating more money to funds awarded 5 Morningstar globes and less money to funds with only one globe.[4]
3. The lower expected returns can be offset by increasing exposure to factors with higher expected returns (such as size, value, momentum, and profitability).
4. Markets are becoming more efficient, quickly incorporating information as to sustainable risks into prices.
5. If you are going to make sustainable investing a core of your investment philosophy, thorough due diligence is required before committing assets. That due diligence should not only include the screening methodologies but also a careful examination of factor loadings, industry concentrations, and expenses. And finally, investors are best served by assessing investment implications of sustainable strategies on a fund-by-fund basis.

It is also important to note that in its 2018 research report, "Big Data Shakes Up ESG Investing," Deutsche Bank estimated that the share of sustainable invested assets would increase from about 50 percent in 2020 to about 95 percent in 2035.[5] That means we may not reach a new equilibrium for quite some time. Supporting this view is that the authors of the 2020 study "ES Risks and Shareholder Voice" found that a majority of ESG proposals have not been supported by shareholders, and in particular by institutional investors, suggesting that today's investors care predominantly about performance. With a shift toward more concerns about sustainability, this could change in the near future.[6] The result could be that until that new equilibrium is reached, sustainable investors could have their cake and eat it too, as the benefits from increased cash flows could drive up valuations of green companies relative to brown companies. If that were the case, sustainable investors might realize higher returns while experiencing less risk. How long this trend lasts will depend on the speed with which investors adopt sustainable strategies. It is also possible that sustainable investors could benefit if an unexpected increase in ESG demand reinforced demand for green products, boosting the profits of green firms at the expense of brown firms.

In Chapter 7 we reviewed the evidence on how sustainable investors are impacting companies and their employees. The key takeaway is that the academic research has found that companies that adhere to positive environmental, social, and governance principles have lower costs of capital, higher valuations, are less vulnerable to systemic risks, and are more profitable. By expressing their values through their investments, sustainable investors are positively impacting companies as they seek the advantages of lower costs of capital and the benefits of a more satisfied and motivated workforce.

We also demonstrated that ESG investors are providing societal benefits through their impact on asset prices. By pushing green asset prices up (lowering the cost of capital) and brown ones down (raising the cost of capital), investors' tastes for green holdings induce more investment by green firms and less investment by brown firms. The more investors care about ESG, the greater the positive environmental impact as emissions are reduced, and the greater the social impact as well.

The bottom line is that sustainable investing is no longer a niche movement. We are witnessing a convergence between corporate sustainability and sustainable investing that is a major force driving market change as investors increasingly focus their attention on sustainability factors.

In Chapter 8 we discussed the practical aspects of building a sustainable investment portfolio. We began by noting that nothing about sustainable investing changes the fundamental principles of investing and that these should be your guiding principles: Markets are efficient (invest systematically, not based on opinions); broad global diversification across unique sources of risk is your friend; invest for the long term (stay disciplined, adhering to your plan and ignoring the noise of the market); and control expenses (while noting that the lowest-cost funds may not be the best choices). We then discussed how to construct a portfolio that meets your unique financial situation and values, including an in-depth look at how to choose managers.

We have also included some valuable appendices, including a history of SRI, a guide to help you select the best vehicles to implement your plan, a resource guide, a guide to help you interview investment managers, and a questionnaire to help you decide whether you should be a do-it-yourself investor or hire a professional advisor, one who acts as a fiduciary (so is required to give advice solely in your best interest). It also includes specific criteria to help you select an advisor if that is the choice you make.

Our greatest hope is that you have not only enjoyed your journey with us through the sustainable investment landscape but have gained the knowledge you need to allow you to integrate your values into your investment strategy.

Finally, we want you to know that we are both happy to answer questions from readers. You can reach Sam at sam@vertasset.com, and you can reach Larry at lswedroe@buckinghamgroup.com.

APPENDIX A

The History of SRI

THE EARLIEST PRECURSORS of socially responsible investing date back to the Pentateuch—the first five books of the Bible, believed to have been written by Moses as early as 1500 BC. The books refer to a Jewish concept called *tzedek* (justice and equity) and how it should govern all aspects of life. Tzedek aimed to correct the imbalances that humans inevitably generate, including the benefits one would receive from ownership. Owners had rights and responsibilities in how holdings were used, one of which was to prevent any immediate or potential harm.

This principle formed the genesis of socially responsible investing, providing religious and indigenous cultures with a set of criteria on how to generate financial returns ethically and sustainably.

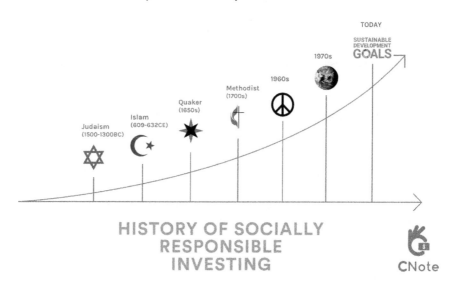

Source: www.mycnote.com/blog/the-history-of-socially-responsible-investing/

Note: The above image provides a cursory summary of some of the movements and institutions that have shaped SRI investing as we know it today. It is not intended to be an exhaustive list.

Religious Roots and Origins of Socially Responsible Investing

Despite a consensus that ethics were an essential consideration for investment decisions, the application of the principle varied: Some groups used it as a guideline, others required it by law. The basis for SRI varies between religious groups, leading to many different interpretations of the subject.

Judaism (1500-1300 BC)

Judaism sees a need for justice/equity in all aspects of life, including government and economic activity. Jewish law states that investments make us property owners, giving us the responsibility to use our holdings to prevent immediate and potential harm.[1]

While most biblical and rabbinical sources refer to single owners or small partnerships, Jewish religious figures eventually addressed the ethics of shareholder responsibility. Since shareholding is a form of ownership, investors must consider the ethical responsibilities of a company before investing. This prevented followers from investing in immoral companies.

Islam (609-632 CE)

The Quran established guidelines surrounding investments based on the teachings of Islam, now known as Shariah-compliant finance. This philosophy aims to govern the relationship between risk and profit along with the responsibilities of institutions and individuals. It states that money should be a medium of exchange, not an asset that grows over time. One of the governing principles in the Quran is *riba*, which aims to prevent exploitation through the use of money. It prohibits the payment or receipt of all forms of usury, including all sorts of interest payments, gambling, or uncertainty. The Quran also forbids any Islamic institution or individual from investing in alcohol, pork products, immoral goods, gold and silver, and weapons.

Quaker (1650s)

Based in England, Quakers are members of a group called the Religious Society of Friends. While the group is primarily interested in Christianity, it is also known for its opposition to slavery and war. In 1758 the Quaker Philadelphia Yearly Meeting prohibited members from participating in the slave trade, marking one of the first occurrences of SRI in its current form. Eventually, some Quakers went on to establish two of the largest financial institutions in modern history: Barclays and Lloyds.

Methodist (1700s)

Established in 1703, the Methodist movement was led by John Wesley, one of the most articulate early adopters of SRI. During a sermon titled "The Use of Money," Wesley outlined his stance on social investing: Avoid industries that have the potential to harm workers and any business practices that might harm your neighbor. Followers eventually resisted investments in sinful companies such as those involved in tobacco, firearms, and alcohol. This was a prelude to modern exclusionary investment screening.

Modern Era: The Rising Popularity of SRI

The modern version of SRI in the U.S. really took hold in the mid-1900s when investors began to avoid sin stocks—companies that dealt in alcohol, tobacco, or gambling. In 1950 the Boston-based Pioneer Fund, established in 1928, doubled down on this movement, becoming one of the first funds to adopt SRI principles. The avoidance of sin stocks in the 1950s marked the beginning of the rise of modern socially responsible investing, with each subsequent decade bringing forth an influx of socially concerned investors.

1960s

Socially responsible investing in the 1960s was largely driven by politics and concerns about the Vietnam War. Protestors boycotted companies that provided weapons for the war, while groups of students demanded that university endowment funds no longer invest in defense contractors. Meanwhile, civil rights, environmental, and labor movements raised awareness about social, environmental, and economic issues, bridging the gap between corporate and investor responsibility. In support of these movements, trade unions like the United Mine Workers and the International Ladies' Garment Workers' Union deployed targeted investments into medical facilities and union-built housing projects.

1970s

In April 1970, 20 million Americans convened for the first Earth Day celebration, opening the door for a cascade of environmental and consumer protection legislation in the early 1970s. As society reacted to war, sweatshops, apartheid, climate change, human trafficking, and a number of other political and cultural issues, socially responsible investors followed suit. Supported by consistent efforts from both investors and corporations, it was clear that the SRI movement was here to stay. A growing number of new funds combined social and environmental consciousness with financial objectives, reflecting the prevalence of aspirational progressive values. The Pax World Funds and the First Spectrum Fund were established in 1971, followed by the Dreyfus Third Century Fund.

1980s

In the wake of the Bhopal, Chernobyl, and Exxon Valdez disasters, concerns about the environment and climate change were at the core of SRI in the 1980s. This led to the launch of the Social Investment Forum in 1984, since renamed US SIF, The Forum for Sustainable and Responsible Investment, which has become one of the largest resources for SRI and impact investing. The standardized approach to SRI in the 1980s involved building a portfolio that behaved like the traditional market while avoiding investments in alcohol, tobacco, weapons, gambling, and environmental pollution. Firms paired these avoidance screens with a commitment to shareholder activism, a practice that allowed shareholders to leverage ownership to improve a company's behavior.

1990s

By 1990 the popularity of SRI mutual funds and socially conscious investing had hastened the need for a way to measure performance. Launched in 1990, the Domini 400 Social Index (now the MSCI KLD 400 Social Index) was composed of 400 U.S. publicly traded companies that met certain social and environmental standards.

2000s and Beyond

Socially responsible investing continued to gain supporters alongside the introduction of many major initiatives and funds. In 2006 the United Nations Principles for Responsible Investment was launched, establishing guidelines for mainstream investors to incorporate ESG issues into investment practices. Many socially conscious investors are going beyond SRI to seek out investments that prioritize a positive impact, sparking a rise in ESG and impact investing. This forward-thinking approach was reinforced in 2015 by the UN Sustainable Development Goals. These goals, backed by all UN member states, are an urgent call to solve the world's most pressing development challenges.

Summary

Socially responsible investments now account for one-third of all assets under professional management in the U.S., and with increased interest from the millennial generation, that number is only expected to rise. Despite the involvement of large investment firms and funds, socially responsible investments are not exclusive to institutional investors. There is a range of retail impact investment options that allow anyone to invest ethically and responsibly. The history of socially responsible investing demonstrates that what's old is new again. We can see that this growing movement shows no signs of slowing, making for an even larger impact as more investors get involved.

APPENDIX B

Should You Hire a Financial Advisor?

WHETHER WE ARE talking about home repairs or investing, individuals can be categorized into two broad groups: those who hire professionals and the do-it-yourselfers—those who do not want to pay professionals for something they believe they can do just as well. Of course, there are some who belong to the do-it-yourself group who would be better off hiring professionals. One reason is that if something is not done right the first time, the cost of correcting errors can far exceed the cost of a professional doing it right in the first place. Another is that while you can recover from making a mistake while trying to fix a leaky faucet, the damage done by financial errors can take years to recover from—and can even be irreversible.

If you are considering being a do-it-yourself investor, ask yourself the following five questions:

1. Do I have all the knowledge needed to develop an investment plan, integrate it into an overall estate, tax, and risk management (insurance of all types) plan and then provide the ongoing care and maintenance (rebalancing and tax management) required?
2. Do I have the mathematical skills needed? Investing requires a knowledge that goes well beyond simple arithmetic. You need advanced knowledge of probability theory and statistics, such as correlations and the various moments of distribution (such as skewness and kurtosis).
3. Do I have the ability to determine the appropriate asset allocation, one that provides the greatest odds of achieving my financial goals while not taking more risk than I have the ability and willingness to take? An important part of the planning process includes the use of a Monte Carlo simulator to estimate the odds of achieving your financial goals under various asset allocations, saving, and spending assumptions. Required assumptions include expected returns of asset classes, expected standard deviations of

asset classes, and expected correlations among asset classes. There are many of these programs available, many of which have serious flaws. And because of their complexity, it is easy to make mistakes.

4. Do I have a strong knowledge of financial history? You should be aware of how often stocks have provided negative returns, how long bear markets have lasted, and how deep bear markets have been. Those who do not know their history are likely to repeat past mistakes.

5. Do I have the temperament and the emotional discipline needed to adhere to a plan in the face of the many crises I will almost certainly face? Are you confident that you have the fortitude to withstand a severe drop in the value of your portfolio without panicking? Will you be able to rebalance back to your target allocations (keeping your head while most others are losing theirs), buying more stocks when the light at the end of the tunnel seems to be a truck coming the other way? Think back to how you felt and acted after the events of September 11, 2001, during the financial crisis that began in 2007, and during the COVID-19 crisis. Experience demonstrates that fear often leads to paralysis, or even worse, panicked selling and the abandonment of well-developed plans. When subjected to the pain of a bear market, even knowledgeable investors who know what to do fail to do the right thing because they allow emotions to take over, overriding their brain. This results in what Carl Richards calls "the behavior gap." The term is used to describe the failure of investors to earn the same return as that earned by the very funds in which they invest. Ask yourself: Have I always done the right thing? Have my returns matched those of my investments?

If you have passed this test, you are part of a small minority. Alternatively, you may recognize you do not have the knowledge, temperament, or discipline to succeed on your own. And even if you decide that you meet these requirements, you may recognize that a good financial advisory firm can add value in many ways, including freeing you to focus your attention on the most important things in your life such as time spent with family, friends, or meaningful endeavors. Thus, you may place a greater value on that time than the cost of advice. It is a matter of finding the right balance in your life.

Hiring an Advisor

If you decide to hire a financial advisory firm, because of the impact it can have, that choice will be one of the most important decisions you will ever make. It is critical that you get it right. With that in mind, we offer the following advice.

There are four criteria that should be absolutes when searching for the right advisor:

1. The advisor adheres to a fiduciary standard of care.
2. The advisor invests their own capital in the same vehicles being recommended.
3. Advice is based on science (evidence from peer-reviewed journals), not opinions.
4. The firm integrates investment planning into an overall financial plan.

Require a Fiduciary Standard of Care

There are two standards of care under which financial professionals operate: fiduciary and suitability. Under a fiduciary standard, the finance professional must always act in your best interest. Under a suitability standard, the finance professional only has to buy products that are suitable. Those products do not necessarily have to be in your best interest. There is no reason why you should settle for anything less than a fiduciary standard. And there is no reason you should ever work with an advisor or firm not prepared to meet this standard. The bottom line is this: You must be convinced that the guiding principle of the advisor or firm is that advice offered is solely in your best interest.

There are actions you can take in your due diligence to give you the best chance of receiving unbiased advice.

First, require that the advisory firm serve as a fee-only advisor, which avoids the conflicts that commission-based compensation can create. With commission-based compensation, it can be difficult to know if the investment or product recommended by the advisor is the one that is best for you, or the one that generates greater compensation for the advisor. Avoiding commission-based compensation helps to ensure that the advice you receive is client-centric: The only things being sold are advice and solutions to problems, not products.

Second, you need to make sure that all potential conflicts of interest are fully disclosed. Along with asking questions, you should review the firm's Form ADV—a disclosure document setting forth information about the firm's advisors, its investment strategy, fee schedules, conflicts of interest, regulatory incidents, and more. Careful due diligence helps minimize the risk of an expensive mistake.

Eat Their Own Cooking

You should require that the firm's advisors invest their personal assets (including the firm's profit-sharing and/or retirement plan) based on the same set of investment principles and in the same or comparable securities that they recommend to their clients. While you should expect to see asset allocations that differ from the one that is being recommended to you (as each investor has their own unique circumstances), the investment vehicles should be the same. There is simply no reason to hire any advisor who isn't willing to demonstrate to you that they are investing in the same vehicles they are recommending.

Evidence-Based Advice

You should only consider working with a firm whose investment strategy and advice is based on the science of investing, not on opinions. To demonstrate the wisdom of this advice, consider this situation. You are not feeling well. You make an appointment to visit a doctor your friend has recommended. The doctor's job is to diagnose the problem and recommend treatment. After a thorough exam, he turns around to his bookshelf and reaches for the latest copies of *Men's Health* magazine. Before hearing his advice, you are probably thinking it is time to get a second opinion. Therefore, you make an appointment with another doctor. After her exam, she reaches for a copy of the *New England Journal of Medicine*. At this point you are feeling much better about the advice you are about to receive. The financial equivalents of the *New England Journal of Medicine* are such publications as the *Journal of Finance*. The advisory firm should be able to cite evidence from peer-reviewed journals supporting their recommendations. You should not get your advice from the equivalents of *Men's Health,* such as *Investor's Business Daily* or *Barron's*. Again, there is no reason to hire an advisor who cannot demonstrate that their advice is based on evidence, not personal opinions.

Integrated Financial Planning

Because plans can fail for reasons that have nothing to do with the investment strategy, it is critical that the advisory firm you choose will integrate an investment plan into an overall estate, tax, and risk management (insurance of all kinds) plan, acting as the quarterback on the financial services team, coordinating the efforts of each of the advisors.

It is important to understand that plans can fail even when estate planning is done well. For example, far too often individuals pay for high-powered attorneys to develop well-thought-out estate plans only to have the trusts totally unfunded or funded with the wrong type of assets. Some trusts are designed to generate stable cash flows and should be funded with safe bonds. Others are designed with a growth objective in mind and should be funded primarily with stocks.

Estate plans can also derail because the beneficiaries have not been properly named (resulting from a failure to update documents to address life events such as divorce or death), or because the type or method of asset distribution is inappropriate (for instance, assets being distributed directly to a beneficiary with demonstrated creditor, bankruptcy, or financial management issues). This is another example of why a financial plan must be a living document, one that is reviewed on a regular basis.

It is also critical to understand that estate plans can fail despite the best efforts of top-notch professional advisors. Unfortunately, it is not uncommon for estates to lose their assets and family harmony following the transition of the estate. This occurs because beneficiaries are unprepared, they do not trust each other, and communications break down. While great attention is typically paid to preparing the assets for transition to the beneficiaries, very little if any attention is paid to preparing the beneficiaries for the assets they will inherit. A good advisory firm can add great value by helping to prepare and educate beneficiaries for the wealth they will inherit.

We have already described many ways a good financial advisory firm can and should add value. Following is a partial list of other ways:

- Regular, ongoing communications, especially during times of crisis. Education protects you from emotions taking control over your portfolio.
- Ongoing education about innovations in finance. The knowledge of how markets work advances on a persistent basis. You should be sure that the firm has the depth of resources to stay on top of the latest research.
- The ability to analyze complex financial products, helping you avoid purchasing costly products that are meant to be sold, not bought.
- College funding.
- Selecting investments for 529, 401(k), 403(b), and other employer plans, ensuring they are integrated into the overall plan.
- Gifting to heirs and charities in the most effective manner.
- Home-purchase and mortgage-financing decisions.
- The management and ultimate disposition of large, concentrated positions with low-cost bases (typically the stock of your employer or stock that has been inherited).
- Separate account management of bond portfolios, eliminating the expense of a mutual fund while maximizing tax efficiency and after-tax returns.
- Ongoing performance tracking, measuring the progress versus your plan and recommending adjustments that are necessary to prevent failure.
- Act as an insurance policy in the event of a death of a family member who is responsible for managing financial matters.

Clearly, no single advisor can be an expert in all of these areas. Therefore, when choosing a firm, be sure it has a team of experts that can help address each of these areas. You should also make sure that the firm's comprehensive wealth management services are provided by individuals who have the PFS (personal financial specialist), CFP (certified financial planner), or other comparable designations. Note that the PFS credential is granted to CPAs who have demonstrated their knowledge and expertise in personal financial planning. And once these designations are granted, they must be maintained through required professional development to keep them current.

It is also important to be clear that the firm will deliver a high level of personal attention and develop strong personal relationships. This should be part of your due diligence process as you check the firm's reputation with other local professionals (such as CPAs and attorneys) and client references.

Another part of your investigation should be discovering how the advisor spends time at work. You might ask: Can you please tell me about your average day? What you are looking for is an advisor who spends the majority of their time solving their clients' concerns about such issues as:

- Making smart decisions about money.
- Minimizing income, gift, and estate taxes.
- Transferring assets to the next generation.
- Protection from third parties unjustifiably taking their assets.
- Interest in making significant charitable gifts.

Your investigation should include sharing all your concerns with the advisor. The objective is to develop a deep understanding of how the advisor can help you address these concerns and ensure that you are confident you have a high level of trust in the advisor, his/her support team, and the advisory firm as a whole.

We need to cover one last point. As is the case with the choice of investment vehicles, cost matters. But what really matters is the value added relative to the cost. The lowest-cost investment vehicle may not be the best choice. Remember, while good advice doesn't have to be expensive, bad advice almost always will cost you dearly no matter how little you pay for it.

The choice of a financial advisor is one of the most important decisions you will ever make. That is why it is so important to perform thorough due diligence. The bottom line is that you want to be sure the firm you choose is one in which the science of investing meets true wealth management and that the services are delivered in a highly personalized manner.

APPENDIX C

Implementation: ESG Mutual Funds, ETFs, and SMAs

I N CHAPTER 8 we provided a process for selecting ESG funds. We intentionally avoided building any actual portfolios because we believe this to be a deeply personal exercise, one that should be based on a host of factors, including your own unique ability, willingness, and need to take risk as well as your own unique set of goals and values.

The good news is that the fund industry has responded to the demand for sustainable investment products so that you now have dozens from which to choose. To help with that process, we provide some examples of funds a sustainably minded investor might consider when building an investment portfolio. We have loosely grouped the funds into different categories based on what type of investor they might most appeal to. Note that given our desire to keep the suggestions simple and the fact that the fund industry is persistently introducing new products, this list is not comprehensive. That a particular fund does not appear should not be taken to mean you should exclude it from consideration. Again, we emphasize the importance of doing your own due diligence (Appendix E contains a list of questions to help you with that process).

The Index Fund or Exchange Traded Fund Investor

The investor who prefers passively managed, low-cost strategies that deliver returns close to an index is in luck. There are many options in most asset classes; a few are displayed here.

US Market Equity	Calvert US Large Cap Core Responsible Index	CISIX
	IShares MSCI USA ESG Select ETF	SUSA
US Small/Value Equity	Calvert US Large Cap Value Responsible Index	CFJIX
	Nuveen Large-Cap Value ETF	NULV
	Nuveen ESG Small-Cap ETF	NUSC
	Praxis Small Cap Index	MMSIX
International Equity	Calvert International Responsible Index Fund	CDHIX
	Nuveen ESG International Developed Markets ETF	NUDM
Emerging Markets	Nuveen ESG Emerging Markets Equity ETF	NUEM
	IShares ESG Aware MSCI EM Leaders ETF	LDEM
Real Estate	Vert Global Sustainable Real Estate	VGSRX
Fixed Income	Nuveen ESG U.S. Aggregate Bond ETF	NUBD
	Fidelity Sustainable Bond Index	FNDSX

The Dimensional-Affiliated Investor

Dimensional's ESG offerings are attractive to investors who want market-like performance with modest tilts to the small, value, and profitability factors. While these strategies are generally only available through select financial advisors and platforms, they may also be available to investors inside 401(k), 403(b), and other retirement plans.

US Market Equity	Dimensional US Sustainability Core 1	DFSIX
US Small/Value Equity	Dimensional US Sustainability Targeted Value	DAABX
International Equity	Dimensional International Sustainability Core 1	DFSPX
Emerging Markets	Dimensional Emerging Markets Sustainability Core 1	DESIX
Real Estate	Vert Global Sustainable Real Estate*	VGSRX
Fixed Income	Dimensional Global Sustainability Fixed Income	DGSFX

*The Vert Global Sustainable Real Estate Fund is sub-advised by Dimensional but is publicly available to all investors. Sam Adams, co-author, is CEO of Vert and a portfolio manager of the Vert fund.

The Engagement-Oriented Investor

Investors who want their assets to encourage more responsible corporate behavior might look to fund managers committed to active shareholder engagement.

US Market Equity	Walden Equity	WSEFX
	VOTE ETF	VOTE
US Small/Value Equity	Calvert Large-Cap Value Responsible Index Fund	CFJIX
	Calvert Small-Cap Fund	CCVAX
International Equity	Green Century International Index	GCIFX
	Walden International Equity	WIEFX
Emerging Markets	Calvert Emerging Markets Equity	CVMIX
Real Estate	Vert Global Sustainable Real Estate	VGSRX
Fixed Income	Pax Core Bond Fund	PXBIX

The Balanced Fund Investor

Investors who prefer a single fund might look to these types of funds, which maintain diversified exposure to several asset classes.

30% to 50% Equity	Calvert Conservative Allocation I	CFAIX
50% to 70% Equity	Calvert Balanced I	CBAIX
50% to 70% Equity	Calvert Moderate Allocation I	CLAIX
85%+ Equity	Calvert Growth Allocation I	CAGIX
50% to 70% Equity	Pax Sustainable Allocation	PAVWX
70% to 85% Equity	Walden Balanced	WSBFX

The Target-Date Investor

Target-date funds are meant for the *set it and forget it* investor. If you have money to set aside for a particular future date, these funds adjust the asset allocation through time so you don't have to. Natixis was the first company to launch a set of ESG target-date funds.

Balanced Fund	Natixis Sustainable Future 2020	NSFDX
Balanced Fund	Natixis Sustainable Future 2025	NSFEX
Balanced Fund	Natixis Sustainable Future 2030	NSFFX
Balanced Fund	Natixis Sustainable Future 2035	NSFGX
Balanced Fund	Natixis Sustainable Future 2040	NSFHX
Balanced Fund	Natixis Sustainable Future 2045	NSFJX
Balanced Fund	Natixis Sustainable Future 2050	NSFKX
Balanced Fund	Natixis Sustainable Future 2055	NSFLX
Balanced Fund	Natixis Sustainable Future 2060	NSFMX

The Thematic Investor

ESG investors can more closely align their portfolio to their values by using thematic funds. One approach is to use a themed core fund to provide broad equity or bond market exposure. Alternatively, you can put part of an allocation into an alternative asset class to invest in specific issues.

	Core Equity Funds	
Women	Fidelity Women's Leadership	FWOMX
	Glenmede Women in Leadership US Equity	GWILX
	SPDR SSGA Gender Diversity ETF	SHE
	Pax Ellevate Global Women's Leadership	PXWEX
Sustainable Development	Impact Shares Sustainable Dev. Goals Global ETF	SDGA
Climate/Fossil Fuel Free	Etho Climate Leadership US ETF	ETHO
	Change Finance US Fossil Fuel Free	CHGX
Social Justice	Adasina Social Justice ETF	JSTC
Vegan	US Vegan Climate ETF	VEGN

	Core Fixed Income Funds	
Community Development	CCM Community Impact Bond Fund	CRAIX
Affordable Housing	Access Capital Community Investment	ACCSX
Climate	PIMCO Climate Bond	PCEIX
Green Bond	Calvert Green Bond	CGBIX
	iShares Global Green Bond ETF	BGRN

Alternative Asset Classes		
Renewable Energy	Invesco WilderHill Clean Energy ETF	PBW
	Tortoise Energy Evolution	TOPIX
Water	KBI Global Investors Aquarius	KBIWX
Infrastructure	Pax Global Sustainable Infrastructure	PXDIX
Cleantech	Invesco Cleantech ETF	PZD

Separately Managed Accounts

For those investors who desire to work with a manager who creates separately managed accounts either because they want to create a portfolio that expresses their personal values or to gain the potential benefits of greater tax efficiency, you might consider these providers: Aperio Group, Dimensional, Ethic, JustInvest, and Parametric.

APPENDIX D

Resource Guide

THIS APPENDIX IS a republication of the 2020 edition of the ESG Resource Guide from the Plan Sponsor Council of America (PSCA). It provides readers with a list of resources through which they can further their education and research into sustainable investing. This is not, nor can it be, a complete list of all providers.

The guide is organized in six parts:

1. *Policy & Advocacy*: This section lists prominent, global, nongovernmental organizations and advocacy groups whose mission and resources are devoted to advancing the understanding and adoption of responsible investing principles.
2. *Legal & Regulatory*: The U.S. Department of Labor's Employee Benefits Security Administration rules affecting ESG investments are frequently cited as impediments to adoption by plan sponsors, so direct links are provided for source document analysis. Links to other global regulatory bodies/statutes are also provided for comparison.
3. *Financial Reporting and Standard Setting*: Organizations listed in this section are at the forefront of promulgating new and improved financial reporting standards that incorporate ESG factors into traditional financial reporting. The goal is to provide a more complete picture of a company's financial performance and material risks.
4. *E, S, or G Focused*: This section includes organizations that have a more focused effort on one of the three major ESG factors rather than a broader advocacy or engagement mission. Impact investing is also included.
5. *Index Providers and Ratings Services*: This section lists organizations that provide the definitional framework for ESG investing via the establishment of indices and benchmarks to measure the performance of ESG investments. These indices can be licensed by investment managers to create index-based mutual or exchange traded funds. Also included are major ESG ratings and ranking services that provide critical data and evaluation of companies and industries.

6. *Research & Publications*: Organizations listed in this section have dedicated resources to study ESG issues and provide analysis, commentary, thought leadership, and products and services for asset owners and investors. While some are academically based, many are commercially oriented and provide subscriber-only websites and/or customized software and hardware as part of their service. News organizations are also listed.

We are grateful to the PSCA for this valuable resource and for allowing us to republish it here. In particular, we would like to thank these individuals who created the Resource Guide: Robert E. "Emery" Pike, CFA, AIF; Matthew Luksa, CRPS, CRPC; Tim Kohn, Head of Retirement Distribution, Dimensional Fund Advisors; Meg Voorhes, Director of Research, US SIF; Mona Naqvi, Senior Director, Head of ESG Product Strategy, S&P Dow Jones Indices; Robert Bush, IMC, FRM, CIMA, Director, DWS Research Institute; and Jenny Terry, Graphic Design and Layout.

POLICY & ADVOCACY

These are non-governmental organizations that are advocates and leaders for setting standards in responsible investing, including Environmental, Social, and Governance. This is where organizations of any size and asset managers and owners can subscribe and align with principals, processes, and goals to transform towards sustainable investment practices worldwide.

GLOBAL & SUPRA-NATIONAL NON-GOVERNMENTAL ORGANIZATIONS

Name of Organization	Note / Description
United Nations Principles for Responsible Investing (UNPRI)	The PRI is the world's leading proponent of responsible investment. It works to understand the investment implications of environmental, social and governance (ESG) factors and to support its international network of investor signatories in incorporating these factors into their investment and ownership decisions.
UN Sustainable Development Goals	The Sustainable Development Goals are the blueprint to achieve a better and more sustainable future for all. They address the global challenges we face, including those related to poverty, inequality, climate, environmental degradation, prosperity, and peace and justice. Goals are frequently cited by policy-makers and practitioners.
United Nations Global Compact	Global initiative to encourage companies to align strategies and operations with universal principles on human rights, labor, environment and anti-corruption, and take actions that advance societal goals.
Sustainable Stock Exchanges Initiative	The SSE initiative is a UN Partnership Program organized by UNCTAD, the UN Global Compact, UNEP FI and the PRI. The SSE's mission is to provide a global platform for exploring how exchanges, in collaboration with investors, companies (issuers), regulators, policymakers and relevant international organizations, can enhance performance on ESG (environmental, social and corporate governance) issues and encourage sustainable investment, including the financing of the UN Sustainable Development Goals.

EUROPEAN ADVOCACY ORGANIZATIONS

Eurosif	Eurosif is the leading pan-European sustainable and responsible investment (SRI) membership organization whose mission is to promote sustainability through European financial markets. Eurosif works as a partnership of Europe-based national Sustainable Investment Fora (SIFs) with the direct support of their network which spans over 400 Europe-based organizations drawn from the sustainable investment industry value chain. These organizations include institutional investors, asset managers, financial services, index providers and ESG research and analysis firms. The main activities of Eurosif are public policy, research and creating platforms for nurturing sustainable investing best practices. Promotes sustainability through European markets.

OTHER WORLD-WIDE

Global Sustainable Investment Alliance (GSIA)	Global alliance between Eurosif, RIAA, RIA Canada, UKSIF, USSIF, VBDO, JSFI. GSIA's mission is to deepen the impact and visibility of sustainable investment organizations at the global level. Our vision is a world where sustainable investment is integrated into financial systems and the investment chain and where all regions of the world have coverage by vigorous membership based institutions that represent and advance the sustainable investment community.

OTHER ADVOCACY & THOUGHT LEADERSHIP

Coalition for Environmentally Responsible Economies (CERES)	Ceres is a sustainability nonprofit organization working with the most influential investors and companies to build leadership and drive solutions throughout the economy. Through powerful networks and advocacy, Ceres tackles the world's biggest sustainability challenges, including climate change, water scarcity and pollution, and inequitable workplaces. Its team of financial market, energy and legal experts apply groundbreaking research using leading industry databases to map both risk and opportunity for investors on the path to a low-carbon future.
The Conference Board Center For Corporate Citizenship and Sustainability	Offers research, publications, peer learning and other tools to help member companies transform their corporate citizenship and sustainability thinking and activities into integral, core business strategies, targeting business opportunities that provide maximum economic, environmental, and societal benefits.
US SIF (The Forum for Responsible & Sustainable Investing)	The leading voice in the U.S. advancing sustainable, responsible and impact investing across all asset classes. Its mission is to rapidly shift investment practices toward sustainability, focusing on long-term investment and the generation of positive social and environmental impacts. US SIF is supported in its work by the US SIF Foundation, a 501(C)(3) organization that undertakes educational, research and programmatic activities to advance the mission of US SIF, including offering training for advisors and other financial professionals on the Fundamentals of Sustainable and Impact Investment. Offers online directory of investment managers and mutual funds that self-identify as ESG.
Global Initiative for Sustainability Ratings (GISR)	Launched in June 2011 as a joint project of Ceres and Tellus Institute, both non-profit research and educational entities, the Global Initiative for Sustainability Ratings (GISR) is a public benefit organization aimed at making financial markets agents of, rather than impediments to, achieving the Sustainable Development Goals and broader global sustainability agenda. As a multi-stakeholder initiative with the public interest at its core, GISR's vision is to transform the definition of corporate value in the 21st century such that markets reward the preservation and enhancement of all forms of capital – human, intellectual, natural, social and financial. We work with investors, companies, ESG research and rating organizations, and civil society organizations to improve worldwide access to high-quality sustainability ratings. GISR does not rate organizations. Instead, through a voluntary accreditation process, GISR will accredit sustainability ratings, rankings or indices on the basis of their alignment with GISR's 12 Principles.

ShareAction	UK based non-profit focused on building a movement for responsible investment by connecting foundations, faith groups, unions and NGOs to take action in the investment system. Also focuses on reforming the rules, governance, and incentives inside the investment system, and unlocking the power of investors to catalyze positive social and environmental change.
TIIP The Investment Integration Project	Established the theoretical frameworks for identifying systemic environmental and social challenges best-suited to investor action and developed and disseminated information about effective system-level investing tools. We have since broadened our efforts and are helping to meet industry demand for practical guidance on adopting system-level investing approaches and measuring investors' impacts and influence on environmental and social systems.
World Business Council for Sustainable Development	WBCSD is a global, CEO-led organization of over 200 leading businesses working together to accelerate the transition to a sustainable world. We help make our member companies more successful and sustainable by focusing on the maximum positive impact for shareholders, the environment and societies. Our member companies come from all business sectors and all major economies. Our global network of almost 70 national business councils gives our members unparalleled reach across the globe. Since 1995, WBCSD has been uniquely positioned to work with member companies along and across value chains to deliver impactful business solutions to the most challenging sustainability issues.
World Resources Institute (WRI)	WRI is a global research organization that spans more than 60 countries, with offices in the United States, China, India, Brazil, Indonesia and more. Our more than 1,000 experts and staff work closely with leaders to turn big ideas into action to sustain our natural resources—the foundation of economic opportunity and human well-being. Our work focuses on seven critical issues at the intersection of environment and development: climate, energy, food, forests, water, cities and the ocean.

LEGAL & REGULATORY

Retirement plan fiduciaries and others are required to abide by numerous laws and regulations which vary by geography and jurisdiction. The links below provide quick access to reference examples but is by no means an exhaustive list. It is strongly recommended for any further review or questions to please consult with an attorney.

USA

Federal Register	June 30 2020 publication of proposed Department of Labor amendments to the "Investment duties" regulation under Title I of the Employee Retirement Income Security Act of 1974 (ERISA), as amended , to confirm that ERISA requires plan fiduciaries to select investments and investment courses of action based solely on financial considerations relevant to the risk-adjusted economic value of a particular investment or investment course of action.
U.S. Department of Labor / Employee Benefits Security Administration	June 23 2020 News Release describing proposed new Investment Duties Rule

U.S. Department of Labor / Employee Benefits Security Administration	April 23 2018 Field Assistance Bulletin (FAB) 2018-01 which provides guidance to the Employee Benefits Security Administration's national and regional offices to assist in addressing questions they may receive from plan fiduciaries and other interested stakeholders about Interpretive Bulletin 2016-01 (relating to the exercise of shareholder rights and written statements of investment policy), and Interpretive Bulletin 2015-01 (relating to "economically targeted investments" (ETIs).
Federal Register	December 29 2016 publication that sets forth supplemental views of the Department of Labor (Department) concerning the legal standards imposed by sections 402, 403 and 404 of Part 4 of Title I of the Employee Retirement Income Security Act of 1974 (ERISA) with respect to voting of proxies on securities held in employee benefit plan investment portfolios, the maintenance of and compliance with statements of investment policy, including proxy voting policy, and the exercise of other legal rights of a shareholder. (IB 2016-01)
U.S. Department of Labor / Employee Benefits Security Administration	December 29 2016 Interpretive Bulletin (IB) 2016-01 relating to the Exercise of Shareholder Rights and Written Statements of Investment Policy, including Proxy Voting Policies or Guidelines
Federal Register	October 26 2015 publication that sets forth supplemental views of the Department of Labor concerning the legal standard imposed by sections 403 and 404 of Part 4 of Title I of the Employee Retirement Income Security Act of 1974 (ERISA) with respect to a plan fiduciary's decision to invest plan assets in "economically targeted investments" (ETIs). ETIs are generally defined as investments that are selected for the economic benefits they create in addition to the investment return to the employee benefit plan investor. (IB 2015-01)
U.S. Department of Labor / Employee Benefits Security Administration	October 22 2015 DOL Factsheet on "Economically Targeted Investments (ETI) and Investment Strategies that Consider Environmental, Social and Governance (ESG) Factors"
Federal Register	October 17 2008 publication that sets forth the views of the Department of Labor concerning the legal standards imposed by sections 402, 403 and 404 of Title I of the Employee Retirement Income Security Act (ERISA) with respect to the exercise of shareholder rights and written statements of investment policy, including proxy voting policies or guidelines. (IB 2008-01)
Federal Register	June 23 1994 publication that sets forth the view of the Department of Labor concerning the legal standard imposed by sections 403 and 404 of Part 4 of Title I of the Employee Retirement Income Security Act of 1974 (ERISA) with respect to a plan fiduciary's decision to invest plan assets in "economically targeted investments" (ETIs). ETIs are generally defined as investments that are selected for the economic benefits they create in addition to the investment return to the employee benefit plan investor. In this document, the Department states that the requirements of sections 403 and 404 do not prevent plan fiduciaries from deciding to invest plan assets in an ETI if the ETI has an expected rate of return that is commensurate to rates of return of alternative investments with similar risk characteristics that are available to the plan, and if the ETI is otherwise an appropriate investment for the plan in terms of such factors as diversification and the investment policy of the plan. (IB 94-1)

US Securities & Exchange Commission (SEC)	Landmark 2010 interpretive release providing guidance to public companies regarding the Commission's existing disclosure requirements as they apply to climate change matters.
US Commodity Futures Trading Commission (CFTC)	Sept. 2020 report entitled "Managing Climate Risk in the U.S. Financial System", a first-of-its-kind effort from a U.S. government entity to examine climate-related impacts on the financial system. The report draws from financial markets, the banking and insurance sectors, the agricultural and energy markets, data and intelligence service providers, the environmental and sustainability public policy sector, and academic disciplines focused on climate change, adaptation, public policy, and finance. The report, which presents 53 recommendations to mitigate the risks to financial markets posed by climate change, is anticipated to become the defacto standard reference for US regulatory and legislative action on climate change going forward.

OTHER WORLD-WIDE

European Commission	Report on EU Taxonomy issued June 2019; most advanced effort to provide standard classification system for ESG investments. Focus on climate change and environmental impact. Will serve as basis for EU regulations and model for other countries/jurisdictions.
European Commission	Landmark Directive issued by EU in Dec 2016 requiring pension funds to evaluate ESG risks and disclose information to plan participants/beneficiaries.
European Insurance and Occupational Pensions Authority (EIOPA)	Quasi-regulatory EU agency for pensions issues July 2020 opinion to country regulators on how ESG factors should be taken into account.
French Energy Transition for Green Growth Law (Article 173-IV)	Ground-breaking law on climate change; came into force on 1 January 2016. It strengthened mandatory carbon disclosure requirements for listed companies and introduced carbon reporting for institutional investors, defined as asset owners and investment managers. Introduced "comply or explain" method of implementation.
Japan Financial Services Agency	Japan's Stewardship Code and signatories, with further policy and legal info
UK Financial Reporting Council	UK Stewardship Code and relevant links to UK policies
Existing Global Stewardship Codes	Minerva Analytics list of links to key international codes. Stewardship Codes are usually addressed by institutional investors and outline best practices for engagement with investee companies. Stewardship Codes are generally voluntary and operate on a "comply or explain" or "if not, why not" basis. Stewardship Codes may have an element of regulatory impetus, for example by inclusion in asset manager conduct of business rules. The Stewardship Codes may have been developed by membership bodies or through regulatory bodies.

FINANCIAL REPORTING & STANDARD SETTERS

Producing useful financial reports requires common standards that are accepted and used by all market participants. The organizations listed below are at the forefront of promulgating new and improved financial reporting standards that incorporate ESG factors into traditional financial reporting in order to provide a more complete picture of a company's financial performance and material risks.

Climate Disclosure Standards Board	The CDSB is an international consortium of business and environmental NGOs. We are committed to advancing and aligning the global mainstream corporate reporting model to equate natural capital with financial capital. We do this by offering companies a framework for reporting environmental information with the same rigor as financial information. In turn this helps them to provide investors with decision-useful environmental information via the mainstream corporate report, enhancing the efficient allocation of capital. Regulators also benefit from compliance-ready materials.
Global Reporting Initiative	GRI is an independent international organization that has pioneered sustainability reporting since 1997; maintains GRI Sustainability Reporting Standards to helps businesses and governments worldwide understand and communicate their impact on critical sustainability issues such as climate change, human rights, governance and social well-being.
Impact Management Project (IMP)	The Impact Management Project (IMP) provides a forum for organisations to build consensus on how to measure, assess and report impacts on environmental and social issues. We convene a Practitioner Community of over 2,000 organisations to debate and find consensus (norms) on impact management techniques. We also facilitate the IMP Structured Network – an unprecedented collaboration of organizations that, through their specific and complementary expertise, are coordinating efforts to provide complete standards for impact measurement, assessment, and reporting.
International Integrated Reporting Council (IIRC)	UK based global coalition of regulators, investors, companies, standard setters, the accounting profession and NGOs. The coalition is promoting communication about value creation as the next step in the evolution of corporate reporting.
Partnership for Carbon Accounting Financials (PCAF)	PCAF is a global partnership of financial institutions that work together to develop and implement a harmonized approach to assess and disclose the greenhouse gas (GHG) emissions associated with their loans and investments. Released Global Carbon Accounting Standard in August 2020 to provide financial institutions with shared methodologies and rules for measuring and disclosing the greenhouse gas emissions of their loans and investments.
Sustainability Accounting Standards Board (SASB)	Independent, private-sector standards setting organization based in San Francisco dedicated to enhancing the efficiency of the capital markets by fostering high-quality disclosure of material sustainability information that meets investor needs. Publishes Materiality Map that is the global standard for identifying sustainability issues on an industry by industry basis.

Task Force on Climate-Related Financial Disclosures	The Financial Stability Board (FSB) Task Force on Climate-related Financial Disclosures (TCFD) will develop voluntary, consistent climate-related financial risk disclosures for use by companies in providing information to investors, lenders, insurers, and other stakeholders. The Task Force will consider the physical, liability and transition risks associated with climate change and what constitutes effective financial disclosures across industries. The work and recommendations of the Task Force will help companies understand what financial markets want from disclosure in order to measure and respond to climate change risks, and encourage firms to align their disclosures with investors' needs.

E S OR G FOCUSED

The organizations listed below generally have a more focused effort on one of the three major ESG factors, rather than a broader advocacy or engagement mission.

ENVIRONMENTAL FOCUS

Carbon Tracker	Carbon Tracker is an independent financial think tank that carries out in-depth analysis on the impact of the energy transition on capital markets and the potential investment in high-cost, carbon-intensive fossil fuels. Its team of financial market, energy and legal experts apply groundbreaking research using leading industry databases to map both risk and opportunity for investors on the path to a low-carbon future.
CDP (Carbon Disclosure Project)	CDP Global is an international non-profit organization comprised of CDP Worldwide Group and CDP North America, Inc. CDP runs the global environmental disclosure system. Each year CDP supports thousands of companies, cities, states and regions to measure and manage their risks and opportunities on climate change, water security and deforestation. We do so at the request of their investors, purchasers and city stakeholders. Over the last two decades we have created a system that has resulted in unparalleled engagement on environmental issues worldwide.
Climate Action 100+	Climate Action 100+ is an investor initiative to ensure the world's largest corporate greenhouse gas emitters take necessary action on climate change. The companies include 100 'systemically important emitters', accounting for two-thirds of annual global industrial emissions, alongside more than 60 others with significant opportunity to drive the clean energy transition.
Global Investor Coalition on Climate Change (GIC)	The Global Investor Coalition on Climate Change is a collaboration among four regional partner organizations around the world to increase investor education and engagement on climate change and climate-related policies. Launched in 2012, the coalition provides a global platform for dialogue between and among investors and world governments to accelerate low-carbon investment practices, corporate actions on climate risk and opportunities, and international policies that support the goals of the Paris Agreement. The regional partners work together to produce research reports and public policy statements and support global investor-led climate initiatives and investor-focused climate events.

Greenhouse Gas Protocol	Greenhouse Gas Protocol provides standards, guidance, tools and training for business and government to measure and manage climate-warming emissions. Building on a 20-year partnership between World Resources Institute (WRI) and the World Business Council for Sustainable Development (WBCSD), GHG Protocol works with governments, industry associations, NGOs, businesses and other organizations.
Institutional Investors Group on Climate Change	The European membership body for investor collaboration on climate change. IIGCC's mission is to mobilize capital for the low carbon transition and to ensure resilience to the impacts of a changing climate by collaborating with business, policy makers and fellow investors. IIGCC works to support and help define the public policies, investment practices and corporate behaviors that address the long-term risks and opportunities associated with climate change.
ShareAction AODP (Asset Owners Disclosure Project)	Ranks the climate-related financial disclosures of the world's largest pension funds, insurers, sovereign wealth funds and endowments.
2 Degree Investing Initiative	The $2°$ Investing Initiative (2DII) is an international, non-profit think tank working to align financial markets and regulations with the Paris Agreement goals. Working globally with offices in Paris, New York, Berlin, and London, we coordinate the world's largest research projects on climate metrics in financial markets.

SOCIAL FOCUS

Social (S): Issues relating to the rights, well-being and interests of people and communities. These include: human rights, labor standards in the supply chain, child, slave and bonded labor, workplace health and safety, freedom of association and freedom of expression, human capital management and employee relations; diversity; relations with local communities, activities in conflict zones, health and access to medicine, HIV/AIDS, consumer protection; and controversial weapons.

Global Thinkers Forum	Global Thinkers Forum (GTF) is a non-profit organization with a core mission to promote values-based thinking and accountability in leadership with a focus on women's empowerment and youth development. Global Thinkers Forum has a network of influencers and partners that reach more than 70 countries around the world and engages leaders across business, philanthropy, academia, science, civil society, NGOs and government. GTF has partnered with some of the world's leading brands, organizations and foundations and has an advisory board consisting of social impact focused leaders from over 20 countries.
Human Capital Management Coalition	The Human Capital Management Coalition (HCMC) is a cooperative effort among a diverse group of influential institutional investors to further elevate human capital management as a critical component in company performance. The Coalition engages companies and other market participants with the aim of understanding and improving how human capital management contributes to the creation of long-term shareholder value.
Interfaith Center on Corporate Responsibility (ICCR)	A coalition of faith and values-driven organizations that collaborate and coordinate their advocacy on specific E, S and G issues.

Investor Alliance for Human Rights	The Investor Alliance for Human Rights is a collective action platform for responsible investment that is grounded in respect for people's fundamental rights. We are a membership-based, non-profit initiative focusing on the investor responsibility to respect human rights, corporate engagements that drive responsible business conduct, and standard-setting activities that push for robust business and human rights policies.
JUST Capital	JUST Capital was co-founded in 2013 by a group of concerned people from the world of business, finance, and civil society, led by Paul Tudor Jones II. JUST Capital measures and ranks companies based on the central values of fair pay and equal treatment for all workers in pursuit of a mission to build an economy that works for all Americans. Guided by the priorities of the public, our research, rankings, indexes, and data-driven tools help measure and improve corporate performance in the stakeholder economy.
Thirty Percent Coalition	We are the Coalition for U.S. board diversity. Our national and international members work to increase diversity in corporate boardrooms across the U.S. The Thirty Percent Coalition was founded in 2011 with these guiding principles: Vision – For senior leadership and board of directors to reflect the gender, racial and ethnic diversity of the United States workforce. Mission – To advocate for diversity on corporate boards, promoting women and people of color. Focus – Collaborating with companies on the demand side.
Workforce Disclosure Initiative (WDI)	The Workforce Disclosure Initiative was founded in late 2016 to address the lack of transparency around workforce policies and practices in companies' direct operations and supply chains. Using the influence of investors, the WDI encourages publicly listed companies to complete a comprehensive annual survey which covers freedom of association, human rights due diligence, diversity, pay ratios and more. This standardised data set, and accompanying resources gives investors additional tools to assess how companies value their workers.

GOVERNANCE FOCUS

Governance (G): Issues relating to the governance of companies and other investee entities. In the listed equity context these include: board structure, size, diversity, skills and independence, executive pay, shareholder rights, stakeholder interaction, disclosure of information, business ethics, bribery and corruption, internal controls and risk management, and, in general, issues dealing with the relationship between a company's management, its board, its shareholders and its stakeholders. This category may also include matters of business strategy, encompassing both the implications of business strategy for environmental and social issues, and how the strategy is to be implemented. In the unlisted asset classes governance issues also include matters of fund governance, such as the powers of Advisory Committees, valuation issues, fee structures, etc.

As You Sow	As You Sow is the nation's non-profit leader in shareholder advocacy. Founded in 1992, we harness shareholder power to create lasting change that benefits people, planet, and profit. Our mission is to promote environmental and social corporate responsibility through shareholder advocacy, coalition building, and innovative legal strategies. Our vision is a safe, just, and sustainable world in which protecting the environment and human rights is central to corporate decision making. We work directly with corporate executives to collaboratively develop business policies and practices that reduce risk, benefit brand reputation, and increase the bottom line, while bringing positive environmental and social change.

Council of Institutional Investors	The Council of Institutional Investors is a nonprofit, nonpartisan association of U.S. public, corporate and union employee benefit funds, other employee benefit plans, state and local entities charged with investing public assets, and foundations and endowments. Our member funds include major long-term shareowners with a duty to protect the retirement savings of millions of workers and their families, including public pension funds. CII is a leading voice for effective corporate governance, strong shareowner rights and sensible financial regulations that foster fair, vibrant capital markets.
European Corporate Governance Center	The ECGI is an international scientific non-profit association providing a forum for debate and dialogue between academics, legislators and practitioners, focusing on major corporate governance issues. Its primary role is to undertake, commission and disseminate leading research on corporate governance. Based upon impartial and objective research and the collective knowledge and wisdom of our members, it can advise on the formulation of corporate governance policy and development of best practices. In seeking to achieve its aim of improving corporate governance, it acts as a focal point for academics working on corporate governance in Europe and elsewhere, encouraging the interaction between the different disciplines, such as economics, law, finance and management.
International Corporate Governance Network (ICGN)	Established in 1995 as an investor-led organization, the International Corporate Governance Network's mission is to promote effective standards of corporate governance and investor stewardship to advance efficient markets and sustainable economies worldwide.
Investor Stewardship Group	The Investor Stewardship Group (ISG) is an investor-led effort that includes some of the largest U.S.-based institutional investors and global asset managers. The ISG was formed as a sustained initiative to establish a framework of basic investment stewardship and corporate governance standards for U.S. institutional investor and boardroom conduct. The result is the framework for U.S. Stewardship and Governance comprising of a set of stewardship principles for institutional investors and corporate governance principles for U.S. listed companies.

IMPACT INVESTING / DEVELOPING WORLD PROJECT FINANCE

Impact investing pursues dual objectives of generating environmental or social returns (effects) and financial gains. It differs slightly from ESG in that the project or investment intentions are stated upfront with clear objectives, and then subsequent measurable results are directly tied to those specific goals.

B Analytics	B Lab helps tens of thousands of businesses, investors, and institutions manage their impact with as much rigor as their profits using the B Impact Assessment and supportive programs and partnerships. The B Impact Assessment is also used to certify B Corporations.
Equator Principles	The Equator Principles (EPs) is a risk management framework, adopted by financial institutions, for determining, assessing and managing environmental and social risk in projects. It is primarily intended to provide a minimum standard for due diligence and monitoring to support responsible risk decision-making.

Global Impacting Investing Network	GIIN focuses on reducing barriers to impact investment so more investors can allocate capital to fund solutions to the world's most intractable challenges. This is done by building critical infrastructure and developing activities, education, and research that help accelerate the development of a coherent impact investing industry. Read the GIIN's latest Op-eds and publications, along with Investor Spotlights, Investment Profiles, and third-party research from other leading impact investing organizations.
ImpactSpace	ImpactSpace helps you connect with companies, investors, deals, and people generating financial returns through the creation of environmental and social value. Our open database, ImpactSpace, aka "CrunchBase for Impact," includes profiles on more than 10,000 impact ventures, funds and deals.
U.S. International Development Finance Corporation (DFC)	Formerly known as the Overseas Private Investment Corporation, the U.S. International Development Finance Corporation (DFC) is America's development bank. DFC partners with the private sector to finance solutions to the most critical challenges facing the developing world today.

INDICES & RATINGS PROVIDERS

These organizations provide the definitional framework for ESG investing via the establishment of indices and benchmarks to measure the performance of ESG investments. Also included are major ESG ratings and ranking services which provide critical data and evaluation of companies and industries.

INDEX PROVIDERS

Calvert Responsible Indexes	"The Calvert Indexes are proprietary indices developed by an early proponent of ESG investing. The indices include companies with strong sustainability profiles that, collectively, may have the potential to meet or exceed the performance of the common broad-market benchmarks."
Institutional Shareholder Services (ISS)	ISS ESG collaborates with index providers globally to develop innovative index solutions based on high quality, reliable, and relevant ESG data. Based on ISS ESG Ratings.
FTSE Russell Sustainable Indices	Designed to meet the diverse environmental, social, and governance (ESG) needs of investors, FTSE Russell offers data and expertise to integrate ESG and investment considerations into a single sustainable investment index solution. With nearly two decades of sustainable investment experience, FTSE Russell provides clients with sustainable investment data models, ratings, analytics, and indexes covering thousands of companies across developed and emerging markets globally.
GRESB - Global Real Estate Sustainability Index	The leading Environmental, Social and Governance (ESG) benchmark for real estate and infrastructure investments across the world. GRESB assesses and benchmarks the Environmental, Social and Governance (ESG) performance of real assets, providing standardized and validated data to the capital markets. ESG data covers USD 4.5 trillion in real estate and infrastructure value and is used by more than 100 institutional and financial investors to make decisions that are leading to a more sustainable real asset industry.

MSCI ESG Indexes	MSCI Inc. is the world's largest provider of Environmental, Social and Governance (ESG) Indexes with over 1,500 equity and fixed income ESG Indexes designed to help institutional investors more effectively benchmark ESG investment performance and manage, measure and report on ESG mandates. MSCI ESG Indexes are designed to represent the performance of the most common ESG investment approaches by including, re-weighting or excluding companies by leveraging ESG criteria.
Morningstar Sustainable Index Series	Leveraging a rich data set of company level ratings, Morningstar offers a range of sustainability benchmarks and indexes focused on specific environmental, social, and governance criteria. The indexes look forward to a changing global economy. Incorporates Sustainalytics Sustainability Scores.
NASDAQ	Nasdaq provides a complete family of environmental indexes, tracking the growing clean-energy sector, also known as the "Green" Indexes. The Indexes are comprised of companies working to enhance economic development based on reduction of carbon usage.
Refinitiv/S-Network ESG Best Practices Indices	The Refinitiv/S-Network ESG Best Practices Indices are a suite of indices designed to provide a benchmark of companies exhibiting best corporate social responsibility practices as measured by their superior ratings in the Refinitiv/S-Network ESG Best Practices Ratings schema. The ratings rank the constituent companies on Environmental, Social and Governance performance and are powered by "dynamic" ratings derived from the Refinitiv ESG database. The indices represent a comprehensive benchmarking system for CSR investors. A universe of over 5,000 companies worldwide are rated in 156 key indicators of ESG performance.
Standard & Poor's ESG Indices	A pioneer of ESG indexing, S&P Dow Jones Indices remains a leader today, combining rigorous company analysis, robust methodologies, and cutting-edge modeling to deliver state-of-the-art indices for a wide range of ESG benchmarking and investment applications. Our solutions range from core ESG and low-carbon climate approaches to thematic and fixed income strategies.
STOXX ESG-X Indices	STOXX provides ESG-screened versions of more than 40 benchmarks that meet the standard responsible-investing criteria of leading asset owners. The suite offers ESG-X versions of global, regional and emerging markets benchmarks, including ESG-X versions of the EURO STOXX 50® and the STOXX® Europe 600. The ESG-X indices incorporate standard norm- and product-based exclusions that aim to limit market and reputational risks while keeping a low tracking error and a similar risk-return profile to the respective benchmark.
TIAA ESG Indices	The TIAA ESG Indexes are designed to reflect the performance of TIAA's strategy that seeks to increase exposure to positive environmental, social and governance (ESG) factors, as well as exhibit lower carbon exposure, relative to their corresponding MSCI Parent Indexes. Construction of the Indexes is also aimed at minimizing the tracking error of the strategy relative to the corresponding Parent Indexes. TIAA is considered a pioneer of ESG investing.
Vigeo Eiris ESG Indices	Vigeo Eiris manages two types of ESG indices, published on financial platforms such as Bloomberg and Datastream: Euronext Vigeo Iris Indices and Ethibel Sustainability Indies (ESI)

ESG RATINGS / RANKINGS / SCORES

Bloomberg ESG Performance Scores	Proprietary ESG score based on public data and Bloomberg analytics; available to Bloomberg terminal subscribers only.
CDP Climate, Water & Forest Scores	CDP's annual A List names the world's most pioneering companies leading on environmental transparency and performance. Our scoring measures the comprehensiveness of disclosure, awareness and management of environmental risks and best practices associated with environmental leadership, such as setting ambitious and meaningful targets.
CSR Hub	CSRHub offers consensus Environment, Social & Governance (ESG) Ratings to benchmark performance, study supply chains, improve reporting, and build portfolios. Transparent ratings and rankings of 19,495 companies from 144 countries, driven by 691 industry-leading CSR/ESG data sources, including ESG analyst, crowd, government, publication, & and not-for-profit data.
EcoVadis CSR Rating	The first and largest collaborative platform in the world for trading partners to share sustainability performance information across four themes: environment, labor and human rights, ethics, and sustainable procurement. Assesses a company's policies, actions and results, as well as inputs from third party professionals and external stakeholders.
FTSE Russell ESG Ratings	FTSE Russell provides investors with the models and data tools necessary to understand a company's operational and product related ESG risks and opportunities. FTSE Russell maintains two core data models: the ESG Ratings and data model assesses operational ESG risks and performance, while the Green Revenues data model classifies and measures revenue exposure to products that deliver environmental solutions. By splitting our data model into these two dimensions users can determine more specifically whether to target ESG issues related to (operational) risk or (product) opportunities.
HIP (Human Impact + Profit) Impact Ratings	Investors, Advisors, and Money Managers are using HIP Investor's unique methodology to rate and rank all types of investments for future risk, return potential and net impact on society. HIP's quantitative analysis systematically identifies environmental, social and governance (ESG) sustainability outcomes at the investment security level. HIP Ratings are a useful tool for investors to fund positive impact solutions – while pursuing optimal risk-adjusted returns.
ISS - Oekom	ISS' ESG ratings on companies, countries and green bonds provide investors with the in-depth insight to effectively incorporate sustainability in their investment decision. Our research is instrumental in helping investors minimize ESG risks, comply with evolving regulatory and stakeholder requirements and seize opportunities. The "ISS Governance QualityScore" for listed equities appears on Yahoo Finance Company "Profile" when available.
MSCI ESG Ratings	MSCI ESG Ratings aim to measure a company's resilience to long-term, financially relevant ESG risks. We leverage artificial intelligence (AI) and alternative data to deliver dynamic investment-relevant insights to power your investment decisions.

Morningstar Sustainability Ratings	The Morningstar Sustainability Rating is a measure of the financially material environmental, social, and governance, or ESG, risks in a portfolio relative to a portfolio's peer group. The rating is an historical holdings-based calculation using the company-level ESG Risk Rating from Sustainalytics, a leading provider of ESG research. It is calculated for managed products and indexes globally using Morningstar's portfolio holdings database.
RepRisk	RepRisk is a global data science company producing quantitative solutions that measure material ESG risks. The RepRisk Index (RRI) measures reputational risk exposure to ESG issues and the resulting RepRisk Rating (RRR) facilitates benchmarking and ESG integration.
S&P Global / RobecoSAM CSA	The Corporate Sustainability Assessment (CSA) is an annual evaluation of companies' sustainability practices. Each year we assess over 7,300 companies around the world. The CSA focuses on criteria that are both industry-specific and financially material, and has been doing so since 1999. The CSA helps companies to understand which sustainability factors are important from an investor's perspective, and which in turn, are most likely to have an impact on the company's financial performance. Thus, the CSA serves as a sustainability roadmap helping participating companies to prioritize corporate sustainability initiatives that are most likely to enhance the company's competitiveness. Recognized globally as the longest running ESG data series.
S&P DJI ESG Scores	S&P Dow Jones Indices has introduced a new set of environmental, social, and governance (ESG) scores, giving investment professionals, analysts, and corporations insight into companies' ESG performance. The scores leverage industry-acclaimed assessment data from renowned ESG data specialist, SAM, part of S&P Global.
Sustainalytics	Global leader in ESG and Corporate Governance research and ratings. Provides proprietary ESG Risk Ratings (scores) for companies worldwide. Scores are used by FTSE Russell, STOXX, and Morningstar to develop and maintain their own suite of ESG indexes. Also used by Morningstar to drive their own ESG Scores ("Globe" rankings). ESG Scores also appear in Yahoo Finance Company "Sustainability" section.
TruCost	Trucost, part of S&P Global, assesses risks relating to climate change, natural resource constraints, and broader environmental, social, and governance factors.
Vigeo Eiris	Vigeo Eiris, a Moody's Affiliate, is a global provider of environmental, social and governance solutions serving the investor and issuer communities.

RESEARCH & PUBLICATIONS

The diverse set of organizations below have dedicated resources to studying ESG issues and providing analysis, commentary, thought leadership and products and services for asset owners and investors.

INDEPENDENT RESEARCH

CFA Institute	Premier global organization for investment managers and financial analysts; offers Chartered Financial Analyst (CFA) designation and others, as well as education and research. Home page for all ESG resources.

Global Sustainable Investment Alliance (GSIA)	The Global Sustainable Investment Review is a biennial report that is the only report collating results from the market studies of regional sustainable investment forums from Europe, the United States, Japan, Canada, and Australia and New Zealand. It provides a snapshot of sustainable investing in these markets by drawing on the in-depth regional and national reports from GSIA members—Eurosif, Japan Sustainable Investment Forum (JSIF), Responsible Investment Association Australasia, RIA Canada and US SIF. This report also includes data on the African sustainable investing market, from the African Investing for Impact Barometer, and on Latin America from the Principles for Responsible Investment.
United Nations Principles for Responsible Investing (UNPRI)	"A Blueprint for Responsible Investing" is the 10 Year Vison and Mission Statement for the UNPRI and all its signatories, and is considered to be the leading reference for guiding and growing the responsible investing movement worldwide.
US SIF (The Forum for Responsible & Sustainable Investing)	The "Report on US Sustainable and Impact Investing Trends" is the flagship publication of US SIF (published biennially), and is the longest running and most widely referenced US report on sustainable investing trends. It provides extensive data on the numbers of institutional asset owners, money management firms and investment vehicles using sustainable investment strategies. It also distills the range of significant environmental, social and governance (ESG) issues that investors consider. It is the only report providing a detailed breakdown of the professional assets under management—across all asset classes—that are engaged in sustainable investing strategies. The report provides valuable market research by identifying and documenting the ESG themes and developments of growing interest to investors. It is widely distributed to policymakers, media, academia and nonprofits.

COMMERCIAL RESEARCH & PRODUCTS

Arabesque	A global group of financial technology companies offering sustainable investment, advisory, and data services through our advanced ESG and AI capabilities. Established in 2013, our story is one of partnership between leaders in finance, mathematics, AI, and sustainability working together to deliver a new approach to capital markets. We believe economic value creation can and should be combined with environmental stewardship, social inclusion and sound governance. Through our companies, we leverage cutting-edge technology, research and data to deliver sustainable, transparent financial solutions for a changing world.
Bloomberg	Annual Impact Survey + other resources
Center for Social & Sustainable Products (CSSP)	CSSP is a European based independent consulting and research house with a focus on ESG (Environmental, Social and Governance) and Carbon risk and its impact on investments. We help our clients to assess and better understand the ESG and climate related risks and opportunities in their investments providing comprehensive reporting and advisory services to our clients. Offers yourSRI.com products and services also .
Forum Ethibel	Our objective is to facilitate and accelerate the transition to a sustainable society. To achieve this, we want to create an impact by actively promoting Corporate Social Responsibility (CSR) and Socially Responsible Investing (SRI). We seek to achieve this by developing specific services and products, such as quality labels, audits, and certification of financial and non-financial products.

Global Sustain	Global Sustain offers innovative online and off-line services related to sustainability, corporate responsibility, responsible investing, green economy, business ethics and excellence, transparency, human rights and accountability. Its members include corporations, non-governmental and non-profit organizations, municipalities and local authorities, academic institutions, media, professional bodies, service providers, chambers, think tanks and other public or private entities.
ISS - Oekom	Provides corporate and country ESG research and ratings that enable its clients to identify material social and environmental risks and opportunities, including through advisory services. The "ISS Governance QualityScore" for listed equities appears on Yahoo Finance Company "Profile" when available.
MSCI	Global leader in sustainability research & index construction
Morningstar	Global leader in sustainability research & index construction
Robeco SAM	Founded in 1995, RobecoSAM is an investment specialist focused exclusively on Sustainable Investing. Serving institutional asset owners and financial intermediaries, the company's research and investment strategies are designed to make a measurable environmental or societal impact and actively contribute towards meeting the UN Sustainable Development Goals (SDGs). 25 years of sustainability research insights powers RobecoSAM's investment process and impact measurement capability. Furthermore, RobecoSAM was first to treat ESG as a standalone factor using its Smart ESG methodology.
S&P Global	Global leader offering ESG data, analytics, and research through Ratings, Market Intelligence, S&P Dow Jones Indices, Platts and Robeco SAM divisions.
S&P Dow Jones	ESG considerations—from the impact of climate change and carbon emissions to equality and human rights—are creating unpriced risks in financial markets. A global transition is now underway to finance a more resilient, sustainable global economy, which may bring with it significant growth opportunities. A growing body of evidence also indicates that a company's dedication to ESG could be an important driver of risk management and returns. More and more investors around the world are taking an interest in the opportunities and risks, and integrating ESG into their strategies.
Thomson Reuters	ESG Peer View proprietary data on EIKON workstation
True Value Labs	Truvalue Labs™ amplifies the research capabilities of investment firms by leveraging artificial intelligence to analyze and interpret massive amounts of unstructured data at a speed and scale never before possible. Our team is composed of industry thought leaders, data scientists, content experts, academics, financial services experts and technology specialists committed to building innovative ESG-focused products for the investment community.
Vigeo Eiris	Vigeo Eiris, a Moody's Affiliate, is a global provider of environmental, social and governance solutions serving the investor and issuer communities.

ACADEMIC RESEARCH

Center for Responsible Business	Part of the Institute for Business & Social Impact at the Haas School of Business, University of California, Berkeley. Our mission is to develop leaders to redefine business for a sustainable future.

The Earth Institute, Columbia University	The Earth Institute was founded in 1995 and is made up of scholars spread out across dozens of research centers and programs at Columbia University. The purpose is to advance the basic understanding of earth science and to apply that knowledge to decisions made by governments and businesses around the world.
The European Centre for Corporate Engagement (ECCE)	ECCE at Maastricht University's School of Business and Economics is the world's leading research institute on sustainable finance and responsible investing. We offer high-quality research on the impact of environmental, social, and governance (ESG) standards on the pricing of assets in financial markets. Moreover, we study the different ways investors can engage with the companies they invest in. ECCE can be regarded as a "lab for responsible investment" utilizing a multidisciplinary research network. ECCE helps practitioners and scholars understand how businesses and financial markets can promote sustainable development by considering (ESG) issues.
MIT Sloan School / Sustainability Initiative	The mission of the MIT Sloan Sustainability Initiative is to deliver the best education, apply academic rigor to real world problems, and empower leaders everywhere to take action, professionally and personally, so that humans and nature can thrive for generations to come. Includes SHIFT, an online platform that allows you to navigate the sea of sustainability tools and quickly carve out the path to implementation that's right for your organization.
SSRN	SSRN is devoted to the rapid worldwide dissemination of research and is composed of a number of specialized research networks. SSRN´s eLibrary provides 950,067 research papers from 502,177 researchers in more than 50 disciplines.
Sustainable Investment Research Initiative Library	The Sustainable Investment Research Initiative (SIRI) Library is a searchable database of academic studies to learn about the impact of sustainability factors on risk and return.
Wharton School of Business	The Business, Climate, and Environment Lab supports cutting-edge research, provides thought leadership, and brings together stakeholders from academia, government, communities, and the private sector to design smart public and private sector policies related to topics such as climate change, renewable energy, air and water pollution, waste disposal, biodiversity, and deforestation.

OTHER

Environmental Finance	Environmental-Finance.com is an online news and analysis service established in 1999 to report on sustainable investment, green finance and the people and companies active in environmental markets.
Environmental Leader	Publication informing execs about energy, environment, and sustainability news.
Responsible Investor	Comprehensive news source on SRI investing; free and timely reports and latest research
Green Money	Publishes monthly eJournal and website with relevant news featuring top writers from the world of sustainable business, impact investing, renewable energy, organic agriculture, and ethically-made products.
Social Funds	SocialFunds.com is the largest personal finance site devoted to socially responsible investing. It features over 10,000 pages of information on SRI mutual funds, community investments, corporate research, shareowner actions, and daily social investment news.

APPENDIX E
Fund Manager Interview Guide

THE BEST WAY to learn the quality and strength of a fund manager's strategy, as well as their commitment to engagement and sustainability in general, is to interview them. Here are questions you should ask:

ESG Quality

- What data sources does the strategy rely on?
- Do you perform any proprietary data collection or research?
- How do you use ESG ratings from ESG researchers?
- How is ESG materiality evaluated for this strategy?
- Do you factor transition and physical climate-related risks into the investment analysis process?

ESG Tilt

- To what degree do you invest based on ESG criteria?
  1. ESG Consideration: ESG factors considered after fundamental criteria applied.
  2. ESG Integration: ESG factors considered alongside other criteria.
  3. ESG Focused: ESG as the determinant of selection using both positive and negative screens.
- What are the most important ESG themes in your portfolio?
- What is your expected tracking error?
- Do you produce ESG or impact reports regularly for this strategy?

Engagement

- What is your engagement strategy?
    1. Proxy Voting: Do you have a separate proxy voting policy for ESG strategies?
    2. Direct Dialogue: Do you engage in direct dialogue with portfolio companies?
    3. Shareholder Resolutions: Do you file or co-file resolutions?
    4. Coalitions and Collaborations: Do you collaborate with other investors on engagement?
- How do you identify the issues for your engagement campaigns?

Commitment

- What industry bodies or affiliations are you a member of?
- How does your firm help build capacity for sustainable investing in financial services?
- What ESG initiatives does your firm practice internally? Please elaborate.
- Do you regularly produce ESG or sustainability reports for your firm?

GLOSSARY

Active management: The attempt to uncover securities the market has either undervalued or overvalued and/or the attempt to time investment decisions, i.e., invest more heavily when the market is rising and less so when the market is falling.

Alpha: A measure of risk-adjusted performance relative to a benchmark. Positive alpha represents outperformance; negative alpha represents underperformance. Positive or negative alpha may be caused by luck, manager skill, costs, and/or wrong choice of benchmark.

Anchoring: A form of cognitive bias in which people place inordinate importance on certain values or attributes, which then act as a reference point, and inappropriately weight the influence of subsequent data to support their initial assessment. For example, some investors will tend to hang on to a losing investment because they are waiting for it to at least break even, anchoring their investment's present value to the value it once had.

Anomaly: Security returns that are not explained by risk considerations per the efficient market hypothesis (EMH).

Arbitrage: The process by which investors attempt to exploit the price difference between two securities that are exactly alike (or very similar) by simultaneously buying one at a lower price and selling the other at a higher price (thereby avoiding or minimizing risk). The trading activity of arbitrageurs eventually eliminates these price differences.

Asset allocation: The process of determining what percentage of assets should be dedicated to specific asset classes; also, the end result of this process.

Asset class: A group of assets with similar risk and expected return characteristics. Cash, debt instruments, real estate, and equities are examples of asset classes. Within a major asset class, such as equities, there are more specific classes, such as large- and small-cap company stocks and domestic and international stocks.

Barra Long-Term Global Equity Model: Global multifactor equity model that provides a foundation for investment decision support tools via a broad range of analytics for developed, emerging market, and frontier market portfolios. It includes 34 industry factors and 11 style factors.

Basis point: One one-hundredth of 1 percent, or 0.0001.

Benchmark: An appropriate standard against which mutual funds and other investment vehicles can be judged. Domestic large-cap growth funds should be judged against a domestic large-cap growth index, such as the S&P 500 Growth Index, while small-cap managers should be judged against a small-cap index, such as the Russell 2000 Index.

Beta: The exposure of a stock, mutual fund, or portfolio to a factor.

Book-to-market value (BtM): The ratio of the book value per share to the market price per share, or book value divided by market capitalization.

Book value: An accounting concept that reflects the value of a company based on accounting principles. It is often expressed in per-share terms. Book value per share is equal to book equity divided by the number of shares.

Brown assets/firms: Securities/companies with poor environmental, social, and governance ratings.

Capital asset pricing model (CAPM): The first formal asset pricing model. It uses a single factor (market beta) that describes the relationship between risk and expected return, and is used in the pricing of risky securities.

Commodity: A physical good (such as corn, oil, or gold) that is supplied without significant qualitative differentiation.

Confirmation bias: The tendency to search for, interpret, favor, and recall information in a way that confirms one's preexisting beliefs or hypotheses while giving disproportionately less consideration to alternative possibilities.

Default: Failure to pay principal or interest in a timely manner.

Diversification: Dividing investment funds among a variety of investments with different risk–return characteristics to minimize portfolio risk.

Duration: The expected percentage change in the price of a bond given a percentage change in the yield on that bond. A higher duration number indicates a greater sensitivity of that bond's price to changes in interest rates.

Efficient market hypothesis (EMH): A theory that, at any given time and in a liquid market, security prices fully reflect all available information. The EMH contends that because markets are efficient and current prices reflect all information, attempts to outperform the market are essentially a game of chance rather than one of skill.

Emerging markets: The capital markets of less-developed countries that are beginning to acquire characteristics of developed countries, such as higher per-capita income. Countries typically included in this category are Brazil, Mexico, Romania, Turkey, and Thailand.

Environmental, social, and governance investing (ESG): An ESG investor explicitly considers the environmental, social, and governance risks and opportunities that companies face when building a portfolio. ESG investors want to consider how a company manages its environmental footprint and its impact on stakeholders. This process usually requires collecting information and data beyond what companies provide in standard financial disclosures. The goal of an ESG investor is to incorporate into their portfolio additional information about company sustainability performance.

Equilibrium: A condition or state in which economic forces are balanced. In effect, economic variables remain unchanged from their equilibrium values in the absence of external influences.

Event risk: The risk that something unexpected will occur (war, political crisis, flood, or hurricane), negatively impacting the value of a security.

Exchange traded funds (ETFs): For practical purposes, these funds act like open-ended, no-load mutual funds. Like mutual funds, they can be created to represent virtually any index or asset class, but they are not mutual funds. Instead, these new investment vehicles represent a cross between an exchange-listed stock and an open-ended, no-load mutual fund. Like stocks (but unlike mutual funds), they trade on a stock exchange throughout the day.

Ex-ante: Before the fact.

Expense ratio: The operating expenses of a mutual fund expressed as a percentage of total assets. These expenses are subtracted from the investment performance of a fund to determine the net return to shareholders. They cover manager fees, administrative costs, and in some cases, marketing costs.

Ex-post: After the fact.

Externalities: The production or consumption of a good or service resulting in a cost or benefit to an unrelated third party.

Factor: A numerical characteristic or set of characteristics common across a broad set of securities.

Four-factor model: Differences in performance between diversified equity portfolios are best explained by the amount of exposure to four factors: the risk of the overall stock market, company size (market capitalization), price (book-to-market, or BtM, ratio), and momentum. Research has shown that, on average, the four factors explain approximately 95 percent of the variation in performance of diversified U.S. stock portfolios.

Global Industry Classification Standard (GICS): A method for assigning companies to a specific economic sector and industry group that best defines its business operations. It was developed jointly by Morgan Stanley Capital International (MSCI) and Standard & Poor's and is used by the MSCI indexes.

Green assets/firms: Securities/companies with good environmental, social, and governance ratings.

Green bond: A fixed-income instrument that is specifically earmarked to raise money for climate and environmental projects. These bonds are typically asset-linked and backed by the issuer's balance sheet, so they usually carry the same credit rating as their issuers' other debt obligations.

Greenium: The idea that bond issuers are able to obtain a cheaper cost of funding by issuing debt with a specified use of proceeds that have positive environmental and/or social impacts compared to traditional bonds.

Greenwashing: The process of conveying a false impression or providing misleading information about how a company's products are more environmentally sound.

Growth stocks: The stocks of companies that have relatively high price-to-earnings (P/E) ratios or relatively low book-to-market (BtM) ratios—the opposite of value stocks. The market anticipates rapid earnings growth relative to the overall market.

Hedge fund: A fund that generally has the ability to invest in a wide variety of asset classes. These funds often use leverage in an attempt to increase returns.

Index fund: A passively managed fund that seeks to replicate the performance of a particular index, such as the Wilshire 5000, the S&P 500, or the Russell 2000. The fund may replicate the index by buying and holding all the securities in that index in direct proportion to their weight (by market capitalization) within that index. The fund could sample the index—a common strategy for small-cap and total market index funds—and/or use index futures and other derivative instruments.

Initial public offering (IPO): The first offering of a company's stock to the public.

Kurtosis: The degree to which exceptional values, much larger or smaller than the average, occur more frequently (high kurtosis) or less frequently (low kurtosis) than in a normal (bell-shaped) distribution. High kurtosis results in exceptional values called *fat tails*. Low kurtosis results in *thin tails*.

Large-cap: Large-cap stocks are those of companies considered large relative to other companies, as measured by their market capitalization. Precisely what is considered a large company varies by source. For example, one investment professional may define it as having a market capitalization in excess of $2 billion, while another may use $5 billion.

Leverage: The use of debt to increase the amount of assets that can be acquired (for example, to buy stock). Leverage increases the riskiness as well as the expected return of a portfolio.

Liquidity: A measure of the ease of trading a security in a market.

Long side: The securities owned versus sold short (the short side), in a long-short portfolio.

Management fees: Total amount charged to an account for the management of a portfolio.

Market beta: The sensitivity of the return of a stock, mutual fund, or portfolio relative to the return of the overall equity market. Because this was the original form of beta, some refer to market beta as just *beta*.

Market cap/market capitalization: For an individual stock, this is the total number of shares of common stock outstanding multiplied by the current price per share. For example, if a company has 100 million shares outstanding and its current stock price is $30 per share, the market cap of the company is $3 billion.

Maturity: The date on which the issuer of a bond promises to repay the principal.

Monotonic: Changing in such a way that it either never increases or never decreases.

Monte Carlo simulation: A tool used to model the probability of different outcomes in a process that cannot easily be predicted due to the intervention of random variables. It is a technique used to understand the impact of risk and uncertainty in prediction and forecasting models.

Mutual fund: An investment vehicle consisting of a portfolio of stocks, bonds, or other securities.

Nasdaq: The National Association of Securities Dealers Automatic Quotation System, which is a computerized marketplace in which securities are traded, frequently called the *over-the-counter market*.

Negative correlation of returns: When one asset experiences above-average returns, the other tends to experience below-average returns and vice versa.

NYSE: The New York Stock Exchange, which traces its origins to 1792, is the world's leading equities market. A broad spectrum of market participants—including listed companies, individual investors, institutional investors, and member firms—participate in the NYSE market.

Passive asset class funds: Mutual funds that buy and hold common stocks within a particular domestic or international asset class. The amount of each security purchased is typically in proportion to its capitalization relative to the total capitalization of all securities within the asset class. Each stock is held until it no longer fits the definition and guidelines established for remaining in that asset class. Passive asset class funds provide the building blocks needed to implement a passive management strategy.

P/E ratio: The ratio of stock price to earnings per share. Stocks with high P/E ratios are considered growth stocks; stocks with low P/E ratios are considered value stocks.

Principles for responsible investment (PRI): Originally conceived by the UN, the PRI is now an independent body that promotes responsible investment and sustainable markets. Members sign on to six principles that define responsible investment as a strategy and practice to incorporate ESG factors in investment decisions and active ownership.

Principle 1: We will incorporate ESG issues into investment analysis and decision-making processes.

Principle 2: We will be active owners and incorporate ESG issues into our ownership policies and practices.

Principle 3: We will seek appropriate disclosure on ESG issues by the entities in which we invest.

Principle 4: We will promote acceptance and implementation of the Principles within the investment industry.

Principle 5: We will work together to enhance our effectiveness in implementing the Principles.

Principle 6: We will each report on our activities and progress towards implementing the Principles.

Prudent investor rule: A doctrine imbedded within the U.S. legal code stating that a person responsible for the management of someone else's assets must manage those assets in a manner appropriate to the beneficiary's financial circumstances and tolerance for risk.

Rebalancing: The process of restoring a portfolio toward its original asset allocation. Rebalancing can be accomplished either through adding newly investable funds or by selling portions of the best performing asset classes and using the proceeds to purchase additional amounts of the underperforming asset classes.

Real estate investment trust (REIT): A company that owns or finances real estate. As represented by REITs, real estate is a separate asset class. REITs have their own risk and reward characteristics as well as relatively low correlation with other equity and fixed income asset classes. Investors can purchase shares of a REIT in the same way they would purchase other equities, or they can invest in a REIT mutual fund that is either actively or passively managed.

Risk premium: The higher expected (not guaranteed) return for accepting a specific type of non-diversifiable risk.

Salience theory: The hypothesis that decision makers exaggerate the probability of extreme events if they are aware of their possibility, giving rise to subjective probability distributions and undermining rationality.

Securities and Exchange Commission (SEC): A government agency created by Congress to regulate the securities markets and protect investors. The SEC has jurisdiction over the operation of broker-dealers, investment advisors, mutual funds, and companies selling stocks and bonds to the investing public.

Sharpe ratio: A measure of the return earned above the rate of return on a riskless asset, usually one-month U.S. Treasury bills, relative to the amount of risk taken, with risk being measured by the standard deviation of returns. For example, the average return earned on an asset was 10 percent. The average rate of a one-month U.S. Treasury bill was 4 percent. The standard deviation was 20 percent. The Sharpe ratio would be equal to 10 percent minus 4 percent (6 percent) divided by 20 percent, or 0.3.

Short selling: Borrowing a security for the purpose of immediately selling it. This is done with the expectation that the investor will be able to buy the security back at a later date (and lower price), returning it to the lender and keeping any profit.

Short side: The securities sold short versus bought (the long side), in a long-short portfolio.

Skewness: A measure of the asymmetry of a distribution. Negative skewness occurs when the values to the left of (less than) the mean are fewer but farther from it than values to the right of (more than) the mean. For example, the return series of -30 percent, 5 percent, 10 percent, and 15 percent has a mean of 0 percent. There is only one return less than 0 percent, and three higher;

but the negative one is much farther from zero than the positive ones. Positive skewness occurs when the values to the right of (more than) the mean are fewer but farther from it than values to the left of (less than) the mean.

Small-cap: Small-cap stocks are those of companies considered small relative to other companies as measured by their market capitalization. Precisely what is considered a small company varies by source. For example, one investment professional may define it as having a market capitalization of less than $2 billion, while another may use $5 billion. We are interested in a stock's capitalization because academic evidence indicates that investors can expect to be rewarded by investing in smaller companies' stocks. They are considered to be riskier investments than larger companies' stocks, so investors demand a risk premium to invest in them.

Socially responsible investing (SRI): Investment strategies that incorporate the investors' individual values and ethics into the portfolio construction process. SRI investors often avoid investing in companies that make or sell controversial products like alcohol, tobacco, gambling, adult entertainment, and guns. They might also emphasize investing in companies that share their particular values, such as social justice and gender equality, or that conform to their religious beliefs. The goal of an SRI investor is to have their portfolio match their individual values.

Spread: The difference between the price a dealer is willing to pay for a bond (the bid) and the price a dealer is willing to sell the bond (the offer).

S&P 500 Index: A market-cap weighted index of 500 of the largest U.S. stocks, designed to cover a broad and representative sampling of industries.

Sin stocks: A company involved in or associated with an activity that is considered unethical or immoral. Sin stock sectors usually include alcohol, tobacco, gambling, sex-related industries, and weapons manufacturers.

Standard deviation: A measure of volatility or risk. The greater the standard deviation, the greater the volatility of a security or portfolio. Standard deviation can be measured for varying time periods, such as monthly, quarterly, or annually.

Stranded assets: Physical assets recorded on a corporate balance sheet whose investment value cannot be recouped and must be written off due to the transition to a low-carbon economy.

Sustainable development goals (SDGs): A collection of 17 interlinked global goals designed to be a blueprint to achieve a better and more sustainable future for all. The SDGs were set up in 2015 by the United Nations General Assembly and are intended to be achieved by the year 2030.

Sustainable Investing: An inclusive term used to describe any investment approach that considers impacts on people and the planet. It takes many forms, including environmental, social, and governance (ESG) investing, socially responsible investing (SRI), and impact investing.

Systematic risk: Risk that cannot be diversified away. The market must reward investors for assuming systematic risk or they would not take it. That reward is in the form of a risk premium, a higher expected return than could be earned by investing in a less-risky instrument.

Tail risk: The chance of a loss occurring due to a rare event as predicted by a probability distribution. In general, a short-term move of more than three standard deviations is considered a tail risk event. While tail risk technically refers to both the left and right tails, investors are most concerned with losses (the left tail).

Three-factor model: Differences in performance between diversified equity portfolios which are best explained by three factors: the amount of exposure to the risk of the overall stock market, company size (market capitalization), and price (book-to-market, or BtM, ratio) characteristics. Research has shown that, on average, the three factors explain more than 90 percent of the variation in performance of diversified U.S. stock portfolios.

Tracking error: The amount by which the performance of a fund differs from the appropriate index or benchmark. More generally, when referring to a whole portfolio, it is the amount by which the performance of the portfolio differs from a widely accepted benchmark, such as the S&P 500 Index or the Wilshire 5000 Index.

T-stat: Short for t-statistic, it is a measure of statistical significance. A value greater than about 2.0 is generally considered meaningfully different from random noise, with a higher number indicating even greater confidence.

Turnover: The trading activity of a fund as it sells securities and replaces them with new ones.

Utility/disutility: The aggregate amount of satisfaction/dissatisfaction a consumer receives through the consumption of a specific good or service. Total utility is often compared to marginal utility, which is the satisfaction a consumer receives from consuming one additional unit of a good or service.

Value stocks: The stocks of companies with relatively low price-to-earnings (P/E) ratios or relatively high book-to-market (BtM) ratios—the opposite of growth stocks. The market anticipates slower earnings growth relative to the overall market. They are considered to be riskier investments than growth companies' stocks, so investors demand a risk premium to invest in them.

Volatility: The standard deviation of the change in value of a financial instrument within a specific time horizon. It is often used to quantify the risk of the instrument over that period. Volatility is typically expressed in annualized terms.

Weight: Percentage value of a security or asset class held in a portfolio relative to the value of the total portfolio.

NOTES

Introduction

1. UN Development Programme. 2021. People's Climate Vote. https://www.undp.org/publications/peoples-climate-vote.
2. Donella H. Meadows, Jorgen Randers, and Dennis L. Meadows, *Limits to Growth: The 30-Year Update*, Chelsea Green Publishing; 3rd edition, June 2004.
3. Paul Hawken, Amory Lovins, and L. Hunter Lovins, *Natural Capitalism: Creating the Next Industrial Revolution*, US Green Building Council; October 2000.
4. Paul Hawkin, *The Ecology of Commerce*, Harper Business, March 2010.

Chapter 1

1. Global Sustainable Investment Review 2020, Global Sustainable Investment Alliance. https://www.unpri.org/pri/a-blueprint-for-responsible-investment.
2. Report on US Sustainable and Impact Investing Trends 2020, US SIF.
3. "Who Cares Wins," UNEP FI, 2005.
4. Global Sustainable Investment Review 2020, Global Sustainable Investment Alliance.
5. "Companies worth $15 trillion revealed on CDP 2020 'A List' of environmental leaders," CDP, December 8, 2020, https://www.cdp.net/en/articles/media/companies-worth-15-trillion-revealed-on-cdp-2020-a-list-of-environmental-leaders.
6. Lawrence D. Brown and Marcus L. Caylor, "Corporate Governance and Firm Valuation," *Journal of Accounting and Public Policy*, Vol. 25, No. 4, 2006.
7. Sustainable Funds US Landscape Report 2020, Morningstar.

Chapter 3

1. Global Sustainable Investment Review 2020, Global Sustainable Investment Alliance.
2. The One Planet Sovereign Wealth Fund Framework, July 2018.
3. Government Pension Investment Fund ESG Report 2019.
4. J.G. Simon, C.W. Powers, and J.P. Gunnerman, *The Ethical Investor: Universities and Corporate Responsibility*, Yale University Press, 1972.
5. Yale Chief Investment Officer Letter to Managers, August 27, 2014.
6. Pope Francis, "'Laudato Si': On Care for Our Common Home," 2015.
7. https://www.gatesfoundation.org/our-work/programs/global-health/malaria.
8. UBS Sustainability Report 2020.
9. Sustainable Funds U.S. Landscape Report 2020, Morningstar Manager Research.
10. Fink Letter 2020. https://www.blackrock.com/corporate/investor-relations/larry-fink-chairmans-letter
11. Fink Letter 2021. https://www.blackrock.com/corporate/investor-relations/larry-fink-chairmans-letter
12. 2019 ESG Proxy Voting Trends by 50 U.S. Fund Families, Harvard Law School Forum on Corporate Governance. http://Corpgov.law.harvard.edu/2020/03/23/2019.
13. Report on US Sustainable and Impact Investing Trends 2020, US SIF.

Chapter 4

1. Morgan Stanley Institute for Sustainable Investing, "Sustainable Signals: New Data from the Individual Investor," 2019.
2. Meir Statman, *Finance for Normal People*, Oxford Press, 2017.
3. Michael Mauboussin, *More Than You Know: Finding Financial Wisdom in Unconventional Places*, Columbia University Press, 2008.
4. Daniel Esty, Feb. 10, 2021, Presentation at Climate One, Commonwealth Club, San Francisco.
5. NYU Stern Center for Sustainable Business, Research on IRI Purchasing Data, March 11, 2019.
6. "Our Common Future," U.N. World Commission on Environment and Development, 1987.

Chapter 5

1. Report on US Sustainable and Impact Investing Trends 2020, US SIF.
2. CDP Media Fact Sheet April 2021. https://www.cdp.net/en/media.
3. "The Materiality of Social, Environmental, and Corporate Governance Issues to Equity Pricing," *UNEP Finance Initiative*, 2004.
4. UNPRI Annual Report 2020. www.unpri.org/annual-report-2020/how-we-work/building-our-effectiveness/enhance-our-global-footprint.
5. Florian Berg, Julian Koelbel, and Roberto Rigobon, "Aggregate Confusion: The Divergence of ESG Ratings," May 2020.
6. Steve Lydenberg, Jean Rogers, and David Wood, "From Transparency to Performance: Industry-Based Sustainability Reporting on Key Issues," 2010.
7. Nasa website. https://climate.nasa.gov/scientific-consensus/.
8. Larry Fink letter to CEOs. www.blackrock.com/corporate/investor-relations/larry-fink-ceo-letter. https://www.cnbc.com/2020/12/16/blackrock-makes-climate-change-central-to-investment-strategy-for-2021.html.

Chapter 6

1. Florian Berg, Julian Koelbel, and Roberto Rigobon, "Aggregate Confusion: The Divergence of ESG Ratings," May 2020.
2. Monica Billio, Michele Costola, Iva Hristova, Carmelo Latino, and Loriana Pelizzon, "Inside the ESG Ratings: (Dis)agreement and Performance," June 2020.
3. Ralf Conen, Stefan Hartmann, and Markus Rudolf, "Going Green Means Being in the Black," July 2020.
4. Elroy Dimson, Paul Marsh, and Mike Staunton, "Divergent ESG Ratings," *The Journal of Portfolio Management*, November 2020.
5. Pension & Investments, "Norway wealth fund misses out on returns due to divestment, Norges says." March 22, 2017.
6. Greg Richey, "Fewer Reasons to Sin: A Five-Factor Investigation of Vice Stocks," July 2017.
7. Harrison Hong and Marcin Kacperczyk, "The Price of Sin: The Effects of Social Norms on Markets," *Journal of Financial Economics*, July 2009.
8. Elroy Dimson, Paul Marsh, and Mike Staunton, "Exclusionary Screening," *The Journal of Impact and ESG Investing*, Fall 2020.
9. Daniel Kaufmann, Aart Kraay, and Massimo Mastruzzi, "The Worldwide Governance Indicators: Methodology and Analytical Issues," Policy Research working paper, World Bank (2010).

10. Rocco Ciciretti, Ambrogio Dalò, and Lammertjan Dam, "The Price of Taste for Socially Responsible Investment," Centre for Economic and International Studies Papers, 2017.

11. Rocco Ciciretti, Ambrogio Dalò, and Lammertjan Dam, "The Contributions of Betas versus Characteristics to the ESG Premium," 2019.

12. Lubos Pastor, Robert Stambaugh, and Lucian Taylor, "Sustainable Investing in Equilibrium," December 2019.

13. Olivier Zerbib, "A Sustainable Capital Asset Pricing Model (S-CAPM): Evidence from Green Investing and Sin Stock Exclusion," 2019.

14. Jason Hsu, Xiaoyang Liu, Keren Shen, Vivek Viswanathan, and Yanxiang Zhao, "Outperformance through Investing in ESG in Need," *The Journal of Index Investing*, Fall 2018.

15. Patrick Bolton and Marcin Kacperczyk, "Do Investors Care about Carbon Risk?" 2020.

16. Maximilian Görgen, Andrea Jacob, Martin Nerlinger, Ryan Riordan, Martin Rohleder, and Marco Wilkens, "Carbon Risk," August 2020.

17. Maximilian Görgen, Andrea Jacob, and Martin Nerlinger, "Get Green or Die Trying? Carbon Risk Integration into Portfolio Management," *The Journal of Portfolio Management*, February 2021.

18. Alexander Cheema-Fox, Bridget Realmuto LaPerla, George Serafeim, David Turkington, and Hui (Stacie) Wang, "Decarbonization Factors," *The Journal of Impact and ESG Investing*, Fall 2021.

19. Bradford Cornell and Aswath Damodaran, "Valuing ESG: Doing Good or Sounding Good?," *The Journal of Impact and ESG Investing*, September 2020.

20. Giovanni Bruno, Mikheil Esakia, and Felix Goltz, "'Honey, I Shrunk the ESG Alpha: Risk-Adjusting ESG Portfolio Returns," April 2021.

21. Wayne Winegarden, "Environmental, Social, and Governance (ESG) Investing: An Evaluation of the Evidence," 2019.

22. Jan-Carl Plagge and Douglas Grim, "Have Investors Paid a Performance Price? Examining the Behavior of ESG Equity Funds," *The Journal of Portfolio Management*, February 2020.

23. Hao Liang, Lin Sun, and Melvyn Teo, "Socially Responsible Hedge Funds," May 2020.

24. Soohun Kim and Aaron Yoon, "Analyzing Active Managers' Commitment to ESG: Evidence from United Nations Principles for Responsible Investment," March 2020.

25. Rajna Gibson, Simon Glossner, Philipp Krueger, Pedro Matos, and Tom Steffen, "Responsible Institutional Investing Around the World," May 2020.

26. Meir Statman and Denys Glushkov, "Classifying and Measuring the Performance of Socially Responsible Mutual Funds," *The Journal of Portfolio Management*, Winter 2016.

27. Alex Edmans, "Does the Stock Market Fully Value Intangibles? Employee Satisfaction and Equity Prices," *Journal of Financial Economics*, September 2011.

28. Jeroen Derwall, Nadja Guenster, Rob Bauer, and Kees Koedijk, "The Eco-Efficiency Premium Puzzle," *Financial Analysts Journal*, 2005, Vol 61, Issue 2.

29. Alexander Kempf and Peer Osthoff, "The Effect of Socially Responsible Investing on Portfolio Performance," *European Financial Management*, November 2007.

30. André Breedt, Stefano Ciliberti, Stanislao Gualdi, and Philip Seager, "Is ESG an Equity Factor or Just an Investment Guide?" *The Journal of Investing, ESG Special Issue 2019*, 28 (2) 32–42.

31. Simon Glossner, "ESG Risks and the Cross-Section of Stock Returns," November 2017.

32. Simon Glossner, "ESG Incidents and Shareholder Value," February 2021.

33. Bei Cui and Paul Docherty, "Stock Price Overreaction to ESG Controversies," April 2020.

34. Fabio Alessandrini and Eric Jondeau, "ESG Investing: From Sin Stocks to Smart Beta," *The Journal of Portfolio Management Ethical Investing 2020*, 46 (3).

35. Michael Halling, Jin Yu, and Josef Zechner, "Primary Corporate Bond Markets and Social Responsibility," August 2020.

36. Jie Cao, Yi Li, Xintong Zhan, Weiming Zhang, and Linyu Zho, "Carbon Emissions, Institutional Trading, and the Liquidity of Corporate Bonds," July 2021.

37. Martin Fridson, Lu Jiang, Zhiyuan Mei, and Daniel Navaei, "ESG Impact on High-Yield Returns," *The Journal of Fixed Income*, Spring 2021.

38. David Larcker and Edward Watts, "Where's the Greenium?" *Journal of Accounting and Finance*, April–May 2020.

39. Wei Dai and Philipp Meyer-Brauns, "Greenhouse Gas Emissions and Expected Returns," October 2020.

40. Brad M. Barber, Adair Morse, and Ayako Yasuda, "Impact Investing," *Journal of Financial Economics*, January 2021.

41. Zacharias Sautner and Laura Starks, "ESG and Downside Risks: Implications for Pension Funds," June 2021.

42. Emirhan Ilhan, Zacharias Sautner, and Grigory Vilkov, "Carbon Tail Risk," *Review of Financial Studies*, March 2021.

43. Tinghua Duan, Frank Li, and Quan Wen, "Is Carbon Risk Priced in the Cross Section of Corporate Bond Returns?" August 2021.

44. Peter Diep, Lukasz Pomorski, and Scott Richardson, "Sustainable Systematic Credit," September 2021.

45. Ravi Bansal, Di Wu, and Amir Yaron, "Is Socially Responsible Investing A Luxury Good?," September 2019.

46. Lasse Heje Pedersen, Shaun Fitzgibbons, and Lukasz Pomorski, "Responsible Investing: The ESG-Efficient Frontier," *Journal of Financial Economics*, November 2020.

Chapter 7

1. Guido Giese, Linda-Eling Lee, Dimitris Melas, Zoltán Nagy, and Laura Nishikawa, "Foundations of ESG Investing: How ESG Affects Equity Valuation, Risk, and Performance," *The Journal of Portfolio Management*, July 2019.

2. Kyle Welch and Aaron Yoon, "Do High Ability Managers Choose ESG Projects that Create Shareholder Value? Evidence from Employee Opinions," April 2021.

3. T. Clifton Green, Ruoyan Huang, Quan Wen, and Dexin Zhou, "Crowdsourced Employer Reviews and Stock Returns," *Journal of Financial Economics*, October 2019.

4. Lubos Pastor, Robert Stambaugh, and Lucian Taylor, "Sustainable Investing in Equilibrium," December 2019.

5. Madelyn Antoncic, Geert Bekaert, Richard Rothenberg, and Miquel Noguer, "Sustainable Investment—Exploring the Linkage Between Alpha, ESG, and SDG's," July 2020.

6. Robert Novy-Marx, "Fundamentally, Momentum is Fundamental Momentum," March 2015.

7. Tiziano De Angelis, Peter Tankov, and David Zerbib, "Environmental Impact Investing," April 2020.

8. Marco Ceccarelli, Stefano Ramelli, and Alexander Wagner, "When Investors Call for Climate Responsibility, How Do Mutual Funds Respond?," April 2019.

9. Itzhak Ben-David, Yeejin Jang, Stefanie Kleimeier, and Michael Viehs, "Exporting Pollution: Where Do Multinational Firms Emit CO_2?," November 2020.

10. Harshini Shanker, "Preferences of Investors and Sustainable Investing," 2019.

11. David Blitz, Laurens Swinkels, and Jan Anton van Zanten, "Does Sustainable Investing Deprive Unsustainable Firms from Fresh Capital?," December 2020.

12. Aneesh Raghunandan and Shivaram Rajgopal, "Do ESG Funds Make Stakeholder-Friendly Investments?," April 2021.

13. Samuel Drempetic, Christian Klein, and Bernhard Zwergel, "The Influence of Firm Size on the ESG Score: Corporate Sustainability Ratings Under Review," *Journal of Business Ethics*, November 2020.
14. Florencio Lopez de Silanes, Joseph A. McCahery, and Paul C. Pudschedl, "ESG Performance and Disclosure: A Cross-Country Analysis," January 2020.
15. www.sec.gov/files/esg-risk-alert.pdf.
16. Davidson Heath, Daniele Macciocchi, Roni Michaely, and Matthew Ringgenberg, "Does Socially Responsible Investing Change Firm Behavior?," May 2021.
17. Alessandro Fenili and Carlo Raimondo, "ESG and the Pricing of IPOs: Does Sustainability Matter?," June 2021.
18. Elroy Dimson, Oğuzhan Karakaş, and Xi Li, "Active Ownership," *The Review of Financial Studies*, August 2015.

Chapter 8

1. Kevin Grogan and Larry E. Swedroe, *Your Complete Guide to a Successful and Secure Retirement*, Harriman House, 2021.

Conclusion

1. Doron Avramov, Abraham Lioui, Yang Liu, and Andrea Tarelli, "Dynamic ESG Equilibrium," October 2021.
2. Ibid.
3. Philippe van der Beck, "Flow-Driven ESG Returns," September 2021.
4. Samuel M. Hartzmark and Abigail Sussman, "Do Investors Value Sustainability? A Natural Experiment Examining Ranking and Fund Flows," *The Journal of Finance*, August 2019.
5. Deutsche Bank, "Big Data Shakes Up ESG Investing," 2018.
6. Yazhou He, Bige Kahraman, and Michelle Lowry, "ES Risks and Shareholder Voice," September 2020.

Appendix A

1. Rabbi Lawrence Troster, "Beyond the Letter of the Law: The Jewish Perspective on Ethical Investing and Fossil Fuel Divestment," December 3, 2014.

INDEX

Note: Page Numbers in *italic* refer to Figures

CPSIA information can be obtained
at www.ICGtesting.com
Printed in the USA
BVHW040446300122
627304BV00006B/7